THE FIRST POLICEWOMAN

A History of the Salinas Police Department

LISA EISEMANN

© Copyright 2005 Lisa Eisemann.
All rights reserved. No part of this publication may be reproduced, stored in a retrieval system, or transmitted, in any form or by any means, electronic, mechanical, photocopying, recording, or otherwise, without the written prior permission of the author.

Note for Librarians: A cataloguing record for this book is available from Library and Archives Canada at www.collectionscanada.ca/amicus/index-e.html
ISBN 1-4120-7548-3

Printed in Victoria, BC, Canada. Printed on paper with minimum 30% recycled fibre. Trafford's print shop runs on "green energy" from solar, wind and other environmentally-friendly power sources.

Offices in Canada, USA, Ireland and UK

This book was published *on-demand* in cooperation with Trafford Publishing. On-demand publishing is a unique process and service of making a book available for retail sale to the public taking advantage of on-demand manufacturing and Internet marketing. On-demand publishing includes promotions, retail sales, manufacturing, order fulfilment, accounting and collecting royalties on behalf of the author.

Book sales for North America and international:
Trafford Publishing, 6E–2333 Government St.,
Victoria, BC V8T 4P4 CANADA
phone 250 383 6864 (toll-free 1 888 232 4444)
fax 250 383 6804; email to orders@trafford.com

Book sales in Europe:
Trafford Publishing (UK) Limited, 9 Park End Street, 2nd Floor
Oxford, UK OX1 1HH UNITED KINGDOM
phone 44 (0)1865 722 113 (local rate 0845 230 9601)
facsimile 44 (0)1865 722 868; info.uk@trafford.com

Order online at:
trafford.com/05-2443

10 9 8 7 6 5 4 3 2

In Memory of
Mabel Marie Eisemann

August 28, 1904 - August 24, 1955

Salinas Police Department	1942-1947
Monterey County Sheriff's Department	1947-1955

The First Policewoman to serve on the Salinas Police Department

"The Salinas Police Department is undermanned but every man on the department is doing his job conscientiously. They are underpaid. Every policeman must learn to take everything from abuse and threats from the public to weather and all the things that are tough going for a lot of people."

Mae Eisemann, December 1947 interview for the Salinas Daily News

Some things never change.

ACKNOWLEDGEMENTS

The writing of this book was made possible by the many former officers, family members and research assistants that gave their time to help gather the information. The information contained in this book came from oral interviews, family records, and newspaper articles. Every effort was taken to insure accuracy. Those who spent many hours alongside the author in the libraries researching the local newspaper articles included the author's parents, Hank and Mary Ellen Eisemann, her husband, Joseph Gunter, and their daughter, Terrin. In addition, Candy Perryman was a tremendous help in completing the newspaper research phase of this project. Emily and Kate Molfino, daughters of Sgt. Tracy Molfino, spent their summer helping with the research. Sgt. Michael Groves spent hours processing photographs used for both the department yearbook and in this book and CSI Mark Babione scanned old newspaper articles and took photos of the old jail at the Monterey County Historical Society, where Mona Gudgel was a great resource and inspiration, providing access to old documents and newspapers with a smile.

Those officers, both formerly and currently with the department, who agreed to oral interviews and provided personal recollections, photographs, and clippings were also instrumental in providing an accurate accounting of the history of the department. Chief Herb Roberson, Dean Seefeldt, Woody Meek, J.W. Wilson, Gary Edwards, Ron Scott, Joe Gunter, John Carr, Art Garcia, Bob Ellis, Steve Perryman, Skeeter Innocenti, Fred Schloss, David Shaw, Vicky Gray, Russ Hauschild, Jesse Gilpas, Guille Cedillo, and Jeanette Reynolds provided many stories never seen in a newspaper. Wayne Schapper and all the Reserve Officers of the Salinas Police Department created an oral tape recording of their hilarious memories. The families of Officers Eddie Smith, Art Barnes, Butch Beevers, Everall Adcock, Phil Crocker, Barney

Abel, Fred Fowles, and Mae Eisemann generously provided both information and photographs.

Lastly, I am indebted to my family and friends for supporting me during the research and writing phase of this project which took well over one year to complete.

Lisa Eisemann
October 19, 2005
Salinas, California

TABLE OF CONTENTS

1. THE MURDER OF MAUD CARSON 1
2. EARLY SALINAS AND THE FIRST POLICE OFFICERS......... 6
3. THE FIRST CHIEF OF POLICE
   & STORIES OF THE EARLY DAYS 11
4. CHIEF STONEWALL JACKSON SMART................... 21
5. CHIEF THOMSON 25
6. CHIEF HISERMAN 32
7. SPECIAL OFFICER NOAH RADER &
   THE BATTLE OF MOSS LANDING..................... 41
8. A METROPOLITAN SALINAS 46
9. CHIEF GEORGE GRIFFIN AND HIS MEN 54
10. THE LAPIERRE ERA................................. 67
11. THE LEGACY OF MAE EISEMANN 81
12. CHIEF GEORGE WEIGHT 88
13. TRAGEDY STRIKES – THE STORY OF
    TRAFFIC OFFICER EDDIE SMITH 95
14. THE LAST OF THE ORIGINALS 100
15. THE GROWTH OF THE DEPARTMENT.................. 103
16. CHIEF RAY McINTYRE 131
17. THE RED LIGHT BANDIT AND
    OTHER STORIES OF THE 1960S 146
18. THE ANNEXATION OF THE ALISAL AND
    MORE STORIES OF THE 1960S 157

19	In the Line of Duty	171
20	Chief Herb Roberson	181
21	Legends in Their Own Time	194
22	A Sunroof for Gary Edwards' Patrol Car	208
23	Red Jackets, Wrecks and Reserves and the 1970s	213
24	The Ferguson Years	227
25	Murders Rock the City and Other Stories of the 1980s	233
26	Chief James Corrigan	242
27	Chief Dan Nelson	251
28	P.C. 187 – The 1990s	261
29	Chief Daniel Ortega	285
30	Gunter's Last Day and A New Era	295
31	The Finest Profession	306

ONE

THE MURDER OF MAUD CARSON

The blood spurted across the room before anyone realized that the young man had shot Maud Carson. Maud had been sitting on the arm of a comfortable chair entertaining several young male guests at her establishment when Howard Hatch entered the parlor, swore viciously at the owner of the house, and fired at her point blank. The double action weapon held five rounds, and with a barrel less than one inch long had been easily concealed in his palm. Maud rose from the chair, the gaping wound in her chest spilling blood as she ran from her attacker. As she stumbled into the adjoining bedroom, through the kitchen and connecting hallway into her own bedroom, shock prevented her from comprehending the irony of the words she had spoken earlier that evening. "Oh, throw that thing away," she had told Howard Hatch earlier that day when he threatened to shoot her in front of several guests.

As Maud collapsed and fell to the floor in her own luxurious bedroom, where she had entertained gentleman callers, she had little time to recall her conversation with the women from other houses who had come to inquire about the man threatening her life that day. She had dismissed him as a threat, telling them that she had known him for about four years and that he was no threat to her, saying, "He's only bluffing." She added that she had been the recipient of other death threats in her time and had always been successful in talking the men out of harming her. "I am expecting when my time comes it will come that way, and that I will be killed by some man, shot to death." Maud smiled grimly at the recollection of the conversation hours earlier. She had not expected to be right so soon. As she stared up at the chandelier above her, she noticed one burned out bulb she had meant to replace and the dainty crystals were in need of a good dusting. Her eyes closed for the last time, her blood staining the carpeting that covered the bedroom floor.

While Maud lay dying in her boudoir, Howard Hatch was chasing the unfortunate young man who had been seated in the chair upon which Maud had perched before being shot. The intended victim had followed Maud's route from room to room, moving swiftly when Hatch's gun refused to continue firing. A game of cat and mouse ensued until the victim, seeing Maud lying on the floor in her room, the blood beginning to pool around her still body, broke out of the house through a back door. Howard Hatch left through the front door. It was one of several recorded murders in Salinas City that year. The date was July 8, 1909.

Patrolman Gus Happ was the first policeman at the scene. One of only three policemen in the city at that time, Happ took over the investigation. Calling the coroner, he started to piece together the events of the night, but could find no apparent motive for the cold blooded murder. Coroner Muller took possession of Maud's remains and took her to the morgue. The next morning, Dr. H.C. Murphy and Garth Parker performed the autopsy. A bullet had entered the chest wall, traveling between the first and second ribs and cutting though the three lobes of Maud's left lung. The bullet had nearly exited her body at the back shoulder and could be seen just under the skin of her right shoulder blade. It was recovered during the autopsy. The entry wound was found to have been discolored by powder burns. The size of a dime, the entry wound showed signs of the weapon being held very close to the victim when fired.

While Coroner Muller called for an inquest to be held the following day, statements were being taken from citizens who had contact with Howard Hatch that fateful day. It was learned that Hatch had been away from his home town for some time before returning only days before the murder. On the afternoon of July 8, 1909, he had stopped in at the Long Green, a house of ill repute after spending several hours drinking at Harbaugh's Saloon, where he told the owner and guests, "I'm going to kill someone before the day is over." At the Long Green, he had asked for Maud and was told she was not there. Upset at not locating Maud, he held an objectionable discussion with one of the house women, after which he took a shot at her through a window. Missing by only eighteen inches, he continued on to the Arno House, where he was entertained by several women until he threatened to kill them with the same weapon later used to kill Maud. He threatened Maud as well, but she dismissed him as an unlikely threat to her and sent him away. Hatch left and returned to the other side of town, choosing this time to continue his drinking binge at the Abbott House Bar. The bartender refused to serve him due to his state of intoxication. Hatch took out the gun and threatened the bartender who threw him out on the street.

By now, Howard Hatch was very drunk, angry, and destructive. He walked back to the Arno House, arriving at 11:00 p.m. When he snuck into the parlor he found Maud entertaining Oscar Redmond, a young man from Parkfield. Following the murder and attempted murder, Hatch returned to Harbaugh's Saloon and confessed his crime, asking the bartender to take the gun and him to jail. Deputy Sheriff Frank Shook was called to the bar and took the murderer into custody. Hatch was quoted in the *Salinas Daily News* as saying, "One thing, a drunken man should never carry a pistol." Hatch later said he had no grudge against Maud and had been friends with her for many years. He could offer no reason for the murder.

The coroner's jury heard testimony from several witnesses at 9:00 a.m. the following morning. Called to hear the case were: M.R. Keef, P. Garrissere, G. Lapierre, A. Walker, C.P. Cooper, W.T. Masengill, John A. Hughes and Martin L. Griffin, all well known citizens of Salinas City. The verdict was published as follows: "We the undersigned jurors summoned to appear before H.V. Muller, coroner of Monterey County, to make inquisition into the cause of death of Clara Walker, sometimes known as Maud Carson, find that the deceased is twenty-five years of age, and that she came to her death in Salinas City, California, on the eighth day of July, 1909, by a gunshot wound, inflicted by Howard Hatch, with murderous intent." *Salinas Daily News, 1909.*

It had been learned during the investigation into the death of Maud Carson that she was from San Luis Obispo. A sister was located and gave Maud's true name as Clara Walker although to many in San Luis, she was known only as "Pearl." There were hints that she had extensive underworld connections and her funeral, held at the Muller Mortuary, was attended by a large crowd which included a number of what were considered to be finer citizens of Salinas City. Buried in the Odd Fellows Cemetery, her grave marker gives her name as Pearl.

The murder of Maud Carson rocked Salinas City and the *Salinas Daily Index* headline read, **"Woman of Underworld Murdered in Cold Blood"** on July 9, 1909. The San Luis Obispo newspaper carried an article saying Maud had been the "proprietress of a house of ill-fame in Salinas," and stating that

Howard Hatch of San Luis Obispo and known to Maud for many years, had "killed her in a drunken frenzy." *Daily Telegram, July 10, 1909.* Detailed accounts of Hatch's actions and the subsequent trial fascinated the citizens of Salinas for months as the trial date was postponed in one of the earliest documented cases of the defense using legal maneuverings to its benefit. It came as some surprise when Hatch chose to plead not-guilty, especially when there were eyewitnesses to not only the murder, but to his statements made earlier in the evening promising to kill someone before the day ended. Defense attorneys P.E. Zabala and Frank J. Fontes challenged all the prospective jurors and made accusations of prejudice against the entire jury pool because of Sheriff Nesbitt's association with the investigation. It became clear during the presentation of the defense case that they hoped to convince the jurors their client was insane, as witnesses were called to discuss the irrational behavior seen in the days before the murder. It wasn't until mid-November that final arguments were made. Judge B.V. Sargent instructed the jury on a Friday afternoon and five hours later the foreman, J.F. Moore, told the judge they had reached a verdict. Howard Hatch was twenty-eight years old when he heard the verdict read. Found guilty of first degree murder, the jury recommended life in prison. Judge Sargent later imposed that sentence on November 24, 1909, ordering Hatch to spend the rest of his life in San Quentin, a term Hatch had not expected. He had been certain of more leniency.

Prison records obtained from the California State Archives told the story of what happened after the sentencing. Hatch's family was wealthy and his sister immediately set about trying to have his sentence commuted. On November 19, 1912, an "Application for Executive Clemency" was filed on behave of Howard Hatch. Notification was sent out to the District Attorney's Office in Monterey County. In 1914, letters were written to Governor Hiram W. Johnson and Warden Hoyle of San Quentin State Prison. Hatch had been a model prisoner, and with no previous history of criminal behavior, was thought to be an ideal subject for a reduced sentence. The Hatch file contains copies of letters from Judge Sargent, recommending commutation of the sentence based on the judge's belief that Hatch did not realize what he was doing when he killed Maud Carson. Other letters were sent from Mr. Bardin, the prosecuting attorney, and from many of the jurors who heard the case and imposed the life sentence. Some jurors felt three years was too short a sentence for the crime, but most agreed to a reduction in the sentence if the governor saw fit to do so. Even Sheriff Nesbitt sent a letter of support for the sentence reduction. Many notes in the file and in the letters indicate that Mr. Hatch had killed a prostitute after she refused to provide him with more alcohol that night.

It was learned that Howard Hatch had a difficult childhood and it was agreed that his mother was less than adequate in her care of him. His father died when Howard was very young and his mother remarried. The new step-father was well set up and Howard was never expected to do much of anything. He had a ninth grade education, which at that time was considered "good," and he had attended some business college classes. He did work briefly at the Zellerbach Paper Company in San Francisco just prior to his arrest. After years of attempts and dozens of letters, it appears that Howard Hatch's sentence was commuted. He was first transferred to a road company in 1917 before being paroled from San Quentin on December 28, 1918. Having arranged for employment with his old employer, the Zellerbach Paper Company at the rate of $3.50 per day, Hatch was released from prison. By the early 1920s, he returned to his hometown of San Luis Obispo, where he worked for Mr. L.F. Sinsheimer, a very well-known and highly regarded businessman and property owner. On November 20, 1923, Mr. Sinsheimer wrote a letter recommending Howard Hatch receive an executive pardon from Governor Richardson. Many other citizens and friends also wrote in support of Hatch's application for a pardon. That, however, was not to be as Howard Hatch died of acute alcoholism on September 11, 1933 at the age of fifty-one. The last entry on his criminal file at San Quentin reads, "Died while on parole." Scribbled across his forehead on the photo in the prisoner record book for prisoner 23946- Howard Hatch is the single word, "DEAD."

TWO

EARLY SALINAS AND THE FIRST POLICE OFFICERS

The discovery of gold in California in 1848 led to an unexpected and rapid influx of settlers to the undeveloped territory of the Salinas valley. San Francisco became one of the top producing ports in the United States, and improvements in technology and the promise of great wealth caused a mass migration to the West. In September 1849, delegates from northern and southern California met in Monterey to hold the Monterey Constitutional Convention and to establish and write a state constitution. On September 9, 1850, California was granted statehood.

By the early 1860s, the town that would be called Salinas had begun to form. The *Salinas Daily News* reported that where once Indians had roamed, there was now "a hotel, a blacksmith, two houses and fifteen citizens, including a town drunk." The proximity to San Francisco made Salinas and nearby Monterey a comfortable destination for travelers, adventurers and criminals alike. The census of 1870 showed 599 residents, but by the time of the next census in 1880, that number had risen to 1,865. The slough that ran through the middle of the little town and served as a cattle lane was responsible for many dead end streets. In 1870, J.D. Carr and two partners drained the area now known as Carr Lake. Carr owned Gabilan Ranch, over 49,000 acres of prime land. There was a livery stable and post office, but it wasn't until the 1880s and 1890s, when Spreckels made the decision to build a sugar factory, that public utilities began to be installed.

There were three wealthy men, all prominent citizens of Salinas who owned much of the property in the fertile valley. Mr. Riker, Mr. Sherwood, and Mr.

Jackson sat down to discuss taking down the fences that separated their vast ranches. They would donate the land which was to become the City of Salinas. Its epicenter was at Gabilan and Main Streets.

Over the course of the years, Salinas would incorporate several times beginning in 1872. The citizens made a bid to become the county seat, voting on Christmas Day 1872. Savvy local citizens and politicians were well aware of the status this would bring the city. That political move would dictate the future of Salinas. As county seat, a courthouse was needed, and a two-story building was erected in the three hundred block of Main Street for a cost of $75,000. Destroyed by fire in 1877, all records kept there perished in the mysterious fire.

By 1872, it had become evident that some law enforcement was necessary to keep the peace in the new city. At the October 14, 1872 meeting of the Common Council of Salinas City, M. Spicer was approved as Marshall and given the title of "Chief of Police and Pound Master." a title the current chief still holds. At a salary of $30 per month, M. Spicer would be assisted in his law keeping by a series of special marshals and deputy sheriffs. It didn't take long for the citizens to realize that the law needed a place to house those who were caught breaking local ordinances. On November 25, 1872, the Common Council voted to build a Town Jail, a "Calaboose." While the town waited for the Calaboose to be built, the city rented part of a blacksmith's shop for $10 per month.

The original jail now stands abandoned at the Boronda Adobe owned by the Monterey County Historical Society
Photo courtesy of SPD

On March 24, 1874, the City of Salinas was formally incorporated. C. Franks was appointed as City Marshall, and John Hay, a city councilman, became a night watchman at a salary of $75 per month. Other marshals of the period included Jim McDougal, L.F. Campbell and James G. Evans. These men protected the city and kept the peace until the appointment of the first Chief of Police in 1903.

The city was growing and its needs included fire service. The Salinas Engine Company was organized in March 1875. By 1878, the new jail was finished. Proudly boasting of the modern jail, it was announced that the new facility could house up to six prisoners. It was located in the three hundred block of Main Street. It can now be seen on the old Boronda Adobe property where it is part of the Monterey County Historical Society's collection.

Bonds were approved and sold, paying in 1888 for the bridges over the Salinas River, which made travel and transportation much easier. In 1899, the Spreckels Sugar Plant opened and by 1900, the population had risen to 3,304 citizens. Salinas High School opened in 1882. According to Robert Johnson, author of *Salinas 1875-1950 From Village to City,* J.D. Carr donated $5,000 in

October 1888, towards the establishment of a library to be located in the Odd Fellow's Hall. It was open one evening each week and for a fee of three dollars a borrower could check out a book. By 1892, there were 3,500 volumes in the privately owned library. Most of the books would later be donated to the public library upon its establishment.

William Joseph Nesbitt was elected Marshall of Salinas City in 1882. Without much assistance and before any officer training classes, the Marshall often relied on citizens to aid in the capture of criminals. In 1883, a horse thief, a stage robber, and his accomplice broke out of the jail by sawing through the bars while police were out to lunch. On the run, they were caught by citizens Frenchy Cayer and George McDougal, both local farmers. A shoot-out wounded both fleeing inmates and they were returned to jail.

The population of Salinas by 1896 amounted to something over three thousand according to the *Salinas Daily News*. There were a volunteer fire department "with two hose companies," good hotels, two banks, and "handsome private residences surrounded by trees and embowered in vines and flowers."

Citizens also enjoyed a number of fraternal organizations such as a Masonic Hall, the Armory Hall, and three public halls for dances and other social events. The Odd Fellows, Native Sons and many others were all represented. Churches and schools served the citizens well. Two city parks, as well as a large number of orchards, were featured as highlights of the town. Salinas was considered an important trade center, connecting north and south, and east and west via the Southern Pacific Railroad. The short gap in the route along fifty-seven miles of the coast of California would be completed soon, making Salinas an important stop for commercial trade.

It was in 1896 that the first three police officers were formally hired to protect the city. On January 6, 1896, the Common Council of Salinas chose two night watchmen after a heated balloting session. The first five ballots proved useless, resulting in continual ties between several men. After a break of five minutes, the balloting continued. It was necessary to have a total of eight ballots before arriving at the first choices for Salinas policemen. There was no police department at that time, but Mr. George Condon and Mr. John Hansen were "duly elected as night watchmen," the Salinas newspaper reported. The next day a third man, J.B. McKenney, was elected as the third night watchman.

The new police officers had only on the job training. On the night of December 13, 1896, George Condon was patrolling his beat when he saw a man prowling around the Burke's yard. Crying out, "Halt!" to the man, the officer approached and gave chase as he fired two shots at him. Salinas residents had been complaining of nighttime "visits" from unwanted people. The suspected thief jumped a fence and made a getaway, with Condon in pursuit. It was suggested by the newspaper that "a few well-directed shots some of these fine nights would cause sounder sleep to our townspeople and no loss to the community." *Salinas Daily Index, December 13, 1896.*

THREE

THE FIRST CHIEF OF POLICE AND STORIES OF THE EARLY DAYS

With the turn of the century, changes were in store for Salinas City and her citizens. It was more than obvious that a fully funded and recognized police department was needed. Three men were listed as "Watchmen," and were paid out of the city's general fund in April 1903. The new watchmen were W.T. Benson, Hugh McKenney, and Thos. Jefferson. They were listed as receiving payments of $14, $33 and $69 respectively as authorized by the Common Council, however, there is no indication of the time period for their service. On July 7, 1903, John Hansen was officially appointed as Chief of Police. Having appointed the above men, on July 16, 1903, the city next passed and signed into law an ordinance establishing a police department, citing a police chief and two officers as staff. They voted to pay the two officers $60 per month, while the chief would receive $70 per month. The council voted to hire special policemen as needed at a rate of $2.50 per day, for no longer than a two week period.

Within months of taking office the new Chief of Police, John Hansen, was making regular appearances at, and reports to, the Common Council. On November 19, 1903, the paper reported Chief Hansen's request to purchase mattresses and cots for the city jail. That same day, twenty-six applications for liquor licenses were granted. Chief John Hansen, having begun his law enforcement career as a night watchman policeman before becoming the first official Chief of Police in Salinas, died February 5, 1928, at the age of sixty-nine. He had resigned earlier. Upon Chief Hansen's retirement, Captain C.J. Fulle took over the duties of chief.

The first recorded "cart-jacking" occurred on a Saturday evening in November 1903, near the corner of Main and Alisal Streets. A ranch hand had received his month's pay and soon spent it all in town. After purchasing a new suit, along with other items, he drank up a lot of "red liquor." In front of the Dashaway Stables, the ranch hand jumped into a cart with the ranch owner, drew a gun and ordered his employer to take him up town. When the employer resisted, the man fired his gun first near the Ross House and a minute later up the street, barely missing a Water and Light Company employee. The cart halted in front of the Jeffery House where a hotel clerk tried to reason with the gun-wielding man. The man was finally subdued after a fight in the mud. He was found to have been sent to Salinas from Castroville under a thirty-day sentence for disturbing the peace in that city. Fortunately, no one was injured by the wild gunfire. *Salinas Daily Index, November 1903.*

The day-to-day expenses for the city were listed in the local newspaper on a regular basis during the early years of the police department. The Night Watchmen, as they were called at the time, were paid out of the general fund. Other services related to the police department included charges for "burying dogs," for which various persons were paid twenty-five cents.

Gus Happ walked the streets of Salinas at night, looking for thieves and robbers. In 1904, along with Officers Croger and Hiserman, Happ arrested five suspects for "highway robbery." An employee of the brewery had been walking home in the early hours of September 29, 1904, after a night of heavy drinking when he was "laid out and robbed" by a group of very young men. The officer had found the youngsters "in dangerously close locality" to the injured victim, who was able to positively identify only one of the men. Denying culpability in the crime, but unable to explain to Happ's satisfaction how they came to have the money he found in their pockets, they were arrested by Officer Happ. *Salinas Daily Index, September 1904.*

Months earlier, Officer Happ had been on foot patrol when he noticed music and noise from a slot machine coming from a saloon he knew to be closed. Venturing down a dark alley, Happ tried to get to the back entrance of the saloon, but saw a man scampering away from the scene. The man "suddenly disappeared as if the ground had opened and swallowed him up." The officer returned to the scene to find a pane of glass broken and a twenty-five cent slot machine rifled. A total of four dollars was lost, but the burglar left his handkerchief in the cup, used to stifle the sound of the coins as they fell. It was thought this evidence might lead to the person responsible. *Salinas Daily Index, March 30, 1904.*

Happ had been born in Germany in 1856, moving to America as a young boy. He worked in the flour mill until John Hays resigned and Happ was appointed the position of night watchman.

In 1905, there were fifty-eight licensed dogs in Salinas. Several hundred were known to be roaming the city. Chief John Hansen seems to have known them all, and then some. His "crusade" to contain the "pestilential dogs" was the subject of some hilarity when, after rounding them up and containing them, someone kicked a hole in the fence, letting the entire group escape. In April, the Chief told the city council he was obeying the city ordinances regarding dogs not in possession of a license tag. Dogs without the necessary tag were held in the pound for three days and, "If the owner does not apply for them in that length of time, they are executed." *Salinas Californian, April 13, 1905.*

Policeman Happ, patrolling the town one evening, noticed a driverless horse. Finding three men asleep under the seat, he removed them and took them to the Calaboose. One fine spring day, Chief Hansen was patrolling his city accompanied by the constable assigned to the city, Constable S.J. Smart. At that time, constables were often appointed or elected to serve in areas not within the city limits. While many worked within the city alongside police officers, they were often regarded at county deputies. The two were cornered by a woman complaining her velvet cape and lap robe had been taken out of her buggy. They headed over to the hobo camp on the other side of the railroad tracks where they soon found a man with a bundle about to enter the Red Front Saloon. He could provide no explanation for his possession of the missing goods and was shown the way to the jail. Constable Smart, who would later become a Salinas chief, was busy making a name for himself early in his career as a lawman. Another local constable had arrested two men, deserters from the Army, who were wanted on burglary charges and for whom a reward from military authorities was offered. When the case resulted in a dismissal, Constable Smart had taken the men to the Presidio and collected the reward. The arresting constable complained that Smart had treated him unfairly and vowed to get the fifty dollars that he felt he earned.

Policeman Croger was on duty in September 1905 when two soldiers on their way to San Francisco, stole two cases of whisky from a local saloon. He was able to arrest one of the suspects while the other was located by sheriff's deputies.

Chief Hansen arrived home one day in a state of dishevelment that caused his wife much worry. The chief, having been in a fight with a drunk, had lost almost all his clothes in the melee. His hat was lost, his coat, vest and trousers were torn before the chief was able to land a blow to the jawbone of the drunken man, thus temporarily disabling him. Not one to hold a grudge, the chief saw that the man had some breakfast before he placed him on a train out of town. *Salinas Californian, April 19, 1905.*

LICENSED TO LIVE

The city in its wisdom, had created a dog law requiring licensing of all dogs believing it could build revenue from the numbers of canines in the city. Charging one dollar per animal, the city advertised the fees at no small cost and spent ten dollars on the tags given out to those citizens who complied with the law. In May 1905, there were exactly forty-two licensed dogs, according to the "License Collector's Office." After paying for the extra time and vigilance of the police officers, the advertising fees, and the tags, it was speculated that the expectations for an increase in revenue by the city fathers would never be seen.

THE LAUNDRY SAFE CAPER

Alerted by the engineer of passenger train number nine, Salinas police found a broken safe lying near the railroad tracks at the Gabilan Street crossing in July 1905. The safe belonged to the Salinas Steam Laundry located on Gabilan Street. It had been placed into a little two-wheeled freight truck after the thieves had kicked in several doors of the business. Rolling the safe out to the sidewalk and down the street, under the arc lights and over to the railroad tracks, the thieves used two sledge hammers and a crow bar to destroy the once burglar and fire proof safe. Two hundred dollars in gold and currency was taken and several hundred dollars worth of checks were left. Law officers speculated and disagreed about the possible perpetrators of the burglary, arresting several hobos without any evidence against them.

Jail guests received new uniforms designed to make escape more difficult. Made of ducking, there would be a shirt and pants. The former would have a black right half and a lighter colored left half, while the latter would have a light right leg and a black left leg. If was felt that this clothing would clearly distinguish prisoners and make them easier to recapture if they escaped.

There were many stories about the city jail. Escapes, visits, and overcrowding were only part of the history. One day, a hobo was discovered passing a bottle through the jail window to prisoners inside. His reasoning was that it was Thanksgiving, a holiday.

By 1907, the mayor had appointed city council members to a police department committee to oversee personnel and payroll issues. There was a Board of Health, a Board of Library Trustees, and a Park Commissioner.

Chief Hansen was warned that juveniles, old enough to know better, were getting into trouble and needed to mend their ways. Since the chief knew the boys, he was ordered to stop the thievery from fruit trees and orchards in the city. The newspaper reported a "Wave of Crime" in the city, stemming from the bold daylight thefts of bicycles, a felony at the time. *Salinas Daily Index, July-August 1907.*

A disturbed baker in the act of frying doughnuts was arrested after much difficulty and placed in a padded cell where he was sedated by the local doctor. Two juvenile jail breakers were sent to the Preston School of Industry as breaking out of jail was, even then, a felony. Horses were stolen with some regularity as they were still the main form of transportation and were often left unattended outside local saloons. Local law enforcement took the theft of any horse seriously and Salinas officers tracked one stolen animal all the way out to the Corral de Tierra area, where they recovered both horse and saddle in September 1907.

At an October 1907 meeting of the city council, the resignation of Chief Hansen was accepted. Mayor Clark announced that he had information of "such a nature that it became necessary for him to ask Mr. Hansen to resign." There is no indication of what that information was, but the names of several men were put forth to fill the two vacancies. The mayor expressed concern that the present salary of $70 per month for the chief and $60 for the night watchmen was not sufficient. The matter was discussed at length, resulting in an ordinance increasing the pay to $90 per month for the chief of police and $75 per month for policemen.

While the city awaited the appointment of a new chief and another officer, the crime wave continued. Policeman Happ, aided by Deputy Sheriff Frank Shook and Constable Hiserman, arrested two Greeks who had been causing a major disturbance in the Gabilan Street area. In a daring robbery, a high school boy walking from the area of the West End school house on Capitol Street, towards his home on Central Avenue, was held up by two men with a pistol. Meanwhile, the hobo problems continued. Policemen Smart and Happ made a "thorough search of the town after the holdup on Capital Street with the result that five specimens of the genus hobo, in all conditions of vagrancy and intoxication, were rounded up and locked up. The combined capital of the quintet was about $10. Two other tramps were shadowed, but managed to escape." *Salinas Daily Index, October 31, 1907.*

With eight more hobos being arrested within the next few weeks, there were now fifty prisoners in the county jail. Known locally as "Hotel Nesbitt", the jail, fondly called after the Sheriff of the time, was at capacity when more hobos arrived from the north. They took over the sand-house near the train station and refused to come out. At 2:00 a.m. on November 15, 1907, the alarm was sounded and Policemen Smart and Happ went running with revolvers drawn. The lawmen surrounded the sand-house, demanding "unconditional surrender." The hobos, fast asleep by that time, were surprised and eventually were arrested. Having given their names and found to have a total of eleven cents between them, James O'Brien, "proudly boasted that an Irishman never goes broke." *Salinas Daily Index, November 15, 1907.*

Finally, the day arrived for the city council to decide who would be the next police chief and what man would become the next officer. W.C. Campbell, who had commanded for a short time as the Acting Chief, was one of the applicants. R.C. Dill, S.J. Smart, C.J. Fulle, and Nis Nissen were read out as candidates. In only two ballets, Smart and Fulle were appointed to the department. The decision about the position of chief would have to wait for the next meeting. On December 17, 1907, the city council voted to establish a dump at the same meeting where they decided on their next chief. Captain Fulle, who carried the title of Captain from his prior military service and not from his duties as a police officer, was voted into office with the first ballot. This action angered S.J. Smart, who resigned, effective immediately, thus creating yet another opening in the fledgling department. Smart would go on to become the Constable of the Alisal Township; while Captain Fulle, as he was known, gave notice that Section 10, Ordinance No. 22, which prohibited bicycle riding on the city sidewalks, would be strictly enforced. He also intended to enforce Section 372A of the Penal Code, regarding spitting on the sidewalk and Sec. 8, Ordinance No. 12 regarding impounding all dogs without licenses attached to their collars. Captain Fulle was a man of military bearing. Having been Captain of the

Troop C, First Squadron of Cavalry, National Guard of California, he owned a white charger. Sitting atop his valiant steed, Captain Fulle made a full reconnaissance of the "suburbs," looking for violations of the sections previously mentioned. The newspaper reported him as being considered not only the chief of police of Chinatown, but also of the moral sections of Salinas. The paper went on to state that, "Captain Fulle, Chief of Police, is on his job and that's all that it is necessary to say, except to suggest his epitaph, the necessity for which, may it be far distant in the future! viz: 'He Seen His Duty and He Done It!'" Salinas *Daily Index, January 9, 1908.*

It was during these mounted patrols that Captain Fulle noticed the local citizens were unable to locate policemen when they were needed. Having heard of the signaling system which had been installed in Santa Cruz, Captain Fulle made a report to the city council requesting a red, glowing light be installed downtown so that any officer seeing it could rush to the nearest phone to receive instructions. That report would lead to the installation of the red lights that summoned officers for the many years before radio communications. It was during this same meeting that Captain Fulle reported the arrests for the prior month, the fines and imprisonments of each violator, and the numbers of cows, horses, and dogs that "fell into the pound master's clutches." The horses and cows were claimed by their owners, but most of the dogs were released from custody by persons unknown. Four were run over in the streets and ten were killed. The General Fund showed an eleven dollar expense for Captain Fulle for, "dog killing." Captain Fulle had his hands full with the stray dog problem and had been housing the extra dogs in the old jail on Salinas Street when he was cautioned by the city council to "remove his canine prisoners from their place of incarceration at the old jail," in March 1908. *Salinas Daily Index, March 3, 1908.*

Shortly after that order, Captain Fulle, still Chief of Police in Salinas, was made an officer of the Monterey County Society for the Prevention of Cruelty to Animals. Shortly thereafter, he was also mentioned as being the secretary of the National Rifle Association and was in charge of applications to the new local branch.

Hate crimes against the Chinese were common during these years and the scare and threat of Smallpox made its way to Salinas. Two cases were known by 1908, both originating in San Jose and being brought to Salinas by travelers. The city, having considered various citizens' offers of property on which to build the public library, finally decided on the Main and San Luis Street location for the future "Carnegie Library" as it was to be called.

Captain Fulle, still active in the military, was called to Rodeo in Contra Costa County to establish a training camp for the state rifle team. He was to be the coach for Troop C, Cavalry. Captain Fulle left to spend his annual vacation in service with the National Guard the same month Orville Wright set the record for flight in both time and distance, flying one hour and twelve minutes. During the six week absence of the police chief, Thomas F. Campbell was appointed as "Acting Chief." Campbell wasted no time sitting in the office but was out and about the town rousting grafters and chasing criminals. Early in the morning on the last day of August 1909, Campbell was watching the suspicious activities of a suspected thief. Keeping him under surveillance, Campbell followed him, watching his path. Sensing he was being followed, the thief grabbed money from the hand of a woman in a store before running swiftly out to the street. The victim screamed, "Stop thief!" and the chase was on. Campbell was joined in his pursuit by helpful citizens who jumped onto bicycles, or into cars, and ran alongside the lawman as he chased the thief around the downtown area. Cornered by the townspeople between Monterey, Pajaro, Gabilan, and Alisal Streets, the thief was captured. The thief, a discharged employee, had stolen a wheel left standing in front of the Waffle Kitchen, his former place of employment.

Captain Fulle returned from his National Rifle Shoot victorious in September 1909. Shortly after his return to duties as the chief, Fulle resigned suddenly stating a desire to do something better with himself. He served as chief from December 1, 1907 until November 1, 1909. It was said that he had accomplished much to "purify the moral atmosphere of the city." *Salinas Daily Index, October 23, 1909.*

Candidates for the newly opened position as chief of police were numerous. O.M. Hiserman, Robert Dill, Nis Nissen, Ramon Laguna, Thomas Meek, J.H. Browne, Al Wilson, S.J. Smart, and T.D. Van Lue all applied for the job. Hiserman received all seven votes of the council and immediately went out and arrested two "knights of the road" for begging and boozing. One was given fifteen days, the other twenty days for disturbing the peace. *Salinas Daily News, November 5, 1909.* Chief Hiserman also began a campaign against juvenile crime, choosing strict enforcement of the curfew and warning parents and youngsters against loitering and malicious mischief.

The great earthquake of 1906 had taken its toll on Salinas City. Many buildings in the city were destroyed. Much of Main Street was lost, but there were no deaths. Communications were difficult and Salinas was essentially cut off from the rest of the world until repairs could be made. The original city hall was damaged in the quake. It had been located at the corner of Gabilan and Salinas Streets. A new city hall was built in 1908 on the site just north of the Salinas Woman's Club and the Armory buildings. Sitting where police cars now can be seen parked, the old city hall was modeled after the Independence Hall in Philadelphia. When the current city hall was built, the old building was destroyed.

J.D. Carr continued his quest for a public library and was instrumental in obtaining a grant from Andrew Carnegie. With the help of the Salinas Civic Club, Carr raised over $4,000 to purchase the land. By 1909, a library stood in Salinas.

BADGE #3 RESIGNED UNDER CRITICISM

Officer Gus Happ, the only remaining officer of the original three men appointed in 1896 when the force was organized, handed in his resignation to Mayor Abbott in 1910. Albert Wilson was appointed in his place as a special policeman, until the Mayor could appoint a permanent replacement. Officer Happ had worked for many years and considered his service faithful and efficient. Apparently, he had been criticized for his acts as a police officer. The exact nature of the criticism was not made public and it was requested he reconsider his resignation. Apparently he did withdraw his resignation as his name appears as an officer until the time of his death in 1915. He even served as acting chief for a time during 1914.

Chief Hiserman made the news with the arrest of a drunken man who wandered into a home on Pajaro Street in April and with another similar arrest in May. On May 10, 1910, Matt Thomson was the Acting Police Chief and along with Constable S.J. Smart, arrested the man who had stolen a pair of ladies boots, then tried to sell them at a second hand store. The acting chief also had a tussle with a drunk, but was able to use force to get him into the jail.

In June 1910, O.M. Hiserman took the job of Chief of Probation for Monterey County. He would take that position on a temporary basis only, as his name had already been tendered by Judge Sargent as the leading Democratic candidate for Sheriff. Many congratulated Hiserman. The chief tendered his resignation in order to put his name on the nomination petition for Sheriff, a race he would lose. His political ambitions continued as he ran for County Assessor in 1914, losing again. He returned to the police department as a night watchman in 1915, replacing Gus Happ after his death.

The pound master of the period was J.D. Berryessa, a man who took his responsibilities seriously. Having received complaints from citizens that two loose cows were creating havoc in the South Main Street grain field, he went after the animals and took them into custody, corralling them at the pound. The owner, Conrad Storm, enraged at the deed, went to claim his cows and refused to pay the customary $1.00 fee to the pound master, who refused to return them without being paid. Mr. Storm returned home to pick up an ax after informing Mr. Berryessa he intended to get his cows. This apparent threat caused pound master Berryessa to scurry off in search of Chief Hiserman and other lawmen for backup. When he returned to his pound and found the cows gone, Berryessa appealed to Hiserman to do something. The gate to the pound had been broken open, no doubt a serious crime; but Chief Hiserman, along with most of the citizens of Salinas, was amused by the story and the spectacle of Mr. Storm having beaten the gate down to retrieve his cows.

FIRST SHOTS FIRED AT SALINAS POLICE

On the evening of December 3, 1910, Mr. and Mrs. Smiley returned to their West Street residence to find a burglar had ransacked their home. Officers made a search, but found no one. Officer Thomson decided to watch the 12:30 train as it pulled out of town. The officer noticed two men jump out of a pile of wood into the blind baggage compartment and immediately gave chase. In response to Thomson's orders to stop, one man jumped off the train and ran with Thomson in close pursuit. Just as the officer was about to make the arrest, the man turned and fired point blank at him, twice, narrowly missing his head. Thomson, taken completely by surprise, had no time to draw his weapon before the criminal escaped in the darkness. The burglars were not found.

FOUR

CHIEF STONEWALL JACKSON SMART

Stonewall Jackson Smart, a local farmer, became Chief of Police in 1910. Assisted by Constables Tom Meeks and Laurence, "Butch" Beevers, Smart could be seen throughout the city, working along side his men. Chief Smart would have an exemplary career as police chief and had a singularly efficient way of handling criminals. Voted into office after serving as Assistant Chief of Police upon the resignation of Chief Hiserman, Chief Smart was unanimously elected by the City Council on July 5, 1910. Shortly after his election, Chief Smart led a raid on a "disreputable resort," as directed by Mayor Francis A. Abbott. Assisted by Officer Matt Thomson and an inspector from the state board of pharmacy, Chief Smart began an investigation into the Long Green. Drug fiends were thought to frequent the Long Green, where opium, cocaine, and morphine were sold.

The officers found ten young boys who had been, "lured to their ruin," according to news reports of the day. The Chinese population in Salinas, as elsewhere, was trafficking poppy juice. Armed with a search warrant, the raid sustained the suspicions of drug use, but no actual product was found. The paper reported, "No more hophead, either Chinese or white, will be permitted in Salinas." *Salinas Daily Index, July 1910.*

The newspapers recorded numerous incidents in which Chief Smart acted as a one-man solution to crime in Salinas. Recognizing a man wanted in San Francisco, the Chief chased the suspect on foot, apprehending him. He caught burglars in the act in the better homes of Salinas, arrested a "loafer" in the alley east of Main Street and broke up numerous fights, drunken brawls, and other petty and serious offences.

Chief Stonewall Jackson Smart

CHIEF SMART'S ROCK PILE

The chief outsmarted many criminals through his perceptive psychological interrogations, getting some to leave town when he had no grounds to arrest them. Hobos plagued the city and took up most of the time of the law enforcement officers. Chief Smart, eliciting the help of Southern Pacific Railroad, set up a rock pile where hobos, after being arrested would have to serve their time working off their fines. The hobos broke up rock which would be used to build and repair streets in Salinas in what was most likely the first "chain gang" or "work detail" to be organized out of the city and county jail systems. The railroad company provided the rock at no cost to the city, and the chief hoped Salinas would gain the reputation among tramps of not being a hospitable place to visit. Without the free food and shelter the jail had previously offered, making incarceration a rather pleasant change for the hobos, Chief Smart felt the work detail would be a great deterrent. So pleased was Southern Pacific Railroad Company with the plan, they offered to provide free rock to any city willing to establish a rock pile that would force tramps to work for their food during their stay in the local jail. The first two candidates for the rock pile detail were Joseph Burns, arrested by Chief Smart himself, and George Wright, arrested by Constable Andrew J. Stirling. Both men made fruitless pleas to Justice Fitch for leniency, and both were denied. The judge let them know of the plans for a rock pile, where they would be allowed to work for some time before their release dates.

A town record was broken by one arrest made by Chief Smart. On March 26, 1912, the chief arrested Agar Davis for stealing a bicycle, then trying to sell it. The arrest and the subsequent appearance at police court netted the suspect a one hundred day sentence in county jail, ten days for each minute the thief had the stolen bicycle.

Through his tenure as chief, Chief Smart continued to be in the news on an almost daily basis as details of his chases and arrests were detailed. Having watched a suspected burglar for some time, Chief Smart was able to make the arrest in March 1913. Apparently, the suspect was not thoroughly searched prior to being placed in the city jail. Informed by other inmates, the chief and officers searched the cell, finding almost all the burgled jewelry, including dozens of rings, bracelets, chains and a gold pin.

Still able-bodied, the chief captured another pair of thieves along with Deputy Sheriff Nesbitt. The two lawmen were surprised when the two thieves, using a language unknown to the officers, coordinated an escape on Church Street, between Gabilan and Howard. Chief Smart was outdistanced by the first suspect, but grabbed a nearby bicycle and rode on until he located the man hiding under a bush near Capitol Street. The man fought, viciously kicking the Chief and was subdued only after the Chief struck two solid blows to the man's head with his revolver.

The cost of living was making it impossible for the two police officers and chief to make a living. In September 1913, the chief, along with Officers Gus

Happ and M.J. Thomson, petitioned for a raise. They claimed the current compensation of $90 per month for the chief and $75 per month for the officers was not sufficient for the men to meet expenses of the day. The matter was referred to the police committee.

FIVE

Chief Thomson

On June 28, 1914, Archduke Ferdinand of Austria and his wife were assassinated on the streets of Sarajevo, the culmination of a Serbian murder plot. By March 1917, the Bolsheviks had taken power in Russia, destroying the Romanov dynasty and pulling out of the war where they had sided with the Central Powers. The United States would not enter the war until April 6, 1917, having watched with some detachment until the stories of horror and poison gas forced action. While the war devastated the world population, advancements in medical care and aeronautical engineering were unexpected positive by-products of the carnage. By the time the Treaty of Versailles was signed, requiring Germany to give up land and pay five billion dollars in reparations, fifty million lives had been lost.

On June 30, 1914, Chief Stonewall Jackson Smart resigned to run for Sheriff of Monterey County. He lost that election and returned to farming, his death certificate listing only "farmer" as his occupation, failing to recognize completely the contribution he made as a law enforcement officer in Salinas. This resignation made necessary the election of first another police officer to fill the vacancy left in the department, and secondly, the naming of a new chief. During the interim until the appointments could be made, Policeman Gus Happ, an eighteen year veteran with Salinas, was appointed as Acting Chief. In July 1914, the council voted to appoint Thomas Meek as policeman. Candidates for the position of Chief included Officers Happ, Meek, and Thomson; one part time substitute officer, Paul Caldwell; and former Chief, O.M. Hiserman. It was Thomson who received the votes that would make him the fifth police chief of Salinas. That fall, the campaign for Constable of the Alisal District was heated. A run off between Butch Beevers, H.A. Andresen and Gregory resulted in Gregory winning the seat, with Beevers in second place.

The Mayor of the City was Feliz and street work was the main discussion of the council meetings. Mayor Feliz also ordered Chief Thomson to "catch more speeders' on Main Street as traffic complaints had been made by members of the council. It was difficult to keep the street lights in working order and the monthly reports of Chief Thomson to the council continued to result in the city reducing the payments they made to Coast Valleys Gas and Electric Company.

One man, wishing to become a police officer, went to the council, offering to serve without pay, willing to assist with certain special events. The council remarked that the city charter would have to be amended and further, that they felt the police force in place was "sufficient to detect violations of city ordinances."

By late in 1914, Chief Thomson was making requests for equipment for his men. In December that year, police telephone boxes were placed at these strategic locations: on the corner of Main and Gabilan Streets, on Main Street between Alisal and San Luis, on East Alisal, and on Market Street. Placed to save police time, the red lights had been installed on top of key high buildings and flashed when an officer was needed. Any officer seeing the flashing lights could go to the box and quickly be in touch with "central." Prior to the placement of the call boxes, officers had to go to a hotel or open restaurant to call central. This method of summoning officers continued into the 1940s.

Chief Thomson believed in continuing his education and began to study the area of "hobo hieroglyphics." Hobos, tramps and vagrants were a large part of the problem for officers during these years. The following translations are the result of the chief's studies.

Large, round circle – No use

Cross in a circle - Good for a hangout

Rectangle, bar and sawtooth – Look out for the dog

"V I n" – Woman in the house

"x" and "n" – Wood to cut

Late in 1915, Chief Thomson used the newspaper to deliver a message to saloon owners. Apparently, there had been many who were serving drunks or habitual drunkards, in violation of the state law. Chief Thomson issued a warning to all saloon owners that those who violated the law would have their liquor licenses "revoked without delay." True to his word, Ruby's Saloon on Market Street was one of the first to lose its license after Chief Thomson and Night Watchman Tom Meek testified about illegal dice games there.

Chief Thomson made a name for himself with local drunks by arresting three agitators who boasted they would never work a day in their lives. Taking them to jail overnight after a foot chase and fight won by the chief, the three were provided with scrubbing supplies and forced to scrub the entire city jail before breakfast. Taken to court later that day, each man was given a fifteen day sentence. The trio was quoted as calling Chief Thomson, "de flippest bull along de line." *Salinas Daily Index, April 2, 1915.*

Drunks, thieves and prostitutes were only part of what the early officers had to deal with. There were murders within the city, vicious killings that were hard to solve due to the transient nature of the hobos and tramps. In July 1915, an elderly cigar maker was brutally beaten with a wagon king bolt and left for dead. Witnesses had seen a man with a German accent carrying the wagon bolt earlier. The suspect had been present in the shop when the victim paid off a bill in cash. Fifteen deep wounds caused the death of J.H. Kaiser. Charles Kohler was eventually arrested, brought to trial, found guilty, and given the death penalty. He had three previous felony arrests.

Former Chief O.M. Hiserman had returned to the force as a night watchman in August 1915, after Gus Happ had passed away, leaving an opening in the department. Happ, the father of three, had fallen victim to a horrible accident in which many large bones were broken. He was considered a faithful city employee and was missed by many. He was fifty-nine years old at the time of his death.

The paving of streets and the improvement of North Main, Blanco, and Alisal Streets were foremost on the agenda of council meetings. The City of Salinas continued to grow during the years before the United States entered World War I. The population nearly doubled during the decade, the rodeo was organized, and the agricultural industry began to boom.

By 1916, news included coverage of the terrible storms and vast flooding in the city and surrounding areas. By February that year, fifteen inches of rain had fallen. The sinking of the Lusitania had begun the shock Americans would continue to get as Germany marched across Europe. Chief Thomson continued to serve the city during 1915 and part of 1916. City officials, at the urging of the police department, were looking into the installation of electrolieres. Plans for fifty electroliers along Sausal, John, and San Luis Streets would mean a safer downtown. Peace disturbances, fights, burglaries and robberies still plagued the area. Granite Rock was working on paving the main streets and the state highway was finished between Salinas and Chualar.

Chief Thomson's reputation with local criminals was well deserved. In January 1916, the chief was in pursuit of a criminal just sentenced to twelve years after the man snuck away after visiting with his wife outside the sheriff's office. Thomson began the hunt for the man by searching the local lumber mill. When a young boy spotted the escapee near Gabilan and Lincoln Streets Thomson, now accompanied by the sheriff, drew his gun, yelling out, "Come out of there quick!" Covered with mud, the two lawmen returned the escaped prisoner to the jail. *Salinas Daily Index, January 24, 1916.*

One day later, at exactly the spot where the escaped suspect was caught by Chief Thomson, Officer Hiserman questioned two men regarding stolen suitcases taken from the train station. Alone with the two suspects, Hiserman was surprised when one man drew an automatic pistol and tried to hit him over the head. Hiserman reacted quickly and was able to disarm the man and arrest him. Both suspects were charged with petty larceny and pled guilty the next morning in front of Justice Wallace. Each received six months in the county jail for their part in the theft of the suitcases. *Salinas Californian, January 25, 1916.*

Constable Cano was a well known and popular officer who served many sections of the county and assisted Salinas police in numerous cases, raids, and searches. In March 1916, Constable Cano was the law in the Pajaro area and was shot in the face by a suspect trying to get away by boarding a train in Watsonville. He lost all the teeth on the right side of his mouth in the attack, but was able to return fire, mortally wounding one of the two men, but the other got away. A $50 reward was immediately offered and a former officer and chief decided to collect. S.J. Smart gathered his family members and said, "Let's take a ride around by Natividad and down to Spence Switch and we'll catch that fellow and get that reward!" While twenty-eight police officers and cavalry volunteers searched on horseback and in autos, Smart set off in his own vehicle. A barbecue was set up at the Alisal grounds, courtesy of Sheriff Nesbitt. Beef, bread, and coffee with cream and sugar was provided for those helping find the suspect. With one of his girls driving, Smart started towards the Natividad area, stopping to get out and check the dirt road for any sign of human crossing. The suspect had been very careful and was aided by the light rainfall of the night before. When Smart spotted the suspect walking in tall grass he cleverly lifted the hood of car pretending to have car trouble and spoke to the man, asking if he was sick and offering to take him for a meal. The man had been shot by Cano's partner and was trying to conceal a limp.

Smart, finding himself with his family and no back up lawmen, found a Greek section hand and enlisted his assistance. Leaving his family waiting at the Spence Switch, Smart then drove the suspect, accompanied by the helpful Greek laborer to town. At the jail, the man asked for food and had to be restrained from eating too much as he had not had a meal in many days. The Sheriff and Troop C Cavalry was notified and returned to town weary and dusty. Smart was given the $50 reward as he clearly deserved it. *Salinas Daily Index, April 3, 1916.*

The injured officer identified the suspect as one of the men who had attacked him. A jury trial was held in May and Cano testified that the suspect was the one who had shot him. On May 25, 1916, the jury instructions were given at 11:45 a.m. A verdict of guilty was returned at 3:30 p.m. that afternoon.

Accompanied by a District Attorney, Chief Thomson, Stony Smart, S. Gregory, Charles Andresen and members of the Sheriff's Department gathered in Monterey for a "raiding party." The Glenwood Inn and The Pacheco were both raided, along with a "Chinese joint." It took four cars to transport the seized items and suspects to Salinas. While Chief Thomson was busy on the Monterey detail, he placed Officer Meek in charge of the department. Meek, not wanting to be outdone, mounted his own raid on Wah Lee's establishment, catching him red-handed with lottery tickets and gambling items. Lee was able to put up the $30 bail set by Justice Wallace. He faced charges of operating a lottery the next day.

After the successful and tiring raids, Chief Thomson and Tom Meek were due for vacation time. Thomson set out with his family for San Francisco while Tom Meek went even further north along the coast. Taking the place of the chief while he was on holiday was former chief S.J. Smart. As Acting Chief, Smart would be in charge of the entire city. He was assisted by Sam Bashline who had been hired to take the place of Tom Meek.

THE EGG THIEF FUGITIVE

When Officer Hiserman came upon a man carrying a bucket containing fifteen dozen eggs and trying to sell them, he was immediately suspicious.

Escorting the man toward the city jail, he was surprised when the man bolted and ran down Gabilan Street towards Salinas Street. Officer Hiserman quickly drew his service revolver and fired three shots in the air towards the fugitive, but the man continued to run. Two citizens directed Hiserman towards the location where they had seen the suspect near the corner of Main and Alisal Streets. Hiserman found his man hiding in the doorway of a tamale shop. The man admitted to stealing the eggs and pled guilty to petty larceny, receiving a sentence of sixty days in the county jail. *Salinas Daily Index, October 3, 1916.*

When On Quong was arrested by Officer Hiserman for selling lottery tickets, it was the surprise of his life. The suspect had wisely been watching for any sign of police activity and believed Officer Hiserman, a night officer, would never come around during the daytime. Hiserman, however, was unaware of the "rules" and was working his detail when he caught Quong selling the illegal tickets. Fined $30, Quong was quoted as saying it "isn't fair for a night cop to work in the day time." *Salinas Daily Index, October 14, 1916.*

THE NICE FAT GOOSE

The chief and his men continued to raid gambling dens in the Chinatown area. They seized lottery tickets, sacks of money, gold, silver and bonds. Their vigilance caused great concern among the illegal gambling establishments in the red light district as they sought to rid the city of undesirables. They also investigated crimes against many of the citizens who tried to help those less fortunate than themselves. When a hobo went into the People's meat market one day, begging for a meal, a generous William Nonneman gave him that and offered him a job plucking a goose. The hobo accepted and began to pluck the goose. Eventually, the feathers were plucked away and the meat began to show. Apparently, the hobo began thinking about a holiday dinner and wrapped the goose up in paper while no one was looking. He snuck out the back door and down an alley where he met up with his friend. When Chief Thomson was advised of the crime, he knew where to look. From his study of hobo habits, the chief felt the two goose thieves would be near the railroad yard. On Central Avenue, two men were spotted, one with a package under his arm. Chief Thomson hid out behind a house until he could reach out and touch them. One man even had goose feathers all over his clothing. In front of the judge, the two stated they wanted a Thanksgiving dinner. Justice Wallace found that excuse lacking and the two were provided with accommodations at the Hotel Nesbitt, (the county jail) where they received both their Thanksgiving and Christmas dinners before their release date just before the new year. *Salinas Daily Index, December 1, 1916.*

Chief Thomson resigned as chief in December 1916, leaving the area for a better paying job in San Francisco. He had served eight years with Salinas, three of them as chief and was said to have had, "a fine record as an efficient officer and competent chief." *Salinas Daily News, December 2, 1916.*

SIX

O.M. Hiserman

*Police Chief
O.M. Hiserman*

Three days after the resignation of Chief Thomson, former Chief Hiserman having returned to the department as a night policeman after Happ's death, was unanimously voted in as the new chief. Charles Andresen was also unanimously elected as policeman, replacing Hiserman. At that time, Andresen was an assistant jailor and had been acting as a special officer during raids and at times when additional manpower was needed. The department and officers continued to battle the hobo problem and drunkenness. Hiserman had previously been an officer, a constable, the chief of probation, twice the chief of police, and a candidate for both Sheriff and Assessor. Between 1907, when his name is first mentioned as a constable in

Salinas, and 1952, when he still held the position of Captain of Detectives, O.M. Hiserman had a remarkable career in law enforcement. He was not a very good driver, and it is said that his wife sometimes refused to ride with him. A large man, he lost a leg to diabetes and had the leg buried at the Oddfellows Cemetery. He was buried there himself in 1952, after dying of coronary thrombosis. The loss of a leg didn't stop the chief from participating in raids in Chinatown. He had officers push him around Chinatown in an old wheelchair, where he assisted and participated in raids on opium dens. Attending a conference with Sheriff Nesbitt, the chief and his men had been given the additional task of enforcing the registration of all men into the armed forces due to the war in Europe. News during these years shows first calm, and then an escalating interest and fear of the events in Europe right up until America entered the war in 1917.

The officers of the Salinas Police Department were a patriotic group. In 1917, the president had issued a proclamation regarding the duties of police officers in enforcing the registration of all male citizens between the ages of twenty-one to thirty in the draft. In what is believed to be the first meeting of all police officers within the county in May 1917, plans were made for one hundred men to come to the aid of city and county lawmen should the need arise. Salinas officers attended that meeting voluntarily and without pay, willing to offer their services in whatever way they could. At the same meeting, a suggestion that the lawmen join the Red Cross was answered with the entire Salinas department stepping forward to donate one dollar each to become supporting members. Present at that historic meeting were, Chief Hiserman, Tom Meek, M.J. Thomson and many of the constables and officers from other departments throughout the county. *Salinas Daily Index, May 21, 1917.*

By mid-1917, the use of weapons in robberies and other crimes had escalated to the point where legislation was needed to control guns and knives. The new law went into effect in July 1917 and prohibiting the carrying of any concealed weapon. The new law also required weapon dealers to keep a record of the sale of any pistol or revolver and to provide a copy of the sale record to the chief of police or county clerk of the jurisdiction where it was sold. The law made the attempt to commit even a minor crime with a concealed weapon a felony. *Salinas Daily Index, July 28, 1917.*

Daylight robberies were common and officers struggled to keep up with a growing crime rate in the city. Often assisted by the sheriff or his deputies, Salinas officers raided establishments in the Chinatown district, making arrests and confiscating money and gambling equipment. Officers also teamed up with city councilmen, the city manager and other citizens who were happy to speed off to chase after fleeing robbers. A favorite escape route was onto the old Sherwood farm in the Santa Rita district, where a slough provided some cover for criminals. Chief Hiserman and his posse of assistants were often successful in capturing the suspects and bringing them to justice. During his first month as chief, Hiserman and his officers made twelve arrests. One of those arrested was George William Hunter, whose only crime, at the moment, was vagrancy. At his arraignment on the morning of September 26, 1918, Mr. Hunter pled not guilty and demanded a jury trial. Taken by surprise at the request, Justice Mitchell set bail at $50 and said he would try to accommodate the request for a trial the following Monday. In the meantime, Mr. Hunter vacationed in the jail, along with Phillip Feeney, who had already been convicted of the same crime and was starting a fifteen day sentence. *Salinas Index, September 26, 1918.*

Traffic Officer Clarence Nuttall was on duty, but in the office when two men in automobiles began a dangerous race on a congested section of what would later be called North Main Street. Finding it necessary to pursue the two men who were racing their respective vehicles at sixty miles per hour, Nuttall himself raced after them, citing them for a court appearance within the five day period required by the law of that time. Officers Meek and Voss were on foot patrol on Sausal Street one night when a train delayed their path. Strolling through Chinatown on a shortcut, the two officers suddenly found a door slammed in their faces and heard the sounds of Chinese language apparently blaring a warning to others. Previously unsuspicious of that particular building, the two forced the door open and found an illegal game in process. Seizing the paraphernalia and $188, they arrested two Chinese for conducting an illegal gambling game. The two pled guilty the following morning, paying fines of $20 each. The lookout, who had shouted the warning out, apparently escaped. *Salinas Index, July 3, 1917.*

By 1918, the City of Salinas issued a new proposed charter to be voted on by the citizens. Of interest in the new charter was Section 54, the description of the police department. "The Police Department of Salinas shall consist of a permanent force of such number of policemen, not less than two as the Council shall, from time to time determine; the Council shall by ordinance provide for its government and control." The charter also provided for judicial power in the form of the police court and a justice court with the power to impose fines and penalties that would be deposited to the city treasurer. *Salinas Daily Index, August 26, 1918.*

In late December 1918, twenty-nine applications for liquor licenses were renewed within the small city. One rejected application was that of a German against whom charges of objectionable language and running a business frequented by enemy aliens were alleged. Chief Hiserman provided evidence of the allegations and the vote to reject the application was unanimous.

O.M. Hiserman was formally appointed Chief of Police on July 22, 1919. He had been acting as chief for some time prior to the formal appointment. Constable Butch Beevers, along with Officer Clarance Nuttall, who would later become a chief, took their cases to Judge David Wallace, who started out as a county recorder and later became Justice of the Peace. Beevers was to be one of the founding fathers of the Salinas Rodeo.

Although the police department had been in existence for many years by 1919, the city council was looking at ways to change the ordinance and create a new city charter, fixing salaries and personnel. On June 14, 1919, a new ordinance created the Salinas Police Department, requiring no less than two officers in addition to the chief, but allowing for additional officers as necessary. The police department was placed under the supervision of the Mayor, with the chief next in line of authority.

The Chinese opium trade was still one of the biggest challenges facing officers in Salinas. Stray dogs were another problem plaguing Salinas. In December 1919, Chief Hiserman told the city council it was impossible to retain a pound master at the current compensation offered, suggesting a return of dog license fees. The council instead decided it was more important to have a "wide awake" pound master and voted to pay him $2.50 per head for all dogs disposed of during the next three months. In July 1920, the city council raised the pay for the chief and officers. The patrolmen were to receive $125 per month, while the chief's raise brought him to $135 per month.

As late as 1919, cattle were still driven through the streets of Salinas with the permission of the chief of police. Sidewalks were being trampled and fences destroyed as cattle stampeded through town. Cattlemen were ordered in December 1919, to obtain permits to run cattle, designating the intended route and limiting numbers. The chief was ordered to place signs in prominent places around town, notifying vaqueros of the new law.

1920 brought the fear of a killer flu to Salinas. So deadly was the flu that Judge Bardin ordered the courts closed for a period of two weeks to avoid assemblage of attorneys, litigants and witnesses who might be infected. Trials were delayed for two weeks as health authorities tried to keep the disease from spreading among adults and children.

Terrible car accidents, both in town and at railway crossings were frequent and often resulted in death. Additionally charged with locating slackers, men who registered for the draft but failed to appear when called, officers struggled with robberies in Chinatown, auto thefts, and the ever present hobos, now armed with guns. Crimes along the railroad were common and Salinas officers often assisted Southern Pacific officers in chasing and apprehending criminals who shot at and fought with police.

Chief Hiserman, assisted by Butch Beevers and Tom Meek made the news regularly, with accounts of fist fights, spectacular chases, and shots fired. Chief Hiserman, being the Sergeant-at-Arms for the California State International Association for Identification, invited the organization to have its annual convention in Salinas. In 1921, the country's top chiefs, fingerprint experts, and policemen attended the convention held in Salinas, sharing stories about cases solved through fingerprint evidence and teaching techniques. Attending were dignitaries from afar, including August Vollmer, then chief of police in Berkeley and the head of the International Police Chief's Association. Butch Beevers of Salinas was at that time known as the "barbecue chef supreme," and prepared a Spanish Colonial meal of luscious meats for the attendees. The convention was a huge success, with credit going to Chief Hiserman for issuing the invitation to the group in the prior year. Chief Vollmer, in cooperation with the university in Berkeley, had set up classes for his men to take, providing them with both scientific and medical educations to help them in police work. They were trained in the use of the "Larsen Lie Machine," which was the first with the ability to record the blood pressure of the subject. Vollmer and his men used the machine with great success during the 1920s.

Not long after the convention ended the chief, along with Beevers, who had been the victim of a theft of coats out of his car, led a raid on 9 Pajaro Street, where Chinese and Mexican criminals were thought to live. It was reported that a large amount of stolen goods was found during the raid and believed that trucks loaded with stolen goods had departed before officers arrived. Arrests were made. A short time later, Acting Chief C.H. Andresen, along with deputy sheriffs and officers Al Wilson, Walter Stone, Tom Meek and N.H. Rader raided 131 Lake Street, where contraband liquor was confiscated and arrests were made.

Officers Tom Meek and Frank Urquidez walked their beat in the Chinatown area in 1922. Always watchful of those establishments where it was thought gambling was taking place, and the two lawmen raided 7 Soledad Street one night in January. Finding four white gentlemen from Monterey engaged in a blackjack game, they arrested the men along with Wong Tott, who claimed no knowledge of the game or any illegal activities. The four men from Monterey were released after a night in the pokey, but Wong Tott had to put up four hundred dollars in cash for bail. Salinas officers had confiscated a large amount of liquor at the Cominos Hotel during the service of a search warrant related to violations of the Vollstead Act. The police court judge had ruled in favor of police, saying the seizure was legal, but after a protracted legal battle, a Superior Court judge was forced to issue an order to Chief Hiserman to return the illegal booze that the higher court had ruled was illegally taken. Chief Hiserman, under orders from the local prohibition enforcement officer, delayed the return of the large amount of liquor. The attorney for the Cominos brothers vowed to take the case to the Supreme Court. The highest court in California refused to grant the writ of certiorari, upholding the validity of the Vollstead Act as enforced by the city. Chief Hiserman then filed federal charges in an attempt to impose further fines on the Cominos brothers. The judge in the federal case, finding the Salinas men had already been convicted in police court and had paid fines totaling $1500, threw the federal case out.

The opening of the Lloyd M. Siebert Field air landing field in March 1922, put Salinas on the map in the important world of air traffic. As one of only two stops between San Francisco and Los Angeles, Salinas aced out Hollister and Watsonville for this honor. Lloyd Siebert, for whom the airstrip was named, had been a Sergeant-Major in the U.S. Cavalry, winning the Medal of Honor during the First World War. A local man, Siebert was the son of a Prunedale rancher and was, in 1922, stationed at the Mexican border with his regiment. The airstrip was being quickly constructed at the site of the old Armstrong Ranch in Salinas.

Salinas Traffic Officer Harry Elasho was on his way home one evening and near the Salinas River Bridge when he saw what he thought were two men coming out of the willows up to the road. Thinking they had run off the road, Elasho pulled over to give aid. As he got out of his car, he found a large revolver in his face as one of the man said, "Hands up!" He complied and the second man, also armed with a gun, reached inside Elasho's pocket and took his "purse." Continuing to pat the officer down, and feeling the club the officer carried in a pocket, the men got excited and ran away. During the pat down search, they had failed to find his gun, which he kept under one arm. Elasho fired at the two men, hitting one with the first shot and missing with his next two shots. Return fire splashed the gravel at the officer's feet up into his eyes, temporarily blinding him and rendering him unable to continue the fight. He began back towards town, but found his sight returning and returned to search for the two robbers. Seeing lights in the distance he tried to follow, but was only successful in finding that their car had been hidden in the willows off Buena Vista Road. A trial of blood was located, crossing the bridge and disappearing where the car had been parked. From the amount of blood present, Elasho told arriving officers his soft-nosed bullets must have torn a large hole in the suspect. Praised for his bravery by Chief Hiserman and Sheriff Nesbitt, the officer was distraught at the apparent getaway of the two robbers.

Death at the hands of others was unfortunately a somewhat regular event in Salinas. During a street fight between two well-known dairymen, which was witnessed by a large number of persons, a strike to the head of one man and subsequent impact with the street, fractured his skull. Having started the disagreement in the Italian Hotel, the two were followed by about thirty onlookers and moved to the Southern Pacific yard off Market Street to end the dispute. Both men had been in the legal system before this date.

In another strange incident, a man who told officers he was in the secret service of Jesus Christ, stabbed and cut a man near Seaside. Officers at the scene telephoned Sheriff Nestbitt and his men who rushed to Seaside to handle the case. With the Sheriff and his deputies long gone, the suspect suddenly appeared at the Claussen Ranch at Davis Crossing. It was left to Chief Hiserman of Salinas to arrest the delusional man.

Reckless driving charges were taken very seriously in Salinas. With the number of injury accidents and fatal crashes, Justice David Wallace dealt out fines to those unfortunate enough to have been caught violating the laws. Three officers were patrolling the main thoroughfare one day in March when Paul Bedolla, a rather well-known man from Gonzales, happened to pass through. Officers Tom Meek, Charles Andresen and Frank Urquidez arrested the man, telling the judge he had been going over fifty miles an hour when they "corralled" him. The fine, imposed on a Saturday evening, was $150. Mr. Bedolla paid it that night. Traffic fines were not the only high cost of living or traveling through Salinas. Chief Hiserman, finding a car loaded with "corn" moonshine, believed the man was making deliveries in town. Going to the ranch owned by the suspect, the chief found barrels of fermenting mash, materials for making mash, corks, bottles, funnels and other "necessary appliances and accessories for a first class moonshiner." He also impounded the car, holding it in a local garage. Pleading guilty to violations of the new county ordinance prohibiting the manufacture of liquor and the sale of the moonshine, the rancher paid $1000, $500 for each of two separate charges. The car was ordered released and the man along with it, but the still, mash, and other evidence of the crime was destroyed. *Salinas Journal, March 13, 1922.*

Judge David Wallace, upset that Paul Parker, editor of the Salinas Journal was not appropriately attired in rodeo "togs," as previously ordered, notified him of the consequences for his misdeed. Giving the man twenty-four hours in which to rectify his misbehavior and disobedience of the judge's prior order, the judge instructed Butch Beevers to see that the clothing was changed or carry out the order to put the man in the jail. Mr. Parker, as part of the publicity committee for the rodeo event, had been one of the first to acknowledge and encourage the order for everyone to dress in cowboy attire. His subsequent inability to abide by the judge's orders came not from disobedience, but rather, from bad luck. Mr. Parker, you see, had loaned his riding boots, sombrero and chaps to none other than Chief of Police Hiserman who had failed, to date, to return them to the owner. Frantic calls were being made to find the chief and obtain the clothing, thus preventing a good citizen from, "languishing in the city bastile." *Salinas Journal, June 14, 1922.*

Domestic problems were nothing new to Salinas officers. Often, problems resulting in divorce actions were made public after court hearings. One local farmer of high standing in the socio-economic life of Salinas, filed suit against his wife of several years. Charging the woman with, "extreme cruelty," he cited her evil ways. During the previous four years of marriage, the woman had been attending classes and ball games, leaving her husband and two children at home alone. She had been attending these activities in Salinas and other surrounding cities, returning home drunk on at least one occasion. Furthermore, she apparently liked to shop and was guilty of "extravagance." The man asked for a decree of divorce and custody of the two children. *Salinas Journal, April 27, 1922.*

By 1924, city traffic officers were issuing tickets to those who sped through the city or chose to leave their cars parked for longer than the allowed time. Traffic Officer Julien Moreau filed forty-five such citations during a one week period in November 1924. Chief Hiserman continued to lead the department with integrity. When a Japanese man tried to bribe Special Officer Noah Rader, Chief Hiserman arrested him in his "drink parlor" in Chinatown, charging him with bribery. Special Officer Rader had resisted several offers of protection money and had set up a trap for the businessman.

Trap doors of varying sizes were found in 1925, in the floor of 22 Market Street, the Oasis drinking establishment. Used to hide bottled goods, the trap doors were discovered by Chief Hiserman, along with Officer Tom Phillips, who also found illegal moonshine whiskey. The proprietor was charged with possession of illegal liquor and fined $400. A powerful Chinese secret society was broken up by Chief Hiserman when he arrested members in Salinas as they made their way in two cars towards San Francisco. They had stopped at the restaurant located at 7 Soledad Street. Hiserman waited outside the building and arrested the members of the Hop Sin Tong.

SEVEN

SPECIAL OFFICER NOAH RADER AND THE BATTLE OF MOSS LANDING

Noah H. Rader spent many years in the military as a member of the Twentieth Infantry and both the Twenty-Second Cavalry and the Fourteenth Cavalry. He served as a Rough Rider under Theodore Roosevelt during the Spanish-American War. Wounded during combat in the Philippines, he was a member of the United Veterans of the Republic. Born in Greenville, Tennessee in 1875, he moved to California in 1900, opening a furniture business in Salinas. Rader found additional work as a Special Officer with both the Salinas Police Department and the Monterey County Sheriff's Department. Both departments often hired extra officers to augment their forces on a regular basis.

When the Eighteenth Amendment was enacted in 1919, prohibition in the United States provided a perfect opportunity for many to make money breaking the law. On the evening of July 6, 1925, Special Officer Rader was on his way home from a meeting of the United Veterans of the Republic when he was summoned by Sheriff Oyer, who was forming a posse. Rader, on his way home to a wife and young daughter, met up with Chief Hiserman, also a posse member. Hiserman armed Rader with a sawed-off shotgun and personally loaded it to its capacity of six shots. Along with Butch Beevers, Henry Livingston, and several others Rader rode towards Moss Landing where it was thought rum runners were landing a shipment of whiskey.

Moss Landing was at the time, just a district located along a country road, but was valued by the rum-runners and bootleggers who found it a convenient harbor where they could off load their liquor. Earlier that evening, Traffic Officer Henry Livingston heard rumors that a shipment was to be landed on the night of July 6, 1925 and had traveled to Salinas to request additional help from the Sheriff Deputies Carl Abbott and Alex Borges. The three returned to the Moss Landing area, driving into a hayfield and parking in the haystacks. As the lawmen walked into the field, they came under fire. One bullet crashed through the windshield of the car, and fragments of glass cut Livingston's face. The officers were able to retreat and returned to Salinas for additional support.

The second trip to Moss Landing that night included Sheriff Oyer, Deputy George Holm, and the men from the Salinas Police Department, Chief Hiserman, Noah Rader, and Butch Beevers. Carl Abbott, Alex Borges and Livingston completed the posse.

Once at the site, officers gathered for a brief consultation, then separated into groups to approach the hayfield where it was thought the criminals were hiding. Sheriff Oyer was in the lead, with Rader following closely behind. Butch Beevers, who had been driven to the scene in a separate car by driver Billy Morrison, was a short distance behind the others.

Suddenly, from the dark came the cry, "Shoot em!" The run runners had seen the officers and with no further warning shots rang out. Machine gun fire came at the officers from all sides. Morrison, a cigarette in his mouth, found it shot right out of his lips. Sheriff Oyer fought with one suspect and attempted to arrest him, but he evaded by slipping out of his overcoat, pulling a gun and shooting the sheriff, making his escape. Beevers, hearing Sheriff Oyer cry out that he had been shot, started towards the fallen man, with Rader beside him. With machine gun fire all around, Beevers saw Special Officer Rader fall to the ground, hit by a bullet intended for Beevers. Finding Rader beyond help, Beevers continued on to Sheriff Oyer, pulling him back to safety and taking him to the Jim Bardin Hospital in Salinas. Livingston had been hit in the leg, but would survive.

Beevers later made the long trip back to Moss Landing, returning for the body of the fallen officer and taking him home to Salinas for the last time. When Beevers arrived in Moss Landing, he found Special Officer Noah Rader lying where he had fallen, shrouded in the mist of the fog. His gun was still clasped in his hands.

In response to the murder of Rader, National Guardsmen and police from Salinas and Watsonville rushed to the scene in Moss Landing. They patrolled until dawn, capturing four men and learning the incident had been an ambush.

The machine guns, rifles, and shotguns used by the criminals were protected by barricades and were located in four vantage points around the hayfield. It was clear by the placement of the weapons that an ambush had been planned and the intent was to kill all the members of the posse. The manhunt was successful and resulted in a number of arrests as Officer Rader's family made funeral arrangements.

The confession of a suspect in San Francisco, the commander of a large gasoline launch, provided further information about those responsible for the events that led up to the death of Noah Rader. In a ten page, typewritten confession taken by authorities in San Francisco, Eugene Koehler gave the details of the shipment that was to be off loaded that night and the names of those in both San Francisco and Monterey County who were responsible for the ambush.

Three warrants were issued, charging murder on July 14, 1925. Identifications had been made and suspects were talking. By July 15, 1925, federal agents arrived in Monterey County to begin investigating the alleged conspiracy violations of the federal prohibition laws. The coroner's jury issued a statement, proclaiming, "City and County officers in the future are to be properly equipped with armored cars and machine guns to adequately combat law breakers." It was learned that Rader had died fighting, his weapon containing only one round when recovered from his hands which still held it when his body was recovered.

In late November, the Preliminary Hearing began, with attorneys from San Francisco and Salinas representing the five men accused of murdering Noah Rader. There were clashes between the defense attorneys and witnesses over the theory that Rader had been killed by the posse members rather than the smugglers. It was learned that Rader had been summoned to duty by Sheriff Oyer with the words, "Hey, come on Rader." Beevers and Livingston testified as to how bullets started to fly when they approached the hayfield that night and how Rader had fallen, mortally wounded. With no felony murder rule, the case against one defendant was dismissed. He had not been present at the time the shots were fired, but would face federal conspiracy charges at a later date.

Rader's widow filed a claim with the State Industrial Accident Commission, winning a judgment which would be set aside when she could not produce a marriage certificate. Refiled on behalf of the minor daughter, Nellie Rader, an award of $5,000 was made ordering the county to pay. The county appealed, but the State District Court of Appeals upheld the decision, saying the words of Sheriff Oyer, "Hey, come on Rader," were sufficient to deem him a county employee at the time of his death. Nellie Rader was awarded $4,900.

The murder trial began in Monterey County in 1926, with one hundred potential jurors called. By March 3, 1926, eleven men and one woman, along with several alternates, sat in the jury box. Only six jurors remained from the original jury pool. Over more than three weeks, twenty-six witnesses testified, some more than once and twenty exhibits were entered into evidence. Ill feelings arose between the prosecutor and one of the defense attorneys. The two men had come to blows in the courtroom during the preliminary hearing and twice had to be separated by Judge Wallace and Butch Beevers. The judge threatened them both with arrest if they continued. There were allegations of police misconduct, prosecutorial fraud, and witness coaching. District Attorney Warth had to take the stand to deny the allegations.

The trial was expensive, costing the county $785 in the first ten days. The prosecution asked for the death penalty on St. Patrick's Day, and the defense called Butch Beevers, the "hero of the Battle of Moss Landing," believing he had testified truthfully to all he saw and did on the night of July 6, 1925. It was a terrible disappointment for the District Attorney when the judge was forced to declare a mistrial when the jury was hopelessly deadlocked, six for guilt and six for acquittal. A new trial date was quickly set and it was expected that trial would cost over $2,000. The second trial was to end as the first, in a hopeless deadlock, this time ten for acquittal and only two for guilt. District Attorney Warth, devastated with the inability of the jury to accept and understand the evidence, asked the judge for guidance and help in filing a motion for dismissal. He had worked for over one year to bring the men responsible for the murder of Special Officer Rader to justice. Feeling he had presented all possible evidence to two juries, he felt the jurors were unable to believe either the officers who were at the scene or the accomplices to the crime who had been granted immunity for their testimony. Judge Treat replied that he too, believed the evidence presented had shown the guilt of the men accused, but felt it was now in the best interest of the county to dismiss the charges, which he did at that time. Defendant Bube, who was thought to have fired the machine gun that had killed Rader, was freed only to be taken into custody by federal officers and transported to San Francisco to await trial on the federal conspiracy charges. Ed Ferris, the last remaining and only outstanding suspect, was captured during a gun battle with federal officers and received a serious gunshot wound to his hip. Any hopes of bringing him to Monterey County to stand trial on charges of murdering Rader were lost when doctors refused to allow him to travel. While Ferris awaited his turn in federal court, Bube pled guilty to the conspiracy charges and received only a sixteen month sentence. No one would ever serve a day in jail or prison for the murder of Special Officer Noah Rader.

The enforcement of the prohibition law cost the United States over one hundred fourteen million dollars. Three hundred thirty-five law officers died trying to enforce the unpopular Eighteenth Amendment. By 1933, when President Roosevelt signed the Twenty-first Amendment repealing prohibition, organized crime had been born, financed by the sale of illegal moonshine. Bootleggers who had learned to soup up their cars to run liquor without getting caught by the law were responsible for the stock car racing industry that led to America's largest spectator sport of this time, NASCAR. In fact, the first man to win the NASCAR race was Glen Dunaway, who drove a moonshine hauling car to the finish line for the win.

While other law enforcement officers from the Central Coast were killed trying to enforce the prohibition laws, Special Officer Rader, called to duty on a posse while on his way home, is apparently the only Salinas officer to have died at the hands of smugglers while in service to both Salinas and the county. His wife and daughter stayed in the area after his death and Nellie Pearl Rader, who was finally awarded the $4,900 judgment that had been appealed by the county, remained here until her death in 1992. Special Officer Rader lies in a grave in the cemetery on Romie Lane alongside his wife, with only a small headstone giving his name and the date of his death. His memory and story will live on as part of the history of the department. The officers of the Salinas Police Department honor this brave soldier and lawman by acknowledgement of his death at the hands of smugglers. Special Officer Rader's contribution as an officer who protected the citizens of Salinas and Monterey County will not be forgotten by the men and women of the Salinas Police Department who are walking in his footsteps eighty years after his death.

EIGHT

A Metropolitan Salinas

1925 was a challenging year for Salinas officers. With the Battle of Moss Landing heading into the trial stage, police continued to fight a variety of crime in town. Lara's Tamale Parlor, located at 59 Soledad Street, was the scene of arrests for liquor possession. Lara pled guilty to the charge and paid a $300 fine. From arrest to payment was less than one hour. Chief Hiserman had been accompanied by Officers Tom Meek, Frank Fontes and O.D. Eastwood.

Officers pose in Chinatown
Courtesy of the Monterey County Historical Society

Not one to wait for crimes to come to him, the chief was out and about the town when he came upon a man with a handbag belonging to someone else.

Taking the man in front of Justice W.F. Buttle, the man pled guilty to vagrancy. The suspect, a lettuce buyer from Los Angeles, was in the company of a female drug addict. Both were "sent up" for thirty days. *Salinas Daily News, July 1925.*

Traffic was by far, the hottest topic of discussion in Salinas. With both city and now, state traffic officers pulling cars over for violations, citizens complained. The editorial in August 1925 was entitled, "The Traffic Cop," and suggested the motorist look upon traffic officer as a friend rather than enemy. "He is frequently the subject of abuse and insult: he risks his life a hundred times a day." *Salinas Daily News, August 13, 1925, Editorial.*

The next day, the newspaper ran a story on the most often used excuses given to officers making traffic stops.

1. "My speedometer must be wrong, officer."
2. "My mother, (father, aunt, sister,) is dying."
3. "I'm trying to keep a date with my wife."
4. "My house is on fire."
5. "I didn't see any speed signs."
6. "I thought all officers rode on motorcycles."
7. This car won't do 40 miles. Try it yourself."
8. "I have an important operation to perform."
9. "I was running short of gas and trying to hurry to the next filling station." *Salinas Daily News, August 14, 1925.*

It was during 1925 that the Board of Supervisors voted for a change in the way traffic officers were hired and worked. Julien Moreau, who had been the Traffic Officer for Salinas for two years was promised a contract with the State Motor Vehicle Department. Moreau, who had served the city so well, was made Captain of the newly formed county-state traffic force. Henry Livingston, the other traffic officer who had been shot during the Battle of Moss Landing, was also to take a new position. Moreau resigned from the Salinas department after the Big Week Fiesta. His services and those of the other traffic officers were badly needed during the rodeo season. That same night, at the meeting of the city council, the pay of Special Police Officers, hired for events like the Rodeo or as needed, was raised to $5.00 per day. The regular officers for the Salinas Police Department were granted a two week vacation following the Rodeo.

Although traffic problems were rampant, burglaries were something of an epidemic. Chief Hiserman received a phone call telling him someone was in a building under construction. He, along with assisting officers, arrived just in time to see Jack Smith, a local barber, leaving the area on his bicycle. They stopped him and found him to have a sack of nails. Friends were surprised to hear the popular barber had stolen the nails and surmised he must have been the "unfortunate victim of kleptomania." *Salinas Daily News, August, 1925.*

It was during this time that the very first appeal was filed in small claims court. The filing of the appeal was of sufficient note and interest to have an article about the suit in the newspaper of the day. That same day in August 1925, two well-known detectives from San Francisco were in town. They were here to confer with our local constable, Butch Beevers. Beevers refused to talk to the press, telling them only that the secret would make for sensational news at a later date.

A man incapacitated by the consumption of Jamaican ginger jag booze was charged with drunk and disorderly conduct after he was found lying on the sidewalk of Gabilan Street. Another man committed suicide by drinking cyanide and was cremated according to his wishes.

Tom Phillips, the popular and long time officer for Salinas, had long coveted the sheriff's job. He announced his campaign and was said to have a great deal of relevant experience. Just days before his announcement, Officer Phillips had arrested John Haines, thought to be the elusive "Jack the Strangler." The serial killer was wanted for the murders of several women in the San Jose area.

Butch Beevers had made a reputation for himself not only as a policeman, but as a founder of, and director of the Rodeo. So competent was Beevers that he was offered a contract with the Fresno rodeo, which he accepted. Butch Beevers was still with the department that year and went after Paul Doll when he fled to San Luis Obispo, bringing him back to face charges of passing worthless checks.

Butch Beevers with his favorite dog
Courtesy of the Beevers family

Chief Hiserman and Officer C.C. Rogers arrested two men who had been committing burglaries throughout the city. Elections were held in September 1926, for both state and county positions. Sheriff Oyer remained popular and Officer Phillips would not win that race. It was a close count for District Attorney, and Albert Warth held a small lead over Russell Scott. The judge in the Moss Landing case ran unopposed and kept his place on the bench. Butch Beevers easily won reelection as the constable for the Alisal District. Former city traffic officer Julien Moreau, made captain of the newly founded county-state traffic squad, was demoted for unknown reasons late in 1926 and replaced by Henry Livingston, one of the men shot during the Battle of Moss Landing.

On September 9, 1927, suspect Lowell Wade led a group of eight inmates in a jailbreak. After beating jailer Ralph Plaice, the group stole a vehicle owned by the Sheriff, Carl Abbott, making a clean getaway. Plaice, badly injured, played dead to avoid further injury. Plaice eventually recovered and went on to become an officer for Salinas. *Salinas Daily Index, January 1927.*

Four boys serving time in the detention ward under the courthouse dug a tunnel and were within hours of escape when they were caught. The jail was full of hobos, twenty-one of them, when Hiserman brought four more in from the railroad yards. Chief Hiserman and C.C. Rogers then raided a shack in the alley off El Sausal, between Monterey and Pajaro Streets. Neighbors complaining of an "all-night rumpus" had contacted the station. The lawmen arrested all three found in the shack, charging them with possession of liquor and obscene photographs and vagrancy. Two days later, all three pled guilty to their various crimes. The liquor possession resulted in a $100 fine, the obscene photos and vagrancy charges, $25 each. Hiserman was on a roll and began a campaign to rid the city of "undesirables." According to news reports in 1927, most of the unwanted folks were "in the Mexican section of the Oriental quarter." Scores of "drug habitues" were arrested and sent to county jail and others left town with suspended sentences. It was believed that much of the crime in Salinas was due to the "lewd women," the drug users and those who were attracted to the area by them. Following the clean-up, it was expected that peace disturbances and petty thefts would decline considerably. *Salinas Daily Index, February 1927.*

It was during this period that C.H. Andresen, a veteran officer since 1915, and a former acting chief resigned. To replace him, the council chose T.E. Phillips, another former officer who had resigned a year earlier in order to run for sheriff. Phillips would stay with the department for many years and feature prominently in the history of Salinas and the police department.

During the 1920s, the biggest crime problem was drunkenness. Officers still had no training, nor did they have much equipment. In January 1928, a new set of rules was imposed on the officers. Previously, officers were fairly independent of supervision while on duty. Beginning in 1928, police were required to "report their whereabouts" at all times, whether on duty or off and to be available for emergency calls. Officers were also ordered to "keep their uniforms and equipment in proper condition." The new rules included requiring officers to report to the office when going on duty or off duty, and to "scan the bulletin board for information of happenings prior to taking post." It was Chief O.M. Hiserman who implemented these new rules under the direction of V.J. Barlogio, the police commissioner.

Shortly after receiving their new rules, the four Salinas officers were called into the office of Chief Hiserman. That day, officers C.C. Rogers, Frank Fontes, Tom Phillips, and O.E. Eastwood were confronted by the chief who demanded they turn over their badges. Placing their badges on the chief's desk, thinking a big shake-up was in store, the officers watched the chief break into a laugh as he reached behind the counter and presented each officer with a new, numbered seven-point star. The *Salinas Daily Index* reported the police force was, "becoming more metropolitan."

The department began to grow during the prohibition years, a result of the need to curtail the liquor trade. On March 12, 1928, Officers Lapierre, Rodgers, and Moronu raided a restaurant at 47 Soledad Street, seizing a gallon jug of "brew" which they threw over a fence.

By late in the year 1928, reports of drunkenness and disorderly conduct were foremost in the news. Officer Fontes and Sergeant of Police Marcel Lapierre made arrests of soldiers and others in violation of the local laws. Robberies were also common. In June 1928, three men were captured by Officer Frank Fontes and Constable L.A. Beevers on Lake Street twenty minutes after robbing a man near the El Sausal railroad crossing. The three robbers, Gonzales, Sambranno, and Martinez, pled guilty and were sent to San Quentin to serve indeterminate sentences.

Injuries to officers were common. Traffic Officer Frank Gruver was badly injured while attempting to make an arrest at Central Park. Confronted by a man and a large crowd, Officer Gruver was badly beaten with a billy while attempting to arrest the Jacobsen brothers. The brothers were eventually arrested and charged with felony assault. Gruver's injuries led to hospitalization in the Murphy hospital, with wounds to his face and hands.

There were not many houses built in the city in the 1920s. Teachers earned an average annual salary of $2,400. One house, listed as having seven rooms and being on a paved street, was offered for sale at $3,550. The Salinas Rodeo had an attendance of four thousand people in 1912, and had grown to over thirty-five thousand by 1929. It was a major part of life in the city. The first airport was established, a new post office built, and the old city hall was sold during the 1920s. A new firehouse was built, and there was talk of a highway bypassing the downtown area. Merchants wanted the traffic to go through the city, afraid their business would decline. The decision was made to widen Monterey and Main Streets.

The unexpected fall of the stock market in October of 1929, led to the Great Depression, and forced many millions of Americans into instant poverty and joblessness. For five years, businesses failed, homes were lost, and starvation was common. President F.D. Roosevelt's New Deal eventually led the way for recovery from the economic devastation in America.

The end of the 1920s brought additional officers to Salinas. Officer C.C. Rogers and Traffic Officer Bernard Abel joined the force. Without any pension plan or insurance, officers in Salinas formed the Benevolent Association of the Salinas Police Department. The main objective of this organization was to accumulate funds which could be used to assist or care for sick or injured officers. Honorary presidents were named for the organization. They included the Mayor, D.A. Madeira, Police Commissioner Vic J. Barlogio, Police Judge Ernest Bedolla and City Attorney Russell Scott. Officers of the Benevolent Association were all members of the Salinas Police Department. C.C. Rogers was elected president; O.D. Eastwood, Vice-President; M.A. Lapierre, Secretary-Treasurer; and T.E. Phillips, Sergeant-at-Arms. A grand ball was planned for February 9, 1929, as a fundraiser for the organization. Efforts to advertise the event were led by Chief Hiserman, who along with Lapierre, Rogers, and Phillips, left town in a new Oakland, All-American six sedan to travel over 350 miles in surrounding counties, distributing window cards advertising the Policeman's Ball.

With the addition of the "Black Maria," officers were now able to transport fourteen to twenty "guests" at a time to the city jail. The new van, a Chevrolet six-chassis wagon, brought the Salinas department up to the category of a "metropolitanized" department, according to the news stories of the day. The ability to transport more prisoners enabled officers to make more arrests and the police judge to fine more offenders.

The early part of 1930 brought arrests for vagrancy by Officers Fontes and Phillips. They rounded up men from the depot area and Chinatown. The only woman to spend the beginning of the year in custody was Betty Davis, arrested at 34 California Street. Several months later, Trigg Phillips would investigate the burglary of Roosevelt School.

Robberies and traffic accidents continued to shock officers and citizens into the 1930s. Mrs. Abbott owned and operated a malt-syrup shop at 351 Main Street. She was gagged, bound hand and foot, and made to lie in a back room while two men rifled through the cash register after threatening to kill her. Officers also had their hands full with violent drunks who were often arrested for disturbing the peace. One man took his anger out on the city jail's patrol wagon, breaking the porthole window. Pedestrian injuries, multiple vehicle crashes, and drunk drivers were also the cause of many serious injuries and deaths. Some were purely accidental. Off duty Captain F.D. Fontes struck a young boy who ran out in front of his car at Capitol and Market Streets. During these early years, it was common for injured people to be transported to the hospital in a police car or the vehicle which had hit them. Witnesses stated the accident was unavoidable as the boy had run out in front of the officer's car. Captain Fontes, who knew the neighbor boy, was said to be "shaken with grief" over the incident.

Two men registered at the Hotel Cominos in February 1929, tried to rob the hotel. They succeeded only in giving the bellboy a serious beating with a blackjack before escaping down the fire escape. They were never caught.

State Traffic Patrolman Karl Lauridsen had just finished a night of relief duty for his friend, Officer Earl Griffin and had parked his roadster in front of his home at 406 Soledad Street. Hearing his roadster start up just as he got in bed, he redressed and got onto the trail of the thief. The city was quickly cordoned off by Salinas officers, sheriff's deputies, and state traffic officers. The suspects escaped the Salinas area and made it to San Jose where police shot the tires out of Lauridsen's vehicle, apprehending the crooks .

NINE

CHIEF GEORGE GRIFFIN AND HIS MEN

Chief George Griffin

George Griffin was appointed Chief of Police in April 1930. A smooth transition between Griffin and Hiserman was due to Hiserman continuing with the department as Captain of Detectives. The two men were shown shaking hands as they discussed their new jobs. After nineteen years of service, many as chief, Hiserman, who had become an expert in fingerprinting and forgery, wanted a chance to build a detective bureau that would be modern and efficient. He began his first day at his new job by asking for the installation of "vis-a-film" so that he could begin a rogues gallery to help officers identify crooks. Hiserman, who had served twice as constable of Alisal township, as a police officer, as chief and in other capacities in his five decade career, was to continue as a law enforcement officer until only months before his death in 1952. He was a member of the local peace officer's association and a past president of the International Footprinters. Officers Adcock and Ray McIntyre were among the men who served as pallbearers at his funeral. He had lived at 127 Pajaro for most of his adult life, having been born on the family ranch which was the site of the Spreckels Sugar Company. His death certificate would sum up his life's work as it listed his occupation simply as, "Police Officer."

Chief Griffin openly declared war on the underworld of Salinas stating, "Crime in this city must be curbed and it is going to be curbed." *Salinas Index Journal, May 1930.* He ordered his officers to visit all underworld locations looking for burglars and other criminals. Salinas was experiencing a wave of both residential and commercial burglaries.

Meanwhile, newly named Captain of Detectives Orley M. Hiserman was given the honor of being asked to speak at the annual convention of the California State Association for Criminal Identification. Choosing his topic carefully, the experienced lawman would speak on "The Detective in the Small City Police Department." While Hiserman planned his speech, Chief Griffin ordered his officers to try to find parking places on a Saturday night in downtown Salinas. Cutting the distance cars could be parked from a fire hydrant, the chief and his officers "found" an additional twelve spaces. Ralph Plaice, the officer who had previously worked in the jail where he was attacked and seriously injured, was now a Sergeant. Along with Captain Fontes, he arrested Harry Killgore for possession of narcotics. Killgore would make a name for himself by pleading to be admitted to a state hospital for treatment for his ten year addiction.

Chief Griffin told the city council his biggest problems at the present time in mid-1930 were those of regulation of traffic through the city and overtime parking. A sub-committee was appointed to study the issue, and the chief provided the names of fifty business people and clerks who were violating the law on a daily basis. Along with traffic and overtime parking, the chief complained that people were double-parking, causing additional traffic hazards. The topic was the subject of much discussion, bringing shoppers, business owners, truck drivers and others to the council meeting.

A photo taken in 1931 showed the department of twelve officers in addition to the chief. The department had many familiar names, such as Chief Griffin, Captain of Detectives O.M. Hiserman, and Patrolman C.C. Rogers. Other well known officers included O.D. Eastwood, Trigg Phillips, Harry Stevens, Marcel Lapierre, Barney Abel, Frank Fontes, Tom Philips, Walter Emery and Ralph Plaice. Several pictured in the photo were to become police chiefs during their career with Salinas. Many, proud of their careers, would die in the upcoming years. Butch Beevers, who had been with the department in the early years, died in 1933. His death certificate listed his occupation as peace officer and constable.

1931 Photo of SPD
Four would become chiefs of police
Courtesy of SPD

C.C. ROGERS

Patrol Officer C. C. Rogers had come to Salinas in 1920, where he married and had a family. His first wife was a long-time resident of Salinas and the family lived at 27 Maple Street. C.C., as he was known to his friends, ran the old Thrift Garage located at the underpass where Bataan Park was built. With his garage gone, Columbus Campbell Rogers, who preferred to be called C.C. for obvious reasons, went to work for Southern Pacific Railroad. But, dissatisfied with the work, he became a city fireman for a time. He transferred to the police department, where he would work for many years while wearing Badge #1. A WWI war veteran, Rogers organized the famous "Musketeers," a skeet and trap team that won competitions throughout Northern California. He remarried after the death of his first wife and moved to Texas, where he lived until his death in 1962.

His body was returned to the city he had served for so many years and in so many ways. He lays at rest in the Garden of Memories.

The chief, suspicious of two Filipino men trying to trade a diamond ring for a used car, assigned Rogers and Hiserman to investigate, but went himself to the car dealership. Interrupting the suspect in the middle of his attempt to swap the ring for a car, Chief Griffin arrested one man while Rogers and Hiserman arrested the other at a restaurant. It wasn't until the jewelry was recovered and the two men under arrest that Mrs. Bullene reported the theft of her property.

The biggest and most daring robbery in the city's history during the 1930s took place in May 1931. Ray Duddy was the manager of the Fox Theater and was bound hand and foot, threatened with death, and forced into a darkened aisle in the theater. The suspects had pointed a gun at Duddy, who was able to make his way outside the theater where two passersby were able to free him and to contact police. The robbers got away with $1,052, but missed a bag containing $348 in coins. Chief Griffin requested assistance from the sheriff and highway patrol, and officers swept through the city in an attempt to locate the dangerous suspects. The robbers were able to escape the massive manhunt. Six years earlier, thieves had managed to steal the safe from the theater. Thirteen hundred dollars was lost in that burglary. The safe was found empty under the Merced River Bridge.

Chief Griffin delivered the annual report of police activities in January 1932, for the year 1931. There were two arrests for murder, one arrest for attempted murder, eleven arrests for burglary, and an increase of felony arrests for the year. There were 2,645 misdemeanor arrests and 1,596 citations and arrests for traffic violations. Other miscellaneous arrests included those for gambling violations, liquor possession, disturbing the peace and petty theft. These were staggering statistics for the twelve man department of 1931.

The Great Depression of the 1930s forced many Midwesterners west. Hundreds settled in "Little Oklahoma," on the east side of Salinas. Hebbron Heights was the first housing development. Amid strikes and the labor problems, larger public works programs managed to get passed. This neighborhood would be the start of the Alisal district which would be the subject of annexation many years later.

Patrolman Robert Cashen was kidded by his fellow officers who told him they were going to enter him in the Olympic trials after he nabbed a shoplifter following a foot race downtown in 1932. The National Dollar Store was located at 257 Main Street and was the scene of the shoplifting of seven pair of stockings. A clerk rushed out to the street screaming at Officer Cashen, who then began his foot pursuit of the suspect. Charles Patten had a half block head start when Officer Cashen started to run north. The suspect vanished behind the Jeffery Hotel at the corner, but Officer Cashen continued. The officer slowly narrowed the suspect's lead until he overtook him and arrested him on Pajaro Street, three blocks from the scene of the crime.

CHIEF GRIFFIN'S DEMERITS

Thinking he could create a department full of integrity and ambition, Chief Griffin devised a plan whereby officers would be given demerits for breaches of conduct. With twenty-five demerits costing an officer one day's pay, twenty-five to thirty-five demerits costing two days' pay and so on, up until one hundred demerits costing six days' pay, he planned to hold practical and written tests to create an eligibility list for promotion. Keeping track of the demerits didn't keep officers and administrators from planning the annual ball. There was to be a Policeman's Ball on February 20, 1932, to be held at the Elks Hall. Salinas still had no pension system for officers and the Mayor urged citizens to support their police by attending the annual social event which benefited the Benevolent Association of Salinas Police Officers.

TRAFFIC OFFICER ABEL

Traffic Officer Barney Abel was seriously injured when a motorist failed to stop when Abel sounded his siren. Abel was following two vehicles on South Main near Chestnut Street. Another officer, Traffic Patrolman Harry Stevens witnessed the accident. The suspect vehicle was traveling about fifty miles per hour with Abel in pursuit. One car stopped at the sound of the siren, the other continued. Abel skidded thirty-eight feet before hitting the first vehicle and smashing his right leg. Had the second vehicle pulled to the curb when the siren was sounded, the accident could have been avoided. Abel was taken by a Struve and Laporte ambulance to Franklin Hospital in San Francisco. Accompanied by Chief George Griffin and his parents, Abel would eventually lose his leg, going through two separate amputation surgeries, but returned to active duty as a police officer. He was, according to the newspaper story at the time, "One of the most popular officers on the local police force." *Salinas Daily News, May 22, 1932.*

Officer Abel recounted many stories to his daughter, Suzanne and her husband, Frank Shute, a Fish and Game Warden. Suzanne recalls her father telling about the time he found a hobo passed out on the train tracks. He used his nightstick to beat on the man's feet, trying to roust him, but the man was out cold. Dragging him into the back seat of the patrol car, Abel started off towards the department. Suddenly, the man awakened and grabbed Officer Abel by the throat, trying to strangle him. Without a radio, the officer had no way to summon help, but thought to activate the car's siren. He was being strangled when a passerby opened the back door to the police car and slugged the drunk in the face. Officer Abel never knew who had come to his assistance.

In another incident, Officer Abel told his family that the department was the scene of its own shooting that day. An officer had gone to use the bathroom. Somehow, his gun dropped to the floor and it went off, sending a round through the wall, into the next room. Miraculously, the bullet just narrowly missed hitting the police chief. Officer Barney Abel left the area for Clear Lake and died in the 1970s. He is buried in Lakeport, at a cemetery near his mother and father's burial place.

Marcel LaPierre was a Lieutenant the day a scraggly looking kitten wandered into police headquarters. LaPierre immediately adopted the three week old kitten, naming him Luke and proclaiming the animal as the department mascot. Within the hour, Luke was provided with a saucer of milk, and gum drops and cough drops and pistol cartridges to play with. The officers were taken by surprise when a small girl walked into the department asking if anyone had seen her kitten. Before returning the kitten, they verified her story of ownership with her mother. Lt. LaPierre growled an order, "Hereafter, we'll have no more mascots, unless it's a glass-eyed owl – something that can't put a guy's heart through the wringer. Whadda they think we're runnin' anyway, the city pound?" *Salinas Daily News, May 24, 1932.*

In 1933, the Salinas Brewery stood on North Main Street. It was the scene of a robbery and threats in July that year. Masked bandits had hidden behind a machine with their nickel-plated pistols and jumped E.E. Smith, the sixty-two year old night engineer, ordering him to, "Reach for the sky, Pop," according to the *Salinas Index, July 19, 1933.* Using telephone wires, they gagged him, smashing open the safe with a sledge hammer to take the cash. After an hour of struggling he loosened the gag and was able to call for help. Chief Griffin dispatched four officers to investigate. They found the robbers had been limited to only $20 in proceeds for their trouble. The brewery had been receiving racketeering threats over the past months.

The California Rodeo brought over 40,000 visitors to Salinas in July 1933. Big Week included round ups of more than just livestock. Salinas police arrested forty-six men on various charges during the weekend of July 24, 1933. At the head of list for charges was drunkenness, with twenty-one arrests. Another nineteen arrests were made for disturbing the peace. Regular Salinas officers received the assistance of twenty special officers who had been stationed around town and at the Rodeo grounds.

The high number of commercial and residential burglaries in the early 1930's was blamed on police administration and in January 1934, the chief was told to "Capture Crooks or Quit." *Salinas Californian, January 13, 1934.* A delegation led by Police Commissioner J. Mitchell went to demand the chief's badge, calling for his resignation. Dozens of skylight burglaries plagued many downtown areas in all cities in California and many were quick to rush to the defense of a chief who had a good record of evidence collection and crime fighting. The accusations would die down as the year progressed and plans for the Seventh Annual Police Ball were in the making by February 1934. All the officers, from the newest patrolman to the chief himself, headed the committees and planned to make the ball, "the most outstanding in the history of the annual affair." *Salinas Californian, February 7, 1934.*

EVERALL ADCOCK

Everall Adcock served seventeen years with the Salinas Police Department as a motor officer. He retired as a Captain in 1945, and when interviewed thirty-three years after his retirement, told reporter Ward Bushee of the *Salinas Californian* that he was concerned about the lack of respect shown to officers in today's department. On a four-speed Harley-Davidson, Adcock could jump a curb to chase a suspect, something no patrol car could do. After retiring from the police department, Adcock ran Cap's Salinas Club, where many police officers, District Attorneys and judges would come to get the "Blue Plate Special." Later, taken over by his son, the club's name would be changed to "Cap's Saloon." When Adcock applied for a position to lead the military police department for the Army, he received letters of recommendation from many local dignitaries, the city manager and Chief Lapierre. He was subsequently given a pass that allowed him into the Salinas Army Air Base, where he and his car could patrol at any time. Adcock was active in the California Police Officer's Association and was president of the local officer's association when he worked at the Salinas Police Department. As president of the Central Coast Counties Peace Officer's Association, Adcock personally invited FBI Director Hoover to speak to the group and received a personally signed response from the director.

Even after his retirement, as he ran his bar, Adcock had a permit to carry a gun. In 1977, while walking by a jewelry store, he heard a woman screaming and saw her struggling inside the store. Pulling his revolver, Adcock went in and told the man to put his hands behind his head. SPD officers arrived very quickly and the suspect was turned over to them. Subsequent investigation showed the man had been looking at wedding rings and putting them in his coat pocket. The female clerk had confronted the man and grabbed the lapels of his jacket, pulling him towards her and reaching into his pockets, recovering the rings.

Everall Adcock, (center) at one of the first FBI training classes in Salinas - Courtesy of The Monterey County Historical Society

THE MULE AND OFFICER ADCOCK

In May 1935, Pound master James Gaynor resigned, leaving the department with no animal control system. Everall, "Mule Skinner" Adcock was on duty on May 7, 1935, when a report came into the department of a mule in a citizen's back yard. Traffic Officer Adcock was detailed to the scene where he found a long-legged Arkansas mule jumping around the yard. The department's desk sergeant got the first call from Officer Adcock fifteen minutes after he had been detailed. The officer, reporting he could not locate the owner, wanted to know what to do with the active mule. He was told to find the owner and began to lead the mule from door to door in an attempt to locate the owner. Another fifteen minutes passed before the second call to the department. According to Officer Adcock, the "blankety-blank mule" was jumping all over the place. Adcock could be heard over the phone, shouting, "Whoa, whoa." The desk sergeant suggested Adcock tie up the mule while he went to locate the owner. Fifteen minutes later, the third and most frantic call was received at the department. The officer could not find a rope and was heard screaming, "Whoa, ouch! He just bit me!" The desk sergeant suggested Adcock ride the mule back to the department, but Adcock wasn't having any of that. Fearing he would be seen by someone, he declined that suggestion. The desk sergeant told Adcock to ride his motorcycle and pull the mule along, but that, too, was vetoed. Screaming for help over the phone, Adcock continued to wrestle with the mule until the desk sergeant came up with an idea. The former Pound Master had been paid $2.50 for every stray dog caught. The desk sergeant suggested Officer Adcock contact the two young boys who had reported the animal in their yard and offer them $2.50 to find the owner. Wondering why it had taken the desk sergeant so long to come up with a plan that sounded good, Adcock did just that. Returning to the police department, he collapsed in a chair and let everyone know how he felt about mules. *Salinas Californian, May 8, 1935.*

*Traffic Officers Adcock, Smith and an unknown officer
Courtesy of Appleby's Restaurant*

By 1936, the rodeo had become big business for Salinas. Police Judge P.J. McLaughlin ordered all businessmen and police officers to attire themselves appropriately in what he described as, "large sombreros, colored shirts, ten-gallon hats, blue jeans and boots." The police department objected to the orders, but apparently feared the judge's wrath as he had made public his intent to "duck in a tub" anyone who did not meet his expectations. The judge was photographed behind a police patrol wagon as he made his orders clear in an article in the *Salinas Daily News, 1936.*

In September 1936, George Griffin was Chief of Police in Salinas when the Salinas-Watsonville Lettuce Strike began. Salinas became a war zone overnight as strikers clashed with police and lettuce growers in attempts to prevent produce from being shipped out of the area. Law enforcement was overwhelmed and Sheriff Carl Abbott put out an order that all able-bodied men over the age of fifteen were to report to the jail for assignment. A street battle on Gabilan Street left several victims with gunshot wounds and other serious injuries. Ray Cato, then chief of the CHP, requested the National Guard be sent in to help stop the rioting. Tempers flared as police, under orders of the sheriff, tried to disperse rioters using tear gas against men armed with pipes, sticks and guns. Citizens were warned to stay off the streets for police could not guarantee their safety. Downtown Salinas was the scene of hand to hand combat between the newly deputized citizens alongside deputies and officers who remained outnumbered. On September 15, 1936, three hundred infantrymen arrived in Salinas to help restore order. Rocks were still being thrown at lettuce trucks trying to leave Salinas and heavy damage was done. Salinas patrolman Everall Adcock was injured in the fighting. Picketers were dispersed only after several tear gas canisters were thrown. During the strike, Colonel Sanborn coordinated all police activities for Monterey, San Benito, and Santa Cruz Counties. Chief Griffin was quoted in the newspaper with a grim prediction. "You must be prepared to defend this city right now. This thing isn't over yet. We have used the most peaceful and modern methods available for quelling violences, but these means won't be successful much longer. This is a most dangerous situation, more so than most of you realize." He continued, "These men, (the strikers), have been carried beyond the point of knowing where to stop by mob hysteria. The fight here has surpassed all expectations, beyond our normal defenses." *Salinas Index-Journal, November 1936.*

Strike Violence in Salinas in 1936
Courtesy of the Monterey County Historical Society

By the end of 1936, Chief Griffin had returned his focus to the traffic safety issues facing the city. He attended the annual meeting of the California Safety Council as both city and state attempted to make highways safer for citizens. The department was not without scandals and problems during these years. Chief George Griffin was sued for defamation by a local man who accused him of inappropriate conduct and public defamation resulting from an incident where the accuser's wife double parked in front of a Main Street hotel, honking her horn to get her husband's attention. The chief won that lawsuit, but problems escalated. Commercial burglaries in the downtown area caused wide concern among citizens and business owners. Gambling, and the associations of criminals connected to the gambling establishments, continued to be something the city council tried to eradicate by ordering police officials to make more arrests. Captain Frank Fontes resigned his rank in March 1931, asking to be reassigned to patrol duty. The unusual request, made public during a council meeting by the seven year veteran of the department, led to a $10 reduction in pay. At that time, a patrolman made only $10 less than a captain. Speculation about charges that Fontes was disobedient was not answered by Chief Griffin. While the chief continued to serve the department, his career was not to end gracefully.

TEN

THE LAPIERRE ERA

*Chief
Marcel Lapierre
1937-1943*

World news of the period included the explosion of the Hindenberg and the beginning of Hitler's reign. The city manager, Barlogio, continued to be a thorn in the side of the police. Citing advanced age, Barlogio requested Captain of Detectives O.M. Hiserman and T.E. Phillips be taken off regular assignment and given routine duties, with a corresponding decrease in salary from $190 per month to $150 per month. City attorney Russell Scott drew up papers for the disposition of the two officers, and Mayor Leach suggested the city establish a pension fund for the two ten year veterans of the force, stating they had, "passed the stage where they can efficiently pursue their duties." The department was further criticized for a "lack of uniform and standard organization in the police force with regard to hiring." There were no age qualifications, no height, weight or other prerequisites for prospective officers. Mayor Leach was of the opinion the department was simply inefficient and ordered an investigation by the city manager. *Salinas Index-Journal, June 13, 1937.*

In 1937, Chief Griffin was removed from office on the charge of insubordination, but was reinstated after a fifteen day suspension without pay. Three months later he was charged with unspecified misconduct and Marcel LaPierre was named as acting chief. A bitter power struggle would take more than one year to play out. Mayor Leach officially named LaPierre acting chief and elevated Officer Trigg Phillips to the position of Lieutenant. After the meeting, the city manager, citing his mistake, asked the city clerk to change the record to reflect the appointment for Phillips as being temporary only. Phillips told reporters his understanding was that his position would be permanent. Later articles indicate Phillips won that battle and the city clerk did not change the record to suit the city manager's request. Hearings continued, with Griffin asking the council to inspect his record as he fought the charges of incompetency, lack of efficiency, and failure to cooperate with city officials. The council unanimously agreed the chief should be removed for the betterment of the department, citing an instance of guns found in the city jail in prisoner's cells. The council met in a secret session and failed to make a record of the meeting in which they voted to request the resignation of the chief. The chief wanted a public hearing and questioned the motives of his accusers. Griffin had begun work as an investigator for the attorney-general's office while he stood accused of, "failing to conduct his department in an efficient manner." The chief fought the charges, stating they were unfounded, and that he had been, "too efficient in the enforcement of gambling laws." In a session that took less than fifteen minutes, the chief's removal was formalized and LaPierre became the next chief for Salinas. *Salinas Daily Index, October 26, 1937.*

The county courthouse was under construction during the 1930s and dedication took place in 1937. The courthouse was built on what had once been large, wild mustard fields, "a playground for games of cowboys and Indians" among the city youth, according to news articles regarding the opening. The county jail was located on the west end of the courthouse. The need for a new courthouse had come about after the mysterious burning of the original courthouse in 1877. Jesse Carr had donated the block to the county for one dollar.

Car crashes claimed thirty-six lives in Monterey County during 1936, and police were desperately seeking ways to lower the death and injury tolls for accidents, both in the city and on surrounding highways. Nearly daily articles detailed horrific injuries and showed photographs of wrecked cars and bodies strewn over the streets. Boy Scouts aided Salinas police by setting up at the main arteries for a traffic count. Police thought they could formulate a traffic plan that would move vehicles through business areas with less congestion. One thought was to eliminate left turns. The main problems with congestion were at Alisal and San Luis Streets and John and Main Streets. Robberies were also daily news as gunmen took advantage of the proximity of the downtown businesses to the railroad tracks and escape routes. Records of arrests show a total of forty-nine felony arrests, nearly two thousand misdemeanor arrests, and over thirty-five hundred traffic arrests for Salinas police in 1935-36. One murder was reported for 1935 and one for 1936. By 1936 and 1937 it was clear that the number of crimes in each category was rising.

With Griffin fired and LaPierre in the position of chief, crime continued within the city. More than one hundred arrests were made during the weekend carnival, with serious injuries incurred by several. A carnival employee, mad at a patron who was teasing the ponies, hit the patron over the head with a pipe after the man pulled a knife on the pony tender. Acting Chief of Police Trigg Phillips warned residents about illegal explosives and begged them to prevent injuries to children from fireworks. A daring commercial burglary at 226 Main Street was believed to be the work of professionals. After cutting a hole into the ceiling of a men's store, $2,000 worth of clothing and shoes were stolen. Skylights and holes cut through walls were also popular ways to burgle businesses. Officer Roy McKenney investigated one such case while Officers George Weight and Robert Cashen worked a second case.

Street peddlers and solicitors troubled the city. Chief Lapierre, Lt. Phillips, and Desk Sergeant Weight attended a county-wide meeting to discuss the problem in 1938. Officer Sheehy successfully arrested two hold-up men wanted for robbery on Bridge Street within fifteen minutes of their latest crime. One was sentenced to five years to life at San Quentin, the other to a five year stint.

A victim/witness in a daylight burglary in Chinatown was able to provide details about the taxi taken by the suspects after the crime. Captain Plaice and Officer Adcock obtained John Doe warrants, while Chief LaPierre learned the two men had taken the taxi to the Gilroy bus station. Learning the men had tickets on a bus leaving in thirty minutes, Sheriff Abbott and Chief LaPierre sped north in time to arrest the two men just before the bus left. Grilled by LaPierre, the two confessed fully. Gambling arrests and raids were also common. The Paradise, located at 4 Soledad Street and the Republic Hotel at 47 Soledad Street, were both the scene of raids where money, silver, and gambling equipment were confiscated.

Traffic continued to be a major problem for law enforcement, and during the rodeo festivities the department and Chief LaPierre appealed to the citizens to obey all laws and signals. Assisted by over thirty highway patrol officers, Salinas officers re-routed traffic and stood at every intersection during the running of the rodeo. During the rodeo burglaries were commonplace. The ransacking of a home on Auburn Street was interrupted by Officer Harry Stevens. As he investigated an open window, Officer Stevens found a burglar and ordered him to surrender. The man ran and the officer fired several warning shots over his head but lost the suspect in the dusk. Chief LaPierre and Officer Weight joined the search and found the suspect hiding behind bushes near the home he had burgled. He was later sentenced to one to fifteen years in Folsom. Sixteen others were arrested the same night for various charges, including a worthless check charge.

It was November 1938, when the FBI held its first class at the city hall. At the request of Chief LaPierre, the FBI had agreed to provide training to officers. The end of the 1930s found the department purchasing the first official vehicle with a one-way radio. FBI training continued for local officers and Hartnell College became the only school in California to offer a police academy course. Chief LaPierre was assisted in his duties by Desk Sergeant George Weight. Statistics for 1939 showed a total of 2,795 persons booked at the City Jail, a "substantial increase," according to the local newspaper. Of that number, 990 arrests were for disturbing the peace. Police had also begun the practice of collecting "blue cards" on suspicious individuals. These cards contained information about subjects involved in traffic accidents, peddling, solicitation, shoplifting and bad check writing.

There were funny stories to go along with the sad and violent daily work. Lt. Trigg Phillips was assigned to pick up a lost boy wandering at a local store. Returning to the police station to make calls about the boy, the Lieutenant was too busy to notice the boy playing with the equipment. As calls began to come into the police department from patrolmen seeing the flashing red beacon lights which were in place to call them to duty, it was learned the young boy had been playing with the light switch that operated the emergency response system of the time. Other officers and supervisors throughout the office kept getting mysterious phone calls that day until they found young Warren Irvine testing the telephone system in the building. It was a busy afternoon for officers who soon found the boy was missing from their care. Officer Harry Stevens was detailed to search for the three year old who was then taken to the juvenile detention facility until his mother was located.

POLICE DEPARTMENT ROSTER FOR 1939

A complete list of police department employees, along with all city employees, was listed in the newspaper in 1939. The list of names started with the chief and ended with the pound master:

Chief of Police Marcel LaPierre, Captain R.H. Plaice, Lt. Trigg Phillips, Desk Officers George Weight, B.I. Abel and William Atwood, Patrolmen O.D. Eastwood, L.T. Gillott, Ray McIntyre, R.M. McKenney, R.M. Cashen, T.E. Phillips, C.C. Rogers, and John Walls; Traffic Officers G. J. Sheehy, Harry H. Stevens, E.L. Adcock, A.W. Skillicorn and Rue Carley; Special Officers James A. "Al" Storm, and Mr. T.L. Miller, pound master. These men were instrumental in forming the "modern" police department of the 1940s and 1950s. All had or would make significant contributions to the people of Salinas, many were seriously injured and returned to work. They included the first father-son combination to serve the department and two men who would become important chiefs, George Weight and Ray McIntyre. O.D. Eastwood and Tom Phillips were first mentioned as officers as early as 1925. Chief LaPierre would become the first chief to hire a female officer. They were a formidable and hardworking group that would forge new ground in police work in the years to come.

In fact, when Don Bates of Centerville, California petitioned the city for permission to open a private patrol business in Salinas, City Manager Barlogio denied the request, saying clearly that the department was, "doing a good job and private patrol was not necessary." *Salinas Californian, August 22, 1939.* Obviously, his evaluation of the police department was correct as, on the night of September 24, 1939, there were no crimes reported and no names listed on the blotter at the station. This event must have been quite notable to have been published in the paper the next morning. What crime they could not prevent, the alert officers often solved quickly. Desk Officer William Atwood, reaching for a paper lost between the wall and a box, found two brand new watches. Two men and one woman had been arrested earlier on charges of shoplifting at a Main Street dress shop. Under arrest, they could not be identified by the jewelry store owner who reported the watches missing after the trio had been in custody for some time. Chief LaPierre solved the mystery, speculating the woman, who had been sobbing and leaning against the desk area, waiting to be searched near the desk, hid the watches while officers were busy with the male suspects. Police Judge P.J. McLaughlin gave the woman and her husband each a ninety day sentence in county jail. The other man was sentenced to thirty days. Upon their release, the trio was picked up by Vallejo officers who saw that they returned to the Bay Area to face shoplifting charges there. *Salinas Californian, October 12, 1939.*

Chief LaPierre, having received a number of complaints about flying embers from bonfires in the city, instructed officers to make courteous requests for citizens to refrain from burning on Mondays. This was so that the ashes and embers would not land on the "spotless linens hung out to dry." *Salinas Californian, October 22, 1939.*

The hard working officers of the night shift successfully ended a crime spree that had begun in Stockton. Night Captain Ralph Plaice, on foot patrol downtown, saw a suspicious young man holding his jacket pocket while locking his car. Taken into custody, a loaded revolver was found in his pocket. Finding he had two other partners in crime, Officers Sheehy and Al Storm began surveillance on the car and an area search for the missing men. Locating the two on a theater balcony, where they quickly dropped a .45 caliber weapon, they soon told officers the truth. Stealing a car in Stockton, then stealing license plates to go with it, they burglarized a service station to get cigarettes. Taking two more cars for parts and gas, they held up two women, stealing purses and diamond rings. Most of the loot was recovered by Salinas officers, including two diamond rings. The boys were turned over to the authorities in San Jose.

Judge McLaughlin signed fifteen bench warrants for citizens who refused to pay their traffic fines. The laws regarding traffic fines had changed and the $1 ticket received, could be increased to $5 or $10 if the person tore the ticket up or refused to pay it on time. Police also had the option of removing the car's license plates for such a violation. Revenue from fines had soared since the implementation of the new law. From fines of $38 in April 1939, to a whopping $359 in October, the message was clear. So intent on compliance with the law was the state, CHP officers operated a "ferry" system, delivering defendants from one county line to the next to get them to court in other cities. *Salinas Californian, November 16, 1939.*

Six Salinas officers attended a fingerprinting class put on by the FBI and held at the Santa Cruz Police Department in December, 1939. The first FBI class had been held in Salinas in 1938, Mr. Nat Pieper, the chief of the San Francisco FBI office presiding. The fingerprinting class students included Chief Marcel LaPierre, Sgt. George Weight, and Officers Sheehy, Adcock, Rogers and Cashen. Another class, to be held in Salinas, would begin early the following year. Pieper would also address the Central Coast Counties Peace Officers Association, speaking on sabotage and espionage investigations at the December meeting in Santa Cruz.

Officers Lloyd Gillott and O.D. Eastwood were on routine patrol in the Maple Park area when they came upon a man on Los Laureles Avenue at 2:30 a.m. in January, 1940. The man was in front of 14 Los Laureles, then the home of Judge Jorgensen. As officers approached and began to question the man, he told them he was walking home after being at a show and lived in Gonzales. He suddenly jumped back, pulled out a gun and told the officers to "Stick it up!" He began to fire point blank at the officers. O.D. Eastwood was holding a gas gun and tried to return fire, but the suspect fled on foot in the Maple Park area. Eleven shots were fired at the two officers, who gave chase through the neighborhood. The suspect jumped over fences onto Santa Lucia and then Carmel Avenue homes, and eventually got away. Neither officer was shot during the fray, but it was believed Officer Gillott may have wounded the man. A cartoon by Eldon Dedini, drawing the path of the chase, was published in the *Salinas Daily News* on January 22, 1940.

Police, Gunman in Shooting Fray

Prowler Shoots At Officers

Police Monday intensified their "shakedown" of Salinas after a gun battle early Sunday in which a prowler suspect made his get-away in a hail of lead after firing point-blank at Police Officers Lloyd Gillott and O. D. Eastwood.

The shooting started on the sidewalk in front of the home of Superior Judge H. G. Jorgensen, 14 Los Laureles avenue, where the officers had stopped in the prowl car to question a suspect about 2:30 a. m. Eleven shots were fired as the man made his getaway in the shrubbery at the Jorgensen home and the adjacent homes of Mr. Bruce Church, 8 Los Laureles avenue, Atty. John A. Murphy, Santa Lucia avenue, and Mr. Lester M. Tynan, Carmel avenue.

The officers came upon the suspect in front of Judge Jorgensen's home, stopping the police car at the curb as Officer Eastwood stepped out to question the man about his being there at that time of the night. The suspect told the officers he lived in Gonzales, had been to a show, was just walking around and had his car parked on the next street and was going home.

Suddenly he jumped back, whipping a pistol from his belt, and ordered the officers to "Stick 'em up!" firing point blank as he barked his command. Officer Eastwood, who was holding a gas club, fired the gas gun simultaneously with the youth's motion in going for his revolver. Both officers jumped aside, the shot passing between them as the youth broke around the shrubs in the Jorgensen driveway.

With the officers in pursuit among the shrubs, the gun-wielder fired twice over his shoulder before vaulting a five-foot wall between the Jorgensen home and the Church yard. Three of the officers' shots ricocheted from the driveway through the Jorgen-

See THUG, Page 10, Column 4.

THIS DIAGRAM by Eldon Dedini sketches the flight of a gunman who escaped in the darkness and shrubbery of Maple Park homes early Sunday in a running gun battle with Police Officers O. D. Eastwood and Lloyd Gillott. The officers stopped the prowler-suspect near the driveway at the home of Superior Judge H. G. Jorgensen. After firing point blank at the officers, the man fled behind bushes along the driveway, firing twice more at the pursuing officers. He vaulted a brick wall to the Bruce Church yard, and again to an adjoining garden, crossing behind the John A. Murphy home and over a fence to the Lester Tynan home, where he gave a whistle and disappeared. Both officers pursued the gunman to the Jorgensen driveway, and Officer Gillott circled around the Church home to Santa Lucia avenue but the suspect was lost in the heavy shrubbery. The policemen are shown in the inset, Officer Gillott, left, and Officer Eastwood.

Eldon Dedini's drawing of the path of the shooter appeared 1-22-40 in the SDN.

Later news articles detail good police work leading to the arrest of the suspect. A description had been provided by the two officers involved in the shootout. An off-duty officer, Officer R.M. McKenney, stopped at a drive-in market on Salinas Street near John and Clay, and noticed a suspicious subject matching the description. He followed the man to the rear yard of the Abbott house, where the officer called the station for assistance. Officer Robert Cashen responded and was able to arrest the suspect. Peter John Vanderbol made a full confession to the crime, along with many others. Officers Gillott and Eastwood positively identified the suspect. Mr. Vanderbol had conveniently kept a diary of his crimes, in which he noted dates and places he burgled.

BADGE #2

Tom Phillips, who had worn Patrolman's badge #2 since 1924, died after a long illness in 1940. Having lived in Monterey County since 1886, he was one of the first men to grow lettuce in the Salinas Valley and was the first driver of an automobile stage in California. Although he had been quite ill for some time, his position was kept open until his death. Throughout the last days of his illness, a patrolman remained on duty and at his side in the hospital to be near him and lend encouragement should he regain consciousness. Officer Phillips was keenly interested in conservation and belonged to a number of associations. He was survived by his wife and sons, and a number of relatives. One of his sons also became a Salinas police officer.

In other city news, Cartoonist Eldon Dedini prepared a cartoon of officers in class for the February 5, 1940, edition of the Salinas paper. Officers were getting ready to attend the second of the FBI courses conducted in Salinas for law enforcement from all over the state. The seventeen week course met at the city hall with more than forty-five officers attending. The peace officers meeting for the central coast counties area was changed to Tuesday nights from the regular Monday night meeting in order to avoid a conflict with the FBI school. Traffic Officer Gerald J. Sheehy of the Salinas Police Department was the association president at that time. The Central Coast Counties Peace Officer's Association represented agencies in Monterey, Santa Cruz and San Benito Counties. In 1940, they met at the Mission Ranch Club in Carmel.

There were glitches in the running of the police department. The time clock at the Salinas Police Department took a holiday in 1940, skipping the Fourth and dating booking sheets as July fifth, causing a bit of a delay in proceedings at the department that day. That didn't keep the officers from making arrests. During the July 22, 1940 weekend, officers made ninety-two arrests. Officer John Walls and others had their hands full with thefts, drunks, fights, and assaults. Still undermanned, the department added three new officers in October 1940. Mr. Marvin York, 28; and Mr. Glenn Smith, 31; and Mr. Olen Vansandt, 20, became "Special Officers" according to Chief Marcel LaPierre. York had formerly been the bartender at the Elks Club, and Smith was a former assistant coach. Mr. Vansandt was only twenty years old and had no work history, but had graduated from Salinas High and Salinas Junior College. According to

Chief LaPierre, the additional officers were needed because of the increased activity in the city resulting from the expansion of Ft. Ord. Assignments at the department were changed to reflect the addition of new positions. Mr. William Atwood, day clerk, was changed to the 3:00 p.m. to midnight shift. Mr. Vansandt took over the day shift and Officer John Walls was assigned to the desk midnight to 8:00 a.m., in place of Officer Barney Abel, who was moved to days to operate the three-wheel motorcycle put in place for checking parked cars. Sgt. George Weight continued in his daytime duties in charge of the office. New Officers York and Smith, along with Vansandt, increased the number of officers in Salinas to twenty-three men.

Officers E.L. Adcock and Gerald Sheehy chased a speeder who tried to outdistance the officers and instead ended the chase in a spectacular crash. The suspect's car, doing at least seventy- five miles per hour failed to make the right angle turn at the end of Central Avenue and overturned after bouncing upwards at least twenty-five feet. Officers were quite surprised that the suspect was able to exit the vehicle and survived with no injuries.

LaPierre and his officers kept crime at bay during 1940. Credited with the proactive results from increased enforcement, LaPierre's department had a thirty-two percent increase in traffic citations and a twenty percent increase in the number of criminal reports filed over the statistics from 1939. Arrests totaled 3,783 for the year and traffic citations were a phenomenal 8,035. Five offenders were sent to state prison and seven hundred ten did county time. Police were proud of their new FBI approved shooting range, located in Toro Park. Chief Marcel LaPierre knew that firearms training was important to his men. Captain Ralph Plaice, the former jailer who had been beaten during an escape at the jail, made the silhouettes for the targets. Traffic Officer Rue Carley was photographed firing at the course and Traffic Officer Barney Abel, one of the best shots in the department, also made the paper. Lloyd Gillott had the highest score, a 97.6. The course, set up by the officers themselves, started from a seven-yard line and had to be completed within six minutes. With practice, the average scores were rising. There were two new weapons for the men to use. One, an H-R. Reising machine gun, was capable of firing up to five hundred rounds per minute. Officers also had new rifles and shotguns. *Salinas Californian, October 12, 1941.*

October was a busy month for officers who took seven hundred forty-three reports and made one hundred seventy-nine arrests. Four hundred twenty-seven traffic citations were issued. The city council allowed expenditures for the police department to replace an ailing old patrol car and add a second car to the department, to be used exclusively for residential areas. The new car cost $1,111.20, and the trade in for the old car was a deal at $499.50.

POLICE BOOK BIG SHOTS

Chief LaPierre took his job seriously. Finding a number of prominent citizens who had failed to pay traffic related fines, he had them brought in on warrants. Embarrassed bankers, architects, and others were forced to have their ages, hair color, and condition of their teeth or false teeth, recorded on booking sheets. Tearing up traffic citations had led these prominent citizens to regret their actions and realize the fine was better than the consequence. *Salinas Californian, January 14, 1941.*

Chief LaPierre attended an FBI national defense training course with some of the Salinas officers in February 1941. Accompanying the chief were Captain Ralph Plaice, Sgt. George Weight, and Officers Glenn Smith, Leo Wade, Marvin York, R.M. McKenney, Ray McIntyre, William Atwood, Al Storm and C.S. Sorenson.

Ralph Plaice had been a jailer before becoming a Salinas police officer on November 1, 1927, when he was appointed as desk sergeant. Since then, he had been promoted to lieutenant in 1930 and had served as a captain in charge of the night shift. No explanation was given in 1941 when Chief LaPierre recommended he be dismissed for "insubordination and conduct unbecoming an officer." He was formally suspended late in 1941, and had plans to fight the order, stating, "My conscience is clear." *Salinas Californian, November 4, 1941.*

Worth Foster, a former Army intelligence officer, was hired shortly after Plaice was suspended. His duties included driving the new patrol car, assigned solely to the residential districts at night. Cratis White was hired to help Traffic Officer Barney Abel patrol the downtown area. A former military policeman who had served in the Army for six years, White rode the second three-wheeled motorcycle, checking for overtime parkers. Also hired as a traffic officer Marvin Roberts, then thirty-three years old, had previously worked at the Rodeo Riding Club. Married, with two children, Roberts had also worked as a special officer for Salinas and for both the sheriff's office and District Attorney's office. He was also a member of the sheriff's posse. Officer Roberts took the place of Traffic Officer Harry Stevens, who had retired in September. *Salinas Daily News, October 6, 1941.*

Traffic Officer on Three-Wheeler
Courtesy of the Salinas Police Department

OFFICER MCKENNEY'S CLAIM

Plain clothes work was new to the city and Officer R.M. McKenney drove around in his own car and in his own clothes doing night patrol. At a city council meeting, he asked to be reimbursed $25 for automobile expenses related to his job. Several council members felt he should have to file a mileage report to the city and refused to vote to approve the expense. Chief LaPierre, having made such a report several months earlier which determined an average monthly mileage of six hundred miles, felt one report was good enough. Two councilmen agreed, stating if the council were to force the officer to make monthly reports, then the other city officials who were receiving a $25 monthly automobile allowance should also have to do so. Officer McKenney's expense was then approved. *Salinas Californian, December 1941.* The argument would become insignificant in the days that followed.

The economic and physical destruction that had ravaged much of Europe after the First World War, along with the anger and newly found nationalism of individual countries, generated the formation of the socialist actions that led to the era of the Nazis. After making demands for the return of land taken away in the treaties after the First World War, Hitler joined forces with Stalin in

1939, before invading Poland. World War II was the aftermath of Hitler's belief that he could control the entire world. Stalin thought he had the Germans in line, having shipped large amounts of food and oil to them, but Hitler attacked in June 1941. Britain promised support for the suffering Balkans and Russia.

On December 7, 1941, the United States was attacked, with heavy losses at Pearl Harbor. Germany, Italy and Japan stood together as the United States joined Britain in the war in Europe. At 4:10 p.m. on December 8, 1941, President Roosevelt declared war on Japan. The war would cost many American lives and change the course the country would take. The Salinas Civil Protection Committee worked with Mayor E.J. Leach on an emergency blackout system. An air raid and blackout signal was installed and businesses were advised to shut off all lights at night. Chief LaPierre canceled all leaves and vacations for officers as Japanese citizens were prohibited from leaving the city. Private planes were grounded and amateur radios silenced as Americans reeled from the losses at Pearl Harbor. The Coast Guard took over Monterey Bay and the wharf, and no ships were allowed into the harbor. Salinas police were "standing by" with the FBI, with specially assigned guards in the Oriental district. A deadline was set for all aliens to turn in any radio equipment. As the radio equipment poured into the police department the line out the door, the chief scrambled to find room to store the big items. Finally, he had to start sending the equipment to the basement. The Sheriff's Department ordered a posse to consist of aerial, motorcycle, and horse patrols as part of a civilian defense plan that had been in the initial planning stages for months. A call for auxiliary members of the police and fire departments went out. Recruits were trained in handling black outs and traffic control and would guard strategic points in the city and county. Blackout instructions were printed in the newspaper and citizens were asked to stay at home. Mass evacuation plans were made and warnings were given to citizens to be silent and not to speak about troop movements. Rules were set forth for Salinas residents. The air raid precautions included orders like, "Extinguish all open fires, such as fireplaces to prevent scattering of hot coals, have sand and a shovel available at all times and keep watch of the roof and attic for fire. Know where your nearest fire alarm box is situated and have a garden hose available or connected at all times. Don't telephone as soon as you hear the alarm-officials need those lines for emergency calls. Cover all windows to prevent flying glass. Keep away from windows, remain on the lower floor and in the center of the house, if possible. Don't stay in the street, get to cover and don't stand up; lie down wherever you are. Have a first aid kit available at all times. Don't light cigarets in the open. And don't peek out of covered windows in lighted room to see what's going on; one flash of light may bring disaster. Keep your head; be calm and sensible." *Salinas Californian, November 10-11, 1941.*

Within days, the United States had also declared war on Germany and Italy. The FBI immediately set up special training classes for police officers in California, holding them in San Jose. Officers from Salinas were sent to study internal security, espionage, sabotage and subversive investigations, spot map maintenance, air raid reports, police communications, traffic control during war time, blackout enforcement, handling of unexploded bombs, evacuation procedures and much more. Chief LaPierre went to training with his men. Joining him were, Sgt. George Weight, Officers McKenney, Skillicorn, C.C. Rogers, and several deputies. Police work had just changed forever.

The city had a residency requirement that prohibited the chief from hiring officers unless they had been living within the city limits for two years prior to their hiring date. In December 1941, the council voted to change that provision to allow hiring of men who had been in schools at Berkeley or other cities. While the Mayor and council always felt local men should be hired first, trained officers were too valuable and important to pass up.

On April 10, 1942, then District Attorney Anthony Brazil, (later a judge), publicly criticized police for a lack of enforcement in Chinatown. He called it a "combat zone where prostitution has been ordered repressed." "That law has not been enforced in Salinas and the police department has not done a sincere job," Brazil was quoted as saying in an article in the *Salinas Daily News*. Most of the problem was due to the military base nearby. Military personnel were later banned from going to the red-light district and a law prohibiting whore houses within twenty-five miles of a military base changed the look of Chinatown.

ELEVEN

THE LEGACY OF MAE EISEMANN,
THE FIRST FEMALE POLICE OFFICER

*Policewoman Mae Eisemann
Courtesy of the Eisemann Family*

Mabel Marie Eisemann was the only daughter of an Irish immigrant father and a full-blooded Cherokee Indian mother. Her mother had been born in Arkansas and was moved to Oklahoma on the "Trail of Tears." Her father was a tin ware salesman and met her mother on a reservation. They participated in the Oklahoma Land Rush, marrying at a very young age. Born in Colorado on August 28, 1904, Mae grew up with five brothers, the family moving to the west coast during her early years. While on a trip to San Francisco, Mae met Henry Eisemann and the two married, moving to Santa Cruz where Eisemann was a lather. The construction industry was booming and Eisemann was highly skilled. Asked to work on homes being built in Spreckels, the couple and their family moved first to

Spreckels, then to 315 North Main Street in Salinas. By then, Eisemann had established himself as a roofer and Mae went to work in the lettuce sheds.

A woman was hired to look after the young family of four children while the couple worked. Mae worked in the sheds at John and Abbott Streets, culling lettuce before being promoted to floor manager. She had only an eighth grade education, but was surprisingly intelligent, hard working, and capable. Still working in the sheds during the lettuce strike of 1936, Mae even took her children to the site of the riots and strikes. In her spare time, Mae, a large woman of two hundred thirty pounds, loved to dance and was quite nimble on her feet. Concerned for the safety of her children should something happen to her, Mae joined the Moose Lodge, working her way up to the position of First Senior Regent for the Salinas Moose Lodge. Her interests had always been in police work and following the lettuce strikes and with her children getting a bit older, Mae applied for a position as Police Matron with the Salinas Police Department.

On May 1, 1942, Mabel (Mae) Eisemann became the first female matron for the City of Salinas. In a handwritten memoir recently found by her son, Mae recounted her start at the Salinas Police Department. She worked as a matron for about six months before realizing she wanted to be able to do more as an officer. She put in her application for a position as an officer under Chief Lapierre. Lapierre was reluctant to be the first to hire a woman, but as luck would have it, there had been a big problem with shoplifters in the downtown area and the uniformed officers had been unable to catch the culprits. Chief Lapierre called Mae into his office one day and hired her as a regular officer. She began her new position just before the Christmas rush season and quickly made a number of arrests of female shoplifters.

Chief Lapierre found Eisemann to be much more capable than he had anticipated and soon assigned her to more challenging beats. As an officer in Salinas, Mae went on to become the first female to have a foot patrol beat in California. She patrolled the 100-block of Main Street, East and West Market streets, Chinatown and Soledad Street without a partner. Her shift kept her on the streets between 6:00 p.m. and 3:00 a.m. She struggled with drunks, arrested prostitutes, broke up fights and mediated domestic disturbances with ease. Her large and statuesque build made her an imposing figure as she walked up and down Main Street and through Chinatown.

Mae's work as a policewoman put a strain on her Moose Lodge relationships. The Moose ran a successful, but not quite legal gambling room and

Eisemann's status as a policewoman placed her in conflict. Judge Anthony Brazil was crusading against gambling, accusing his police department of not following his directions to eliminate the vice from the city. He would play a role in the future of the police department. Much of the gambling in Chinatown would eventually be moved to South County where the long arms of the judge could not reach or influence so easily.

Policewoman Mae Eisemann was formally appointed as a special police officer and her work was highly commended by Chief George Weight during the city council meeting of February 7, 1944. Eisemann also received praise for her value to the city from City Manager Barlogio who proposed she be allowed to conduct follow up investigations on cases she turned over to county juvenile authorities. Chief Weight requested she be given a car allowance so that she could extend her duties to the outlying city districts. Mae never had a uniform during her years as a Salinas officer, but wore Badge #1 throughout her career.

In September 1944, Policewoman Mae Eisemann made headlines again as she solved the mystery of a blood trail found near the Greyhound Bus Station. The blood trail started at a broken window at 135 ½ Monterey Street and stretched to the Greyhound Bus Station. The amount of blood led authorities to speculate that an artery had been cut. Recalling having seen a man with a bandaged hand in a downtown bar that night, Eisemann located the man and "questioned him expertly," according to the *Salinas Daily News* article. The man admitted putting his hand through a shop window, but denied an attempted burglary. Still quite angry, the man had to be forcibly placed in jail by Policewoman Eisemann.

The city's first policewoman was featured in several lengthy articles in the *Salinas Daily News*. Reporter Berniece Batterton spent one night on patrol with Mae Eisemann, writing about her remarkable instinct and compassion. During the quiet night, Eisemann made several arrests, sent several working women and soldiers on their way to avoid arrests and helped break up fights. She responded to an accident and met with locals like "Buck, a real old plantation Negro who was amusing the customers with the drumbo." Buck, and others like him, often provided much needed information that helped police solve crimes and locate wanted persons. Batterton concluded her report saying, "Mae Eisemann, the first policewoman the city has ever employed, is giving the taxpayers their money's worth every night in the week." *Salinas Daily News, 1940s*.

Eisemann's son planned to follow in her footsteps, working as a typist in the department during his summer vacation for experience in law enforcement and choosing to attend the San Jose State police school. For two years he stayed in the police science department, working each summer typing reports for the officers, using earphones and a machine that he worked with his foot. Changing to Penology Studies, Eisemann spent one summer working at the Soledad State Prison as a correctional officer. His early morning shift forced him to count bodies almost constantly and he hated the job, knowing in his heart that law enforcement or corrections was not for him. He persisted, however, until the prison had its first escape. Eisemann received a phone call one night calling him into the prison to assist in the search for the first man to ever escape from Soledad Prison. When he arrived at the prison, he was handed a very large handgun. Eisemann had never handled a gun in his life and had no idea what to do with the weapon. He was taken to Fresno and placed in the home of some people who lived near where it was thought the escaped convict would go for help. He sat for hours and days at a window, watching for the prisoner. After the prisoner was captured in some fields nearby, Eisemann returned to Salinas and eventually, to college. He promptly changed his major to Sociology. The prisoners had known him to be gullible and had taken advantage of his good heart. He knew he would never survive. He received a Bachelor's Degree in Sociology and his parents attended his graduation. Following the congratulations, his father asked him bluntly, "Well, what are you able to do?"

Henry Eisemann returned to Salinas and went to work for his father's business, Eisemann Roofing. He later received teaching credentials, a master's degree, and guidance counseling certifications. After a long career as a teacher, counselor, school principal, and author, he is now retired and continues to live in Salinas with his wife of fifty years, Mary Ellen.

Many of Eisemann's relatives were involved in law enforcement in various ways. One uncle was the chief of police for one of the large movie production houses, MGM or Paramount. Another was the chief of security first for a Saudi Arabian oil company and later for a large oil company in Okinawa.

Mae Eisemann became an officer in the California Women's Peace Officer's Association and served under three different police chiefs before resigning in 1947. In her letter of resignation, which was printed in the newspaper, Eisemann gave the reason for leaving as ill health. The truth was that her beloved daughter, Connie, had been killed while riding a horse during the Rodeo parade the previous year and Mae was never the same after that. She wrote that there was, "not a city on the coast with a chief as honest and as efficient" as George Weight. With an insight into what the future was to hold for the department, Eisemann also commented, "The Salinas department is undermanned but every man on the department is doing his job conscientiously. They are underpaid." She went on to say that, "Every policeman must learn to take everything from abuse and threats from the public to weather and all the things that are tough going for a lot of people." *Salinas Daily News, December 1947.* Her statements remain as true today as they were sixty years ago.

Mae Eisemann returned to police work soon after her resignation, going to work for the Sheriff's Department as a matron. Woody Meek, now retired, recalls the department continuing to call Mae in for special assignments due to her female replacement being unable to do what Mae was capable of in law enforcement. As a matron, Mae's contact with prisoners kept her in the newspaper as she was photographed escorting female murder suspects and other high-profile prisoners to and from court. She set up one of the first education programs at the jail, using her skills as a seamstress and quilter to teach the women skills they could use when released. Her program was a huge success and there were open houses at which the ladies sold the items made while serving their time. She died in service to the Sheriff's Department in 1955 of a heart attack.

Her family remains in Salinas still today. Her granddaughter received a Bachelor's Degree in Criminology and studied Forensic Sciences as a graduate student at U.C. Berkeley. She is a private investigator, dance teacher, and the author of this history and is married to retired Salinas Police Detective Joe Gunter. Mae's great-granddaughter, now fifteen, recently wrote an essay for school in which she was required to write about the person that has most influenced her life. She wrote that, aside from her parents, one a private investigator and the other a retired Salinas homicide detective, the person who has most influenced her life is Salinas Canine Officer Bill Gaston. In her essay, Terrin Eisemann wrote that when she met and spoke with Officer Gaston and his partner, Klief, she knew that was what she wanted to do with her life. Devastated at the death of the police canine, Terrin says nothing will deter her from her goal. Now in high school, and with a clear goal, she knows what she must do to reach that goal and is aware of the history she will make when she achieves that goal.

With the help of her father, Joe Gunter, whose reputation as a homicide detective is legend and begins at the end of the 1960s, the inspiration of her mentor, Officer Bill Gaston, and the support of her mother and many other Salinas officers, Terrin looks forward to walking in the footsteps of her great-grandmother and all the officers of the Salinas Police Department who have gone before her. Where Policewoman Mae Eisemann walked alone on the streets of downtown Salinas and Chinatown, Terrin Eisemann hopes to walk in the company of a canine officer as her partner.

MILITARY DUTY FOR SALINAS OFFICERS

Chief Lapierre assigned Al Storm to oversee the night detail at the police department when Officer McKenney left to do his military tour of duty late in 1942. The resignation of Storm in February 1943, was, according to news articles, due to differences with Traffic Officer Skillicorn. Storm cited his dissatisfaction with continuing to work the night detail as the reason for his resignation. Lapierre appealed to the city council for additional officers, stating a lack of manpower as the cause of increased crime. The current nineteen officers, where formerly twenty-eight had served the department, were simply unable to keep up with the demand for service. With the resignation of several officers and more who had been called to military duty, the police department was understaffed. Only one new officer, Henry Lasserot had been hired to replace an ailing officer forced to retire. Chief Lapierre was subpoenaed before the Grand Jury as they investigated charges against the chief and the department. District Attorney Brazil told the Grand Jury he had lost all confidence in the police department.

The chief discussed the difficulties in closing the gambling casinos located in Chinatown. Accused of friendship with the Chinese, the chief defended himself and his department. He compiled statistics showing 196 arrests and 189 traffic citations issued for the month of March 1943. The Grand Jury convened, calling the chief, Desk Sergeant John Walls and Traffic Officers Marvin Roberts and Rue Carley. The strain of the investigation and the accusations were too much for Chief Lapierre. On May 3, 1943, he resigned, citing stress as the reason. He had served sixteen years with the department, over five as the chief. His resignation was made with dignity, class, and respect for his men. Lapierre had been born and raised in Salinas, had served for two years during World War I, and had joined the police department as a desk sergeant in 1927. Later, he was appointed to the position of Captain and acting chief prior to succeeding Chief George Griffin.

Following the resignation of the respected chief, Lt. Trigg Phillips also resigned the following day. His letter of resignation also showed his respect for the department. Another war veteran, Lt. Phillips entered the Salinas Police Department as a patrolman in 1928. He was appointed Chief of Police in 1937, but after a short time asked to be relieved, recommending Lapierre for the job. He continued to serve as the night detail Lieutenant under Chief Lapierre until 1943. He had been recommended for further promotions over the years, but preferred to continue his duties as the night Lieutenant. His resignation left the top two positions in the department unfilled. The city council was quick to act, putting Captain Weight in place as the acting chief. Sgt. Adcock of the traffic detail was appointed acting in charge of the night detail.

Following the resignation of the two highly respected and top police officials, the city council ordered their new acting chief to "close down" on Salinas. City Manager Barlogio wanted strict enforcement of all laws within the city. The council came up with six recommendations to assist police with law enforcement. These included ordinances barring double doors on businesses, requiring commercial card rooms to close at midnight, requiring licensing of skating rinks, making the use of shills illegal, and requiring licensing for any dance where liquor would be served. This only led to further resignations by police officers C.C. Rogers and Ted Miller. Rogers, the oldest veteran in the department left to accept a position with the war department after twenty years as a Salinas police officer. Miller had served six years and left to go into private business. Within one month of the latest resignations, Salinas had another murder, this time on Lake Street. The stabbing at 13 ½ Lake Street led to the arrest of a farm worker at the Spiegl farm.

TWELVE

CHIEF GEORGE WEIGHT

Chief George Weight

It wasn't until July 1943, that the appointments of Chief Weight, Captain Adcock, Lt. John Walls and Sgt. Sorenson became permanent. When the new pistol range opened on the Salinas Army Air Base in August, Chief Weight, along with other members of the department made the newspapers in a photo showing them shooting next to the commanding officer of the base. His officers wasted no time investigating routine and unusual crimes around the city. During one weekend in September, officers made fifteen arrests and answered many more calls. Four accidents and two thefts, several family fights and two false alarms were reported. There were injured women, speeding cab drivers, and prowlers on Harvest and Church Streets. After a four-day investigation, Salinas police raided two Soledad Street opium dens, finding pipes, fresh opium, metal cans and tar. Arrests were made during the successful search.

Salinas had a population of 13,000 and the department had grown from twelve officers in 1931 to twenty-seven officers in 1943. There was a curfew for juveniles, and two-way radios had been installed in three radio cars and several other police department vehicles. There were no unsolved murders on the books. Chief Weight was an expert in fingerprinting and photography. He was a believer in training for his officers. Weight appointed Ray McIntyre as his Captain and his three Lieutenants included J.C. Yetter, Eldon Fowles, and M.E. Roberts, all experienced officers. Dean Seefeldt was one of two desk sergeants and remains one of the oldest members of the department still alive during the writing of this history. Seefeldt was interviewed during the research phase and provided his memories. Herb Lasserot was also a sergeant, and Jack Wright was the traffic sergeant. Traffic officers at the time included Ray Waters, William McLaughlin, William Barr, and Claude Yetter. Patrolmen were Earl Ashton, A.T. Barnes, W.R. Weichring, L.V. Emery, H.L. Duncan, Vic Taylor, Russell Hill, Dewey Smith, R.E. Taylor, and Quentin Smith. Mrs. Mabel Eisemann was the only female officer, and two females worked as stenographers and clerks.

Chief Weight wrote an article for the *Taxpayer's Magazine* discussing how police problems were caused by the increase in population. Weight's belief in crime prevention and strict enforcement included the need for cooperation among outside agencies, especially the military police. With so many officers in military service, the department was trying to cope with hiring new officers, while holding the positions of those serving overseas for their return. Roy McKenney answered the statements of the chief with bitterness, saying that cooperation between agencies was not new and was taught to all who attended the FBI classes. Mr. McKenney had been an officer and had been temporarily promoted to Acting Captain before his departure for military service. He was angry that he had not been returned to his acting captain position following his return from the war. Having been offered a position as patrolman, he had turned it down. McKenney also praised the work of policewoman Mae Eisemann, who had worked under his supervision at one time. Citing her work as, "highly efficient,", McKenney still believed there were areas in the city where it was not safe for a woman to patrol alone.

John Walls was working at the Salinas Police Department in 1943, when there was a big shake up of personnel. He called his friend, Dean Seefeldt, who had recently moved south to Long Beach to come back to Salinas and join the force. Dean immediately picked up and moved back to Salinas and became a patrol officer. After about one month on patrol, his friend, John Walls, informed him that the way to move up in the department was through "the desk." Dean worked the desk from 7:00 p.m. to 3:00 a.m. for some time until being promoted to days. It was during this time that Dean became very friendly with a number of the officers, including Mae Eisemann.

Dean recalls the department having two black Chevy squad cars, one brown car, and one paddy wagon. Officers purchased their own motorcycles, and Grady Webb loaned money to one officer to help with his purchase. Webb was later arrested for robbing a bank and was sent to prison.

Motor officers of the 1940s
Courtesy of the Salinas Police Department

Dean Seefeldt recalled the old jail had no door handle or lock on it as it was always open. Mae Eisemann would often slam uncooperative women into the door to get them in for booking. In another comical story, Officer Kuykendall went to the "house" of one Beatrice, "Dixie" Shultz. Dixie ran a whorehouse and there was a big fight. Kuykendall and another officer were arresting men and taking them one by one down to the squad car. As they went inside to get another suspect, a friend of the suspects was letting them out the other side of the squad car. As the two officers brought out the last man, they found the car empty of suspects.

Early in 1945, Dean Seefeldt and Officer Harold Duncan were drafted right out of the police department and into the military. The shortage of officers due to their service in the military was a cause of concern. The department held the positions open, awaiting the return of their regular officers, but needed extra manpower. Ney Otis, a seventy-three year old retired probation officer offered to help and went to work for SPD as a Desk Sergeant. According to Chief Weight, he would continue, "until such time as police officers now in service return, or as long as there is need for his services." Dean Seefeldt returned from the service on March 16, 1946, and began his job at the police department full time, also working half days as a lather. He made more money working half days as a lather than he did full time as a police officer, and on December 31, 1946, Dean resigned from the department to work full time as a lather. He cited his career change as necessary to support his wife and two daughters.

Seefeldt recalled attending a large party in Carmel Valley and drinking more than enough champagne. While he was fine at the party and upon his arrival home, he slept only a short time before rising to go to work at the station. Drinking a large glass of water before walking to work, Dean made it only a short distance to a call box located at San Luis and Cayuga Streets. He called in, asking for a squad car to pick up a man "holding up a telephone pole." When the officers arrived, they found one of their own. They took him into the department, holding him up, and placed him in his chair at the desk where he continued to work for the entire day. For many days after, they compared drunks being brought in to his condition that day.

Dean was interviewed at his home in North Salinas on December 13, 2004, about his memories of the department life. His remarkable memory still intact, he was able to identify each and every member of the department in 1943, provide their spouse's names, and tell what became of them after they left the department. Seefeldt also provided a copy of the photograph of the officers of the department taken in 1943. Not pictured in that photo was one of the motorcycle officers who was fired after Mae Eisemann found him having relations with a lady in a jail cell. Although he could not get into the cell, the two had "made arrangements" according to Seefeldt. That officer was fired.

Seefeldt's salary as a Sergeant on the police force at that time was $260 per month. He took home only $238. When he submitted his letter of resignation, the Chief tried to entice him to stay, offering to make him a Lieutenant. Unfortunately, Lieutenants made only $10 per month more and Seefeldt decided to take the more lucrative job in construction.

By early 1944, Salinas police were making almost nine hundred arrests per year. By far the greatest number of arrests was for drunkenness, but assaults, burglaries, robberies and other serious crimes were common. Salinas may have seen its first drive-by shooting that year as Chief George Weight reported the shooting out of windows in a south Salinas home was done from a vehicle.

Truancy from school was blamed on "war restlessness" and the chief urged parents to force their children to attend school as required by the law.

The 1945 Salinas Police Department
Courtesy of Dean Seefeldt

In 1944, 3,233 arrests were made with no murders recorded. The number of actual police reports went down, due to the inadequate number of officers and the inability to work on crime prevention programs, thus allowing more crimes to be committed. Chief Weight stressed prevention through extensive patrolling and direction towards juvenile problems. With only two patrol cars, one wagon, a three-wheeled motorcycle, and four traffic motorcycles, officers were subject to being on call twenty-four hours per day. Training required about one year for an officer to be useful, and eleven police department members were currently in the armed services. Leslie Barker, C.M. Logan, Ed McFadden, Ray McIntyre, Gerald Sheehy, W.A. Skillicorn, Glenn Smith, Walter Weichring, Jack Wright, John Wright, and Herbert Lasserot were in various divisions of the wartime armed services, leaving the department short handed.

The news listed officers on leave in 1945

Officers who were left to patrol the city included W.R. Thornton, who joined the department in September 1943, Joe Yetter, formerly a Greyhound dispatcher who began his law enforcement career in September 1942; and Mae Eisemann, the first female officer for the city and the night foot patrol officer for the red light district and Chinatown. Les Emery had been a driver for a transport company prior to joining up in September 1943, and O.B. Pelley had been with the railroad before his 1945 start date with SPD. Marvin Roberts joined the department in 1941, after working for the Rodeo riding club; and Dean Seefeldt, who joined in 1943, had been a lather. Ed Adams, then seventy years old was the Pound master and a special officer for SPD after his career as a carpenter. Louie Cryts and Len Hansen had been truck drivers before 1943, when they became police officers, and Harold Duncan had been a service station operator before he started in June 1943. Boyd Hunter had run a restaurant before 1944. W.R. Hurley had run a poultry farm and J.T. Kuykendall had been a bookkeeper before their 1943 start dates with the Salinas Police Department.

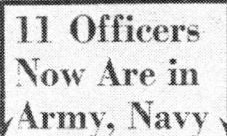

11 Officers Now Are in Army, Navy

Eleven recent members of the Salinas police department are in the armed services, Police Chief George Weight disclosed today.

Leslie Barker, patrolman from February 1942 to October 1942, is a member of the army air corps. C. M. Logan, traffic officer from November, 1942 to February 1943, is a member of the naval shore patrol. Patrolman from April 1942 to September of the same year, Ed McFadden now is a sergeant in the army air corps. Another air corps sergeant is Ray McIntyre, patrolman and traffic officer from March 1938 to October 1942.

Traffic officer from November 1934 to September 1942, Gerald Sheehy now is in the coast guard. W. A. Skillicorn, patrolman from November 1937 to March 1943, now is an infantry sergeant who has returned from the Aleutians to attend officers' school. Glenn Smith, patrolman from October 1940 to March 1942, now is a chief petty office in the navy.

Walter Weichring, patrolman from May 1941 to October 1942, is now a sailor. Cpl. Jack Wright of the AAF, was a patrolman from April 1942 to October of the same year. John A. Wright, patrolman from September 1941 to October 1942, now is an MP in the army. Herbert Lasserot now is serving in the navy.

*Officer Eldon Fowles
Courtesy of the Fowles Family*

Eldon Fowles was a grocer before signing up as an officer in 1944. Born and raised in Hollister, and known to all as Fred, he soon found himself a captain in the department. Captain Fowles was the man who designed the shoulder patch worn by officers to this day. His lettuce fields with the sun rising brought him little fame at the time. A very popular man and officer, he is remembered by his son, Don Fowles, who still lives in Salinas, as a man who, "gave people breaks." He was a highly respected officer who died a little more than one year before retirement. His battle with serious lung cancer that quickly went to his brain, resulted in massive weight loss. His funeral was held with police honors, including a twenty-one gun salute.

Lorraine Fontes joined the department as the typist and clerk after graduating from Salinas High School in June 1944, and Arthur Barnes had worked at a seed company and served his military duties before becoming an officer in July 1944. O.D. Eastwood, at the age of sixty-seven was the oldest member of the department at that time, having become a patrolman in 1927. He was single, lived in a hotel and was formerly a truck driver. Barney Abel joined the department in 1928, as a traffic officer, and Lt. Worth Foster sold insurance before becoming a patrolman in 1941. Claude Yetter worked for a peanut company before 1943 and Ed Smith, who would be dead within one month of the date of the story in the newspaper, had worked for the Elks Club before 1943, when he became a traffic officer. Some were married, others single, many had children and all of them worked with little training, varying levels of education, little or no equipment and only one another to rely on for assistance.

In April that year, Officer Barker returned to duty on the department after spending some time in the army air force. Police Sergeant C.S. Sorensen, a five year veteran of the department filed papers for appointment as the city police judge. Sergeant Sorenson served for three years as the police court bailiff and one year as a sergeant prior to his application. He was appointed to the position after a special meeting of the city council. Lt. John Walls had resigned in December 1944, after several years as a police officer to take over his father's insurance business. With the department since 1939, he was first a patrolman before being promoted to Lieutenant.

THIRTEEN

Tragedy Strikes
The story of Traffic Officer Eddie Smith

Traffic Officer Eddie Smith
Courtesy of the family of Eddie Smith

Edgar Claude Smith was born in a little town in Oklahoma before moving to New Mexico, where he would meet his future bride, Cleo. Known as Eddie his entire life, he moved his family to California when the oil wells in New Mexico dried up and he no longer had work. Eddie Smith brought his family to Monterey in 1939 and his daughter, named Eddie after her father, was born there. The family moved to Salinas in 1940, living first on Pine Street and later on Maple Street. Eddie went to work for Bruce Church, but later decided to try for a job as a police officer. Cleo worked at the Jeffrey Hotel where she worked three split shifts a day as a waitress. When Eddie needed money to purchase the motorcycle for his work as a traffic officer, Bruce Church loaned him the money.

Cleo remembers how Eddie was in charge of changing the signals at the main intersections in town twice a day. From the Jeffrey Hotel, she would see him change the signals in the morning and again in the evening. At that time, signals were manually operated and the flags were changed by the traffic officers to ease traffic flow at different times of the day or night. The couple and their daughter had a wonderful relationship with the other police officers and their families. Cleo recalls the many parties attended by all the officers and their wives. When the Smiths moved into their new home, they had an open house party that was well attended and quite loud. Neighbors called the department to complain, requesting police break up the party. They were told by the only person at the department there was no one to respond because, "All the policemen are at that party!"

Part of Eddie Smith's duties as a traffic patrol officer was to provide crossing safety for the students at Salinas High School. His motorcycle could often be seen parked along Main Street in front of the school as he guided students across the busy street. In his spare time, he loved to fish and would spend hours at the Carmel Beach, fishing, but rarely catching much.

In February 1945, Officer Smith, along with the rest of the Salinas Police Department officers, was featured in an article in the newspaper. Sitting next to him was Mae Eisemann, as had been the case in all department photographs. Eddie used to comment to his wife about how they always sat him next to Mae in the photographs. Easter was the first weekend in April in 1945, and early Saturday morning, six year old Eddie was photographed in her Easter Sunday outfit, sitting atop her father's police motorcycle.

Six year old Eddie Smith on dad's bike
Courtesy of Eddie Smith's family

Her mother recalls how proud the officers were of their big motorcycles and how they all kept them sparkling. The next day, Eddie Smith was killed. Officer Smith had gone to work that morning and found his radio was not operating at all. Larry's Motorcycle Shop was normally responsible for the maintenance of police motorcycles, but it was Easter Sunday, and Larry's was closed. Officer Smith made the decision to head north to the Santa Rita area to get the problem fixed. With the radio repaired, Officer Smith was returning to the downtown area, traveling south on North Main Street, when a car driven by Mrs. Looney turned directly in front of him. Unable to avoid hitting the car, Officer Smith crashed into the vehicle and was thrown from his motorcycle, receiving fatal injuries. His good friend and fellow officer, Joe Yetter was the first to arrive at the scene. Mrs. Smith was at work that day and too busy at first to meet with the two women who had arrived to speak with her. At the insistence of her supervisor, Mrs. Smith went out to meet Officer Mae Eisemann and the wife of one of the other officers. They were there to break the news to her about the death of her husband. She recalls the day, and her thoughts that Eddie would not be changing the signal that evening.

The young mother of then six year old Eddie was grief stricken and in shock. The funeral plans were a blur and she provided a suit for her husband's burial. Later, she would learn that officers criticized her for not burying him in his police uniform, something she says never occurred to her broken heart. Eddie Smith was one of a number of siblings, most of whom were away fighting the war at the time of his death. When the only stateside relatives wanted to attend the funeral, the date for the funeral was postponed as the train was delayed in arrival. The funeral finally took place one week after Officer Smith's death. Mr. Muller of Muller Mortuary had been one of Eddie's many friends and took care of him.

It was the biggest funeral Salinas had seen at the time. Both Cleo and her daughter, Eddie, still remember the overwhelming smell of the flowers that day. They remember the line of cars, the stacks of flowers, and the sadness they felt. Officer Smith's funeral was well attended by Salinas Police Department officers and by then Sheriff Alex Bordges, many deputies, CHP Captain Frank Mills and many members of the highway patrol. Pallbearers included Salinas officers Harold Duncan, Joe Yetter, Len Hansen, Marvin Roberts, Barney Abel and Officer Dean Seefeldt.

Sixty years have passed, but the memories are intact. The family received nothing from the police department as there were no benefits at the time. Cleo sold Eddie's service revolver back to the department for the much needed money. There was no recognition that he had died in the line of duty and the department kept his badge.

After the funeral, Mrs. Smith contacted Bruce Church to let him know she intended to honor the loan and continue the payments for the motorcycle. According to the widow, Mr. Church was the consummate gentleman and forgave the loan, telling her it had already been paid for. Mrs. Smith became the first woman in Salinas to be granted a home loan after the death of her husband. She continued working at the Jeffrey Hotel for a short time until she was able to get other work that paid her better.

Five years after the death of her husband, Mrs. Smith would remarry. Raymond Myers, a decorated war veteran, and Cleo Smith were married in 1950. Mr. Myers adopted little Eddie and the three formed a loving family, staying in the area. Officer Smith's daughter, Eddie Smith-Taylor went on to become a matron for the Del Rey Oaks Police Department. After two years, she decided she didn't have the heart to deal with the victims and resigned. She now lives in Missouri with her husband.

Cleo Myers continues to live in Pebble Beach, where she made her home with her second husband for many years. Shocked and thrilled to learn of the pending recognition for her first husband and Eddie's father, Cleo and Eddie agreed to be interviewed and share their memories of Eddie Smith in the wake of losing their beloved "Bill" Myers. Graciously allowing the interview to be conducted in their home, they shared their memories of Eddie Smith and the police department of the 1940s. They anxiously await the overdue recognition of Officer Eddie Smith for his contribution to the citizens of Salinas and his death in service to the Salinas Police Department. In 2005, Chief Ortega was accompanied to Washington D.C. by Deputy Chiefs Rick Moore and Cassie McSorley. They participated in a ceremony in which Officer Eddie Smith was honored as an officer killed in the line of duty. In a local memorial, Eddie Smith's granddaughter carried a candle in his memory during the 2005 MCPOA Fallen Officer's Service in Marina. In 2006 Traffic Officer Eddie Smith's name will be added to the California Peace Officer's Memorial.

FOURTEEN

The Last of the Originals

Mae Eisemann was often called upon to deliver the news when someone was hurt on duty. When Officer Marvin Roberts was in a bad accident, Mae Eisemann had to make the necessary notifications to the family. Many of the officers, including Barney Abel, Bob Cashen, Johnny Walls and Gullet and Seefeldt, all lived on Katherine Avenue, which, at that time was the last street in the city. O.D. Eastwood lived in a convenience hotel and is thought to have been used only as an extra officer. He "shuffled" along at a very slow pace, according to the memory of Dean Seefeldt.

Les Emory left the department to become a car salesman. Bill Hurley left the department and returned to his native Oklahoma. Joe Yetter left to become the Chief of Police in Gonzales. Marvin Rogers owned the stables located at the rodeo grounds. Bill Thornton ran a second hand furniture store. Herb Lasserot was a carpet layer and never forgave Dean Seefeldt for being promoted to sergeant before him.

Dean Seefeldt's memories include stories about the people who worked at the police department in his time there. Grady Webb was a motorcycle officer at that time. He later owned a hotel located on Avenue B, where the Dean Whitter building now stands. Ray Waters married Evelyn Miranda and was a P.O.W. during the war. Dick Barlogio called the department, "Salinas' Finest" whenever he spoke of his police force. Les Barker, an officer prior to 1942 wartime, returned to work as a Salinas Police Officer after finishing his tour of duty with the Army-Air Force. He was honorably discharged from the service and returned to Salinas to resume his duties as police officer. Barney Abel rode the three-wheeler owned by the department. Although he lost a leg, he continued as a police officer.

Henry Eisemann, son of Mae Eisemann, recalls a day when he was a child. Mae often socialized with other members of the police force and Henry knew them all. One day, while visiting at Barney Abel's house, Henry and his father were waiting while Barney took a shower. Seeing a snake crawling across the floor, Henry's father picked it up, not realizing it was a rattlesnake. Barney, coming out of the bathroom and not yet having his wooden leg attached, saw Mr. Eisemann holding the dangerous snake. He hopped quickly to the table where his service revolver lay and shot the snake's head off as it was held in the hands of Mr. Eisemann. Upon retirement, Barney Abel moved to a lake area up north where he continued to live until his death.

THE SLEEPY SERGEANT

Sgt. "Sleepy" Foster later became a lieutenant. He used to ride with Bill Thornton, who was the driver. Foster would instruct Thornton NOT to drive down Monterey or Main Streets, the two busiest streets in town, wanting him to stay in low visibility areas so he could sleep in the car. So, Thornton would wait until Foster fell asleep, then would parade up and down Main and Monterey Streets so everyone could see Foster sleeping in the patrol car.

Officer Sorenson was first a desk sergeant and later became the city judge. Captain Adcock used to instruct the officers to "Call me at this number," providing them with a particular phone number, but no location. Some research on Seefeldt's part located the phone number at the Fox Theater, upstairs in the projection booth. Apparently, Adcock used to sneak up to the projection room and sleep. The phone, located near his napping place, would alert him that others were looking for him.

The newest housing division in town was Pacific Park. Sorenson, Weight and others bought new houses over near the Santa Barbara Street area. Woody Meek who would begin his thirty-two year career with SPD in 1948, was another officer who purchased a house in that area. Meek, now a widower, still lives in that house, being the only owner, and was able to provide extensive information regarding the department during his years there as well as numerous photographs of interest.

Art Barnes, not present in the photo of 1943, had to go to work in the sheds following his work in the department. In order to earn enough Social Security benefits to live, Art continued to work in the sheds for some time. He and his wife lived on Oak Street. Officer Duncan's personal calling card was found in the purse of a "woman" upon her arrest, causing concern among some of the officers.

Captain Fred Fowles, also not in the photo, later became an assistant chief. He lived in Hollister and he and his friends used to play Cops and Robbers --- with live ammunition! No one was ever shot, but there were several close calls. Boyd Hunter owned the Ritz Bar on Salinas Street, across from the Armory. The current King's Den was then called The Big Hat and was a restaurant.

It was August 6, 1945 when an American Super-Fortress carried an atomic bomb to Hiroshima, dropping it from 30,000 feet. Emperor Hirohito would formally surrender to American General Douglas MacArthur, the Supreme Allied Commander, on September 2, 1945, bringing an end to the war, but only a beginning to the many years of recovery for all the countries and nations that had suffered so much physical devastation and the loss of so many lives. The war had taken its toll on the police department as well, with many officers called away to duty, their lives forever affected by the service to their country.

FIFTEEN

THE GROWTH OF THE DEPARTMENT

SHERIFF'S SOFTBALL TEAM
BEATS SALINAS POLICE

"**H**ard hitting sheriff's office softball team defeated Salinas police department players 16-4 in a four inning game at the Sherwood park diamond Monday night.

High point of the contest, both literally and physically, was Jack Wright's foul blow which landed in a tree along third base line and failed to come down. After Third Baseman Sherman Hendricks of the sheriff's team waited hopefully with hands cupped several minutes for the ball to come down, other measures were taken. First Baseman Pete Witcher started to climb the tree. Somebody else threw a bat at the ball and the bat failed to come down. Then Pitcher Bert Cahoon knocked the first ball out with another, but lost the second ball up the tree trying to get the bat down. Several more shots and Cahoon dislodged both the bat and the ball and the game was resumed.

Witcher's home run with two on in the first inning put the sheriff's team in front 3-0 and they were not headed thereafter. Only uprising for the SPD came in the fourth. Bob Hofer singled, Bill McLaughlin doubled and Chief of Police George Weight and Dean Seefeldt walked, forcing Hofer in with the first run. Then Larry Moore larruped a three bagger. That gave the policemen their only four runs.

Bob Amyx, for the policemen, allowed 15 hits and walked five while the Policemen collect five hits and five free passes off Cahoon's delivery. The game ended abruptly in the fourth when a line drive caught Policeman Second Baseman McLaughlin in the stomach, laying him out. It was dark anyhow by that time." This article was taken from the *Salinas Californian, July 31, 1946*.

Many changes were in store for Salinas over the next few years. The transition to a post-war world impacted the city, its citizens and its police department. New officers were hired and the crime rate grew. Twenty-three year old Stanley Lisk joined the Salinas Police Department after returning from service with the United States Marines. He was assigned to traffic patrol duties.

Salinas Police Patrolman Arthur T. Barnes, Patrolman Earl Ashton, and Lt. Eldon Fowles testified at the robbery trial of Jess Escovedo on July 24, 1946. Escovedo was on trial for the beating and robbery of James De Bacia in the alley of Monterey and Pajaro Streets, north of Gabilan Street, which took place in May 1946.

Chinatown had long been considered the "colorful" part of Salinas. In an article in the local newspaper, the history of Chinatown and its ties to the building of the railroad in the 1870s was noted. Officers and members of the SPD were shown in photos along with Chief Weight and Captain Ray McIntyre. It was noted that Captain McIntyre acted for the Chief in his absence and freed the Chief's time up for "purely administrative matters." *Salinas Californian, June 10, 1947.*

SALINAS POLICE MAKE 47 WEEKEND ARRESTS

The weekend of July 22, 1946, was busy for Salinas officers. A man who tried to stab his wife was found hiding in a pumpkin patch and a woman who stuck her tongue out at officers was arrested and locked up. There were burglaries, thefts, assaults and a variety of other incidents. Alert officers spotted a car near the Pub. Numerous burglaries in the area made this vehicle suspicious and officers investigated. As they approached, the driver began blinking his lights on and off, but before they could reach the car, it sped off down Clay Street. Officers blacked out their vehicle and watched the downtown area. Soon, they saw the men walking and stopping them, they also located the car in which were found burglar tools, punches, sledgehammers, and money. The men had been busy burglarizing a variety of businesses in the area and police interrupted their spree.

Parking meters made their debut in June 1946, raising $1,815 from fines given to violators. The business owners vehemently opposed the meters, which were installed to provide funds to use for finding a solution to the parking problem. Shoppers were not happy about receiving citations. Having received a citation, a woman from Los Angeles sent it back to Judge Sorenson with five cents. She claimed she didn't know how long she would be shopping, so decided to pay upon her return. She was gone forty-five minutes and found the ticket on her car. She calculated how much she figured she owed for her time, sending in the nickel. Another overtime parked driver was furious at receiving a citation, claiming he had put five cents into the meter and placed a nickel under his windshield wiper. He felt the officer should have taken the nickel and put it in the meter rather than leave him a ticket on his windshield.

Chief Weight began demands for new quarters for the police department. The jail, built to hold forty-two prisoners, was often maxed out with fifty-five to seventy in custody. There was no room for questioning suspects. Sketches were made for a new building, with offices and police court on the first floor and a jail on the second floor. The Salinas Police Department had twenty-eight sworn officers, two clerks and one policewoman, (Mae Eisemann). The department also had three cars, each with two-way radio, one patrol wagon with two-way radio, one three-wheeled motor bike, and five motorcycles.

New officers were needed, especially for traffic control and accident investigation. Fortunately, Raymond McIntyre, who had been a traffic officer with SPD before going into the service, returned to duty in Salinas. Having served as a security and intelligence officer during the war, McIntyre returned to Salinas as a patrolman. During the 1946 year, Salinas had 553 accidents, with Market Street claiming the unwelcome honor of having had the most collisions, racking up a grand total of 119 accidents in the one year period, including seventeen injuries, six pedestrians struck and one fatality. The Market Street area was dubbed, "Accident Alley," by Sgt. Jack Wright in 1946. South Main Street fared no better, with forty-two crashes and ten injuries. Two fatalities and seventy-eight injuries were reported as the results of the numerous accidents. Chief Weight warned citizens that, "dangerous carelessness" in their driving was causing the increase in serious accidents within the city.

The Monterey County Peace Officer's Association was founded in 1946. A list of past presidents found in materials provided by Chuck Foster lists Joe Corby of the King City Police Department as the first president of the MCPOA. The following year, Jack Wright of Salinas became president and not until 1951 did another Salinas officer, Ray McIntyre, become the head of the organization. In 1954 and 1968 respectively, Harold Duncan and Tom

Brooks became president. Roy Hanna served as president in 1975 and many other Salinas officers served on the board.

By December 31, 1946, Salinas police proudly reported their conviction rate for drunk drivers in the city. One hundred twenty-three people had been arrested for driving under the influence and one hundred twenty-two were convicted and sentenced. The remaining case was still pending at the close of court that year.

1947 brought new issues related to parking, traffic, the rodeo and rezoning requests. For reasons unknown, Officer Claude Yetter was suspended for thirty days in April and May. Chief Weight had recommended the suspension and hired Officer C.I. White to take his place. Officer White would have a one year probation period to serve before his acceptance as a full time officer. Walter Freylach was also hired. Freylach had been a wartime official with the San Francisco Police Department and took the place of Officer Harold Duncan, who was attending a school in Washington. Soon after he began work as a Special Officer, Freylach made headlines when he shot a Soledad man after an altercation in the La Conga Bar on West Market Street. Off duty at the time, Special Officer Freylach, while at the bar, witnessed a man purposely bumping into a female repeatedly. Freylach first asked the bartender to warn the fellow to stop. That didn't work, and Freylach himself pushed the man away from the woman, telling him he was a police officer. The man then hit Freylach in the face, whereupon the officer drew his gun and told the man to halt. Undeterred, the man continued towards the officer and grabbed the gun. The officer fired during the struggle, the bullet going first through his own hand before entering the arm of the suspect, breaking a bone. It was thought the man would be charged with resisting an officer. *Salinas Californian, June 1947.*

In 1947, the top officers and chiefs met to plan the organization of a local chapter of the California State Peace Officer's Association. Other officers met to plan a field day that would provide training to local junior traffic safety patrols at elementary and junior high schools. In cooperation with other law enforcement agencies and chamber of commerce representatives like Garth Lacey, a local attorney, games, races, and contests were planned with prizes for winning teams donated by local merchants. Two new officers were hired that August. One, a former special officer who had worked during Big Week, was James M. Butler. The second, Willard M. Gilbert, had been the night manager for the Yellow Cab Company before being hired. Other officers were showing off their prize horses at the rodeo grounds. Vic Taylor owned Baby Beautiful, an American Saddle and Arabian horse. Jim Boyer was showing his horse, Caleb Hope, an American saddle bred stallion. Both horses were considered prize animals.

There was talk of annexing the Alisal area, either as a self-contained incorporated city, or into the City of Salinas. In 1947, the Alisal area was the responsibility of the county, with law enforcement duties shared between the Sheriff's Department and the state highway patrol. Six men were assigned to Alisal at that time, and with a population of 14,688, there were 2,448 inhabitants per police officer. Salinas, on the other hand, with a population of fourteen thousand citizens, had twenty-eight officers, one for every five hundred inhabitants. Figuring the optimum conditions for a free and incorporated city, it was believed that Alisal would need a minimum of sixteen officers, including a police chief. Two patrol cars, two motorcycles, a radio station and other equipment would be needed in addition to a station house. It took nearly twenty years before the annexation agreement was made, turning the Alisal District over to the Salinas police department, making it a full and legal part of the city.

City officials were pondering the reduction in revenue from the police court. Declining revenue worried city officials. While one hundred sixty-two persons were arrested in September, only eighty-two paid fines. Parking meter violators paid $328 and fifty-four speeders paid $405 in fines.

Traffic safety issues, as always, were front page news and a "Traffic Safety Boxscore" was printed daily. As of January 9, 1948, it had been one hundred twenty-one days since Salinas had a traffic fatality. Officers of the Monterey County Peace Officer's Association discussed a road blockade system that would coordinate different agencies. Reeling from the recent shooting of Officer Tom Flowers during the chase and capture of two escaped convicts near San Ardo on Christmas Day, officers stressed the importance of adding air support and better radio communications systems.

During the first week of January, 1948, Luther Pilcher joined the Salinas Police Department. Within two weeks, Thomas R. Jones, just returned from active duty with the Navy, was hired as a patrolman. Chief Weight proudly boasted that Officer Jones had experience with the shore patrol. The new officers got to work quickly. Officer Pilcher, with the assistance of military police, chased a stolen vehicle, forcing the thieves to abandon the car on Main Street. Officer Pilcher grabbed one of the thieves, but recognizing him, let him go in order to chase the other two men. The chase led him north on Main to Gabilan and east to the alley at the back of the PGE building. Officer Thomas Jones, who had just checked in at a nearby callbox, nabbed one man. Hearing the firing of warning shots, Officer W.B. Hurley, who had left the side of Officer Jones, ran into the alley from Monterey Street and arrested the second man. Officer Jim Boyer escorted the two suspects to the station and a warrant was issued for the third man who had been recognized by Officer Pilcher. He was later arrested at his home.

Mid-January brought a report of one strong-armed robbery. Salvadore Flores, who resided at the back of the tallow works, told police he had been attacked at Market and Monterey Streets. He claimed the loss of three dollars in cash and one wristwatch, valued at over seventy dollars. Other thefts reported to police that day included a wristwatch taken from a man at the Golden Dragon Café, then located at 13 ½ Soledad Street, and a floor mat stolen from the Muller Mortuary. A mangled body found beneath a train earlier in the week was identified through the use of fingerprints.

A soldier being questioned at the police station in connection to an attack at Market and Monterey Streets attacked Officer D. Smith, who had changed into civilian clothing and was still at the station. Officer Smith was struck in the face before other officers could come to his aid. Other officers were also hit before they subdued the suspect. Originally charged only with disturbing the peace, the suspect was subsequently charged with battery. Officer Ernest Thiele, who had been kicked by the suspect, found that his leg was broken.

The wave of crime in Salinas continued into late January, with burglaries and thefts. Jewelry, watches, radios, clothing and toiletry sets were stolen in a series of hotel and home burglaries. Police questioned two men who had escaped from the stockade at Fort Ord, and witnesses identified the men as those who had tried to sell some of the stolen items. Some citizens conducted their own investigations. Having lost a purse containing car keys during a car burglary, Mr. and Mrs. Perry searched Central Park. Locating first a handkerchief, then an area of disturbed dirt, they dug near the tennis courts and located the purse, minus the cash it had held. Also missing were a pair of stockings, a set of rosary beads and a coin purse. Burglars removed the nuts off a safe at the Great Western Laundry, but were unable to get inside. Reports of numerous burglaries and attempted burglaries filled the news.

Chief Weight asked the city council to pay his way to a national police school to be held in Washington D.C. The chief had graduated from the National Police Academy in 1942, and had paid his own way at that time. The chief had the best of reputations and was selected by his peers as the president of the newly founded Zone No. 7 of the California Police Chief's Association. Comprised of Monterey, San Luis Obispo, Santa Barbara and Ventura counties, Zone No. 7 included seventeen of the 281 incorporated cities in California.

There were small breaks in the action for department members. In August 1947, police reported an, "All Quiet" period of thirty-seven hours, the longest period without a booking in many years. Between 10:47 p.m. on a Wednesday evening and 11:50 a.m. the next day, no bookings were reported, providing a short respite for the hard working officers.

Twenty members of the police department were honored by the presentation of American Victory Medals in the fall that year. Navy veterans received their awards from a naval representative several weeks before the awards were made to the Army veterans. Navy veterans of the department of 1947 included: H.L. Duncan, Sgt. H. Lasserot, W.R. Wiechring, W. J. McLaughlin, C.I. White, Edwin Tregenza, M. Gordon and W.M. Gilbert. A photograph of the Army veterans receiving their awards showed the following men receiving the medals from Master Sergeant Lippincott of the Army: Sgt. Earl Ashton, J.C. Boyer, R.E. Taylor, R.E. Hill, Capt. R. J. McIntyre, J.N. Butler, Chief Weight and Mr. Davies. A.T. Barnes was also a veteran, but was not present for the photograph.

Big Week was over and Chief Weight was looking for new officers to help with the growing crime problem in his city. James M. Butler had worked as a special officer during Big Week and had Army experience, making him a qualified candidate. Along with Willard Gilbert, who had been a night manager for Yellow Cab, he was sworn in as a police officer and scheduled to begin working August 29, 1947. Police court fines for July and August amounted to only $8,076.50, down almost ten thousand dollars from the previous year. Soldiers from Ft. Ord, while welcome in Salinas, were restricted from certain areas because of the history of problems. Without assistance from military police, Salinas officers were not able to control the activities and behavior of soldiers and chose to restrict them from the following areas; 1) All of Soledad Street from East Market to Lake; 2) All of Lake Street from California to Pajaro; 3) All of Bridge Street from Lake to Menke; and 4) All of Carneros Street from California to Bridge.

TRAFFIC OFFICER ART BARNES

Arthur Barnes was thirty-six years old when his motorcycle was involved in a collision with a labor truck on North Main Street. The impact caused a compound fracture of his left leg and shattered the bones in his knee, and the officer had many cuts and bruises. Taken to Salinas Valley Memorial Hospital, the officer was treated as fellow officers investigated the accident. They found Officer Barnes, along with his motorcycle, had been thrown over seventy feet from the point of impact. He had been attempting to cross the street to follow a car traveling the other direction. The truck had been hidden from his line of sight by a lettuce truck. The city would eventually be sued by the drivers of the civilian cars involved in the accident, but the city denied the claim for over five thousand dollars.

The first month of 1948 was rather slow in police court. Only 1,348 cases were handled by the judge, who had heard 2,167 in January 1947. Eighty-six of the 1,348 cases heard in January were for disturbing the peace. Other statistics included; one arrest for rape, twenty for vagrancy, one for assault, two for battery, two for car theft, two for hit and run, and many for miscellaneous charges. While statistics seemed to indicate a drop in criminal activity, the police department continued to be busy. Drunk driving arrests were reported alongside reports of police chasing various animals through town. A possum kept officers busy on Capitol Street, but they were finally successful in capturing the offending animal after a possum hunt. The animal was lodged in the city pound.

The FBI school for officers that year included a mock pursuit using patrol cars, walkie-talkies, and airplanes. Chief of Police George Weight piloted the plane while FBI agents and SPD Officer Weichring scoured the land. The "suspects," one FBI agent and Undersheriff Vic Tibbs, were spotted on Old Stage Road. Abandoning their vehicle, the suspects fled into a lettuce field, but were seen by the officers in the air. Officers closed in on the suspects and held a simulated gun battle. Monterey officers volunteered to serve as a mock jury during the upcoming "trial." Chief Weight believed in training and was the secretary of the Monterey County Police Officers Association. The association had an ongoing interest in, and discussions about, the future development of communications, and hosted guest speakers at their meetings. The chief, also a member of the Exchange Club, was photographed during National Crime Prevention Week at a lecture by an FBI man who discussed his two decades of experience in identification and arrest of criminals on a national scale.

The city council approved the purchase of a new police car from Chevrolet, costing $688.44, after a trade-in. In February 1948, the statistics for arrests during 1947 were available. Police officers made 17,893 arrests, up from the

1946 total of 15,502. Rape cases rose from six to seven that year, burglary from twenty-two to forty-five cases, larceny from sixty-three to seventy-seven and auto thefts from seven to twenty-five. Of these cases listed above, one hundred sixty-eight went to court and one-hundred fifty-eight resulted in convictions. One hundred vehicles were stolen within the city limits and ninety-six were recovered.

'OLD 185'

Main Street was lined with parking meters, the wise city council's solution for rampant parking problems. John Grau was the maintenance man who was responsible for collecting funds out of the meters and was featured in the newspaper with a photo of the most money making meter in town. Parking meter No. 185 was located in the 200 block on the east side of the street, and had a long reputation for the biggest haul. In January 1948, a record $15.02 was taken out of the meter, a one-month record. Averaging between twelve and thirteen dollars each month, the fifteen dollar amount was big news. Other meters on Main Street only produced about ten dollars each month. The lowest producing meter was located at the corner of Lincoln and West Alisal Streets. A free lot nearby was the suspected cause of the underperforming meter. There were 563 meters in operation in 1948 and the city received an average monthly revenue of $4,524.09, all of which was supposed to go into a fund for traffic control.

Police, noticing signs sticking out from the inside of a suspicious car, stopped two men from San Francisco. Both were soldiers. Apparently, the two had helped themselves to a stop sign and a directional sign while in the San Jose area. They were arrested and charged with tampering and possession of highway signs.

The headline in the March 1948 newspaper read, "***Former Policeman Here Held in SF For Bank Robbery.***" Grady Arthur Webb, thirty years old, had been a Salinas police officer between December 1942, and January 1943, and again between May 1943, and August 1943. He had been fired for conduct unbecoming an officer. He had served a sentence of six months for carrying a concealed weapon and threatening people and was released from the Monterey County Jail on November 2, 1947. He had also been arrested by Salinas police in 1946, charged with battery, and served a county sentence. Webb's current charges stemmed from the San Francisco Bank of America robbery where the teller was told by the robber that he was holding a gun on her. The FBI arrested Webb, but credited Chief Weight and Lt. Joe Yetter of Salinas for solving the crime. The Salinas officers, relying on a tip from a local source that Webb's girlfriend was suspicious of his sudden wealth, located her in Las Vegas and got a statement. Webb had netted $7,332 in the robbery and had gone to Detroit, where he lost all the money except for a small amount he had given to a friend for safekeeping. Taking that, he went to Los Angeles, where he was robbed. Unemployed, and without any of the proceeds of the robbery, he had been living in a hotel. In April 1948, Webb was convicted of the bank robbery and formally charged with additional robberies of banks in Long Beach and Santa Monica.

In March 1948, fifty-eight officers graduated from the FBI National Academy in Washington. Six of those were from Northern California and included Chief George Weight and Patrolman Harold Duncan, both of the Salinas Police Department. Two members of the Sheriff's Department had submitted applications for later sessions, but none had attended to date.

Police received a call from a man in the wee hours of the morning of March 30, 1948. After asking for help, the man collapsed. Officers found him weak from blood loss. He was bleeding out from the area where a tooth had been pulled. Rather than waiting for an ambulance, police rushed the man to the Park Lane Hospital where he received a blood transfusion that saved his life.

By the end of March, 380 cases were pending in police court. Four hundred forty-one people were fined during the month, with charges ranging from disturbing the peace to drunk driving and speeding. The number of cases and the amounts of fines had sharply decreased for the same period one year earlier.

Parking problems continued, leading to the hiring of a planning consultant from Los Angeles. After analyzing the city's parking and traffic issues, the expert concluded that downtown business owners, parking in the valuable nearby spaces, were taking up parking needed for shoppers. Finding a total of six hundred possible parking places, he stated Salinas needed six thousand, comparing parking meters to aspirin, saying, "Aspirin gives temporary relief, but is no substitute for an operation when an operation is needed." He jeered at the city's diagonal parking places saying that only added to the traffic flow problem. He suggested all day parking areas for shop owners and clerks, leaving customers the best spots for easier and closer access to the stores.

Daily reports of serious accidents continued to headline the news. Between April 25 – 29, 1948, thirteen accidents injured nine persons within the city limits. County statistics were staggering. The toll for Monterey County during the first four months of 1948 was twelve deaths, 172 injuries and 134 accidents. The death toll for 1947 was forty-nine, with 778 injuries received in 984 accidents. Cars crashed on city streets, at railroad crossings, and into coffee shops.

Car dealers had to go before the city council to request a permit to operate a business. Chief Weight reported during one meeting that violations by one such businessman were still pending in court. The city denied him the needed license. The top money maker in April was revenue from the parking meters. $2,947.50 was collected through fines, the result of 528 tickets issued. Drunk in public and drunk driving fines took second seat to the parking meter violations that month.

Salinas police were faced with more than traffic accidents and drunks. A two-year old boy became trapped between pipes, falling on his head. He was in danger of being crushed when the fire department was called. Police, afraid to await the arrival of the firemen, took matters into their own hands, rescuing the young boy before the fire units arrived.

The El Rey movie theater box office was the scene of an armed robbery in May 1948. With a revolver pointed at her head, the cashier handed over $33 to one of the two robbers, who asked for more. She then handed him eleven additional dollars, asking him if he wanted the change from the till. He did not and the cashier was able to give excellent descriptions of the two robbers to police. Fortunately, the bulk of the theater's money had just been deposited into the safe, and the bandits got away with only the money kept in the till to give change.

Chief Weight, again on the job, confiscated a collection of fighting cocks and sent them to the city pound to be cared for until he could figure out what to do with them. The pound master retuned a note to the chief, telling him he had placed the chickens in the "pond." The chief, not sure whether the pound master had misunderstood his instructions or had just made a spelling error, sent another note asking the officer to, "Either get those chickens out of the pond, or put the "U" back into pound!"

Traffic officers took their duties very seriously and rarely gave warnings or breaks to offenders. One day, finding a car parked in front of a coffee shop with an expired meter, an officer got off his motorcycle to write a ticket. The owner, sitting calmly eating at a table in the restaurant told the officer, "You can't give me a ticket; the sign says," 'Free Parking While Eating!' The officer, instructing the offender, read the rest of the small print on the sign to the man before giving him the ticket. The small print said, "In the rear."

Chief Weight started early recruiting special police officers for the big rodeo week. Notices were put up around town and in all the newspapers. The city council agreed to across the board pay raises for employees. The pay raises, which would take place on July 1, 1948, would increase the salary of the police chief to $460 per month. By way of comparison, the police judge would earn only $402 per month after the increase, and the city manager would make $718.75 with his raise.

The 1948 police department was proclaimed "efficient" by the newspaper in June 1948. With twenty-eight members, the department boasted of Chief Weight, Captain McIntyre, Lieutenants Marvin Roberts, Eldon Fowles and Joe Yetter. Sergeants included Earl Ashton, Herb Lasserot, Jack Wright and Harold Duncan. Lorraine Fontes and June Toney were the clerks at that time. The department operated three patrol cars equipped with two-way radio systems, one patrol wagon with a one-way radio, one three-wheeled motorcycle with a one-way radio and three solo bikes with one-way radio systems. Harold Duncan had only recently been promoted to Desk Sergeant when Officer Thomas Jones resigned. Jones would be seeking employment elsewhere, leaving another opening in the department.

By June 1948, the police court was handling an average of sixty-nine cases per day. More than half the cases were parking meter violations. Two hundred eight criminal cases were filed in May 1948, resulting in fifty-four persons being fined and ninety-two receiving jail sentences. KDON-FM went on the air on June 12, 1948, bringing the new FM radio system to Salinas. Still trying to find enough good men and women to assist Salinas officers during the rodeo season, the chief issued a call for fifty more applicants. Sgt. Jack Wright was elected president of the MCPOA just days before Chief Weight swore in seventy-eight new, special police officers. Their names and addresses were listed in the newspaper that June. One familiar name, and the only female in the group of seventy-eight, was former Salinas officer Mabel Eisemann. Their efforts would result in one hundred thirty persons appearing in Judge Sorenson's police court following the weekend of the rodeo celebration. Charged with disturbing the peace, fighting, malicious mischief, and drunk in public; men and women were fined. Chief Weight praised the work of the special police officers who had held the town together during the four days of the rodeo, which had been attended by 55,000 that year.

With the rodeo over, the chief began a campaign for a safer Salinas. Asking citizens to make sure they had a safe Fourth of July celebration, he warned of the hazards of the season and sought out criminals of all ages. A gang of five young boys, ages six to thirteen, was arrested and held for multiple burglaries around town. Believing the gang was responsible for eleven cases, police questioned the boys, who finally admitted their guilt. Most lived in squalid conditions in the Bataan trailer park. One, along with his mother and five siblings, lived in a one-room trailer. The boys stole cash and candy, dividing it up between them.

The Salinas Junior College was renamed in 1948 after twenty-eight years and was henceforth to be called Hartnell College. The change was made because students from other areas, attending the college in Salinas, thought the name would be more reflective of the variety of students at the college. The original Hartnell College was the first in California and had been located five miles east of town, in the Gabilan mountains.

Sgt. Jack Wright became the president of the MCPOA in July 1948. A barbecue in King City celebrated not only the new officers of the organization, but also its anniversary. The group, originally organized in 1946, held monthly meetings during which important dignitaries would speak to officers from all agencies in the area. At the July 1948 meeting, Opie L. Warner, editor of the Police and Peace Officer's Journal, spoke about his thirty-seven years as a police reporter in San Francisco. The meeting closed with a motion in memory of one of the founders of the MCPOA. L.L. "Doc" Watson, had been a sheriff's deputy and was one of the founding members of the organization.

Still trying to build his police force, the Chief announced the hiring of Buddy E. Wright. Wright had served a trial period with the department and was appointed as a probationary officer in July 1948. Edwin Tregenza, having served his trial period as well as a probationary period, was hired as a regular officer at the same time. A few months later, Chief Weight hired Richard G. Crocker, the son of a county sheriff's office juvenile officer on January 10, 1949. The twenty-one year old Crocker had served in the 11th Airborne Division of the army and had recently been discharged after serving in the Pacific Theater.

The city was growing. Valley Center was under construction, with new stores opening daily. Sears opened in July 1948, followed by Woolworth's and others. The modern displays and large sizes of the stores interested the public, who flocked to the openings. New and more prolific drug dealers were appearing in the city as well as new stores. Ten pounds of marijuana, worth $10,000 was seized by Salinas police. The drugs, located at the Guerrero Camp on Boronda Road, were guarded by a watch dog and the doors had been fortified.

THE BROWN'S DEPARTMENT STORE ROBBERY OF 1948

The biggest robbery in Salinas in recent history took place at 9:35 p.m. on December 21, 1948. Brown's Department Store, located at 320 Main Street, was at that time, one of the only "department" stores in Salinas. While taking the $5,455 day's receipts to the bank that night Mr. Wallen, an employee, was approached by three men as he put his key into the bank depository lock. One man shoved a gun in the face of the victim, while the other grabbed the canvas bag of money. There were no witnesses other than Mr. Wallen, who could state only that the two men were white and well-dressed.

THE POLICE BENEFIT ASSOCIATION SHOW OF 1948

The Salinas Police Benefit Association was busy planning a vaudeville style show that would serve as a fundraiser for local charities. Held at the Salinas High School auditorium in September 1949, the show boasted ten big name vaudeville acts. Benny Rubin, who directed the Abbott and Costello shows and worked in movies as well as radio, would be the Master of Ceremonies. Other sensational acts would include Ames and Arno, comedians, the Morrell Trio, skaters, Johnson and Diehl, jugglers and many other singers, dancers and entertainers. Harold Duncan's wife was in charge.

The possible ramifications of annexing the Alisal District were discussed in 1949. In a question and answer column in the local paper, editors asked what the effect would be upon the police department. The answer, partially quoted below, shows what the department expected. "Consolidation of the Alisal with Salinas will present no special police problems other than recruitment and training of additional qualified personnel for patrol duty." The article went on to explain that no additional administrative or office staff would be needed, but that officers would need equipment such as radio cars and modern radio equipment. Believing that expansion of the Salinas force was preferable to the starting up costs of a brand new police department, a "short adjustment period" was expected. *Salinas Californian, September 14, 1949.* Put to a vote one week after that article, the citizens of Alisal rejected the annexation proposal by a large margin.

TODDLER DEFIES POLICE

A young, three year old girl was picked up by police and taken to the station where she was "interrogated" by six different officers trying to learn where she lived. According to the news report that day, she gave only "evasive" answers. Her father finally arrived to pick her up, telling officers she had crawled out of her mother's car while her mother had been shopping downtown. Hoping her first ride with a policeman would be her last, the father was told that, in the future, she could, "hold out until her lawyer arrived." *Salinas Californian, September 24, 1949.*

The MCPOA had a meeting and barbecue at the posse grounds on Old Stage Road in 1948. It was at that meeting the board voted to include members of the Army Provost Marshall's office, fish and game wardens and the county coroner in the organization. The newly elected president was Sgt. Jack Wright of the Salinas Police Department. In August, statistics from the National Safety Council were published. 32,300 traffic fatalities were reported for 1947, the same day three people were injured in crashes in Salinas. Babe Ruth died that month of cancer, and thousands of fans walked past an open casket located in the rotunda of the stadium known as, "the house that Ruth built." Penney's had opened its first store in Salinas in 1928. The original store, located inside the Cominos Hotel met the local needs until 1948, when the modernized store was built.

In-service training for officers began early in 1949, with firearms training high on the list of things Chief Weight wanted to improve. Two FBI officers led the school, which took place at the old Toro park range. Chief Weight wanted monthly practice sessions after the supervised training was over. The chief made the rounds, speaking at various events, schools and organizations. He delivered a speech at Hartnell about narcotics and the probability of addicts becoming problem criminals. He provided students with a display of opium scales, cans and paraphernalia. No training could prepare officers for the risks they took on a daily basis. One officer had placed a dog into the patrol wagon and taken it to the pound after it bit a little girl in the leg. In attempting to remove the animal from the wagon, the officer received numerous bites to his fight hand and had to be sent to the hospital.

In 1949, the International City Manager's Association came out with a report listing Salinas as having the highest proportion of officers to population in the country. With twenty-nine full time officers on the SPD payroll, figures indicated a 1.96 per 1,000 resident ratio of officers. The national average at the time was 1.89. "The per capita cost of maintaining the Salinas Police Department is higher than in most cities," the study said, costing $6.56 per resident annually, rather than the $4.03 per resident seen in most cities of similar size. The starting salary for patrolmen in Salinas was $2,760 per year, also above the national average of $2,305, according to the survey. *Salinas Californian, January 1949.*

Chief Weight, on a mission to properly train his officers, sent three men to the new Camp Shoemaker Northern California Peace Officer's Training School in February 1949. Officer William A. Miller, Homer L. McNabb and Richard G. Crocker, were all men with little or no previous training. They were the first of the Salinas officers sent to study the four week course. Instruction in report writing, patrol procedures, care of equipment, rules of evidence, interrogation techniques, accident investigation, first aid and firearms, were only part of the course. Officers were also given instruction in courtesy, public relations and the penal code.

While the three officers were away for training, fellow officers had to call in firemen to assist with a downtown call. A four-month old pig was discovered window shopping in the two hundred block of Main Street by one of the motorcycle officers. Unable to contain the animal himself, and calling for much needed backup, the officer soon had help from both the police and fire departments. The round up began with the motor officer shouting directions and officers chasing the renegade pig around the downtown area. With the suspect finally in custody in the brand new patrol wagon, the officers held a conference about their collective lack of exercise and conditioning. *Salinas Californian, February 1949.*

With District Attorney Anthony Brazil appointed to the Supreme Court, Burr Scott was appointed to the position of District Attorney by the board of supervisors. Judge Brazil would be sworn in the same day Judge Henry Jorgensen announced his intention to retire at the end of his term. Jorgensen served for twenty-one years as the county's only Superior Court judge. Two new, 1949 Chevrolet sedans replaced the two, "old" 1948 models in the departments. Equipped with two-way radios, red light and sirens, the cars would be fitted with FM frequency modulation equipment to coincide with the new radio station being installed at the department. The city knew a modern jail and police station were badly needed. The city council discussed the possibility of selling the Clay Street Park in order to raise much needed funding for the new facilities. After a house-to-house survey found many children in the area who used the park, the council voted against the recommendation to sell the park.

The frequency of loose dogs continued to irk local authorities. L.F. Bollegar was the pound man in 1949 and wanted all citizens to be made aware of the laws regarding loose pets. In a brief article in the newspaper, Bollegar wrote, "Here are the rules:

1. Dogs within the city limits must be on leashes.
2. No dogs are allowed on school grounds.
3. No dogs are allowed in public parks."

Continuing, he stated, "All dogs impounded are kept for seventy-two hours for the owners to claim them. If you want your dog back, have $3 bail to pay the standard pound fee." *Salinas Californian, October 19, 1949.*

Overtime parking still managed to be the largest contributor to the city coffers by way of fines. The third quarter of 1949 brought $10,240 from parking fines, peace disturbance cases and drunk driving cases submitted to the police court. It was during this same time that the first instance of probation being granted in a marijuana case was reported. Until that time, the law called for a jail sentence of a minimum of three months for the offense.

C.C. Rogers, a familiar name to Salinas officers, along with a team of Salinas men, won a silver cup at the Arizona Challenge Cup, a prestigious competition for marksmen. Rogers won not only in the team competition, but was overall champion in the .28 gauge individual competition. Rogers had been with the department many years when, in 1939, he was recognized for another of his famous talents. Officer Rogers had invented a home-made quail call that was surprisingly successful. Using old clothes-pins and rubber bands, he constructed an instrument "that really works!" *Salinas Californian, December 8, 1939.*

Commercial burglaries were hurting business all over town. On one night, the Sugar Valley Pet Center, Tynan Lumber, Salinas Farm Supply, Teamsters office and others were all hit. Police believed the six burglaries to be the work of one person, or group. Damage at all the businesses would amount to more than the $95 in proceeds located by the bandits. Store owners were getting bold and one man working at the Palace Liquor Store at 17 W. Market, when confronted by a robber who tried to hold up the store for a bottle of whiskey, ordered him out of the store. The store manager told the robber, "I don't put up with this sort of thing." Some argument ensued, but the robber was scared off when another customer arrived. *Salinas Californian, September 8, 1948.*

Burglaries were bothersome, but violence was also soaring in town. Police discovered an unconscious man at the Shell station at Main and Soledad Streets one night. The man had been stabbed by a female acquaintance and had tried to make his way for help before collapsing. An argument resulting from two men who disagreed about who was going to drive a car, led to one removing a screw driver from the glove compartment and viciously stabbing the other, resulting in a charge of assault with a deadly weapon.

Introduced by Chief George Weight in September 1948 at a meeting of the Rotary Club, FBI agent Scott Werner spoke on crime statistics. Blaming much on the end of WWII, a period of lawlessness and a tendency towards organized crime, the agent informed the Salinas audience that there was now "one major crime committed in the United States every eighteen seconds." *Salinas Californian, September 15, 1948.*

Major crimes aside, police were constantly taking accident reports. Seven accidents in one weekend resulted in some citations, several injuries and much damage to vehicles. Police were to get a new patrol wagon as soon as the city council approved the $1,442.28 needed to purchase the much needed conveyance from Richardson Motor Company. Training of officers was also discussed at the city council meeting that evening. Concerned over the hiring of Patrolman M. D. Kert, hired on a probationary status, Councilman John Meyenberg gave his opinion that officers should be trained before being hired. Responding, Chief Weight reported that without funding, it was not possible. Once hired, recruits were tutored by fellow officers who had more experience. He also spoke about wanting to send some of the younger men to a training program and was instructed to get the details and costs for council members to review, approving the appointment of Officer Kert that night.

Chief Weight's Drunkometer

Claiming that many metropolitan police agencies were now using the machine, Chief Weight told the city council of the "drunkometer," a reliable device used to test the extent of one's intoxication. He had a list of equipment for the modern police department, including the new, "Black Maria" wagon which would replace a ten year old wagon. A wire recorder and shot gun as well as an adding machine had been requested. The chief would also need to replace some officers as former police officers Robert Taylor and Charleston White, Jr. moved to the Highway Patrol. *Salinas Californian, October 23, 1948.*

The November 1948 meeting of the MCPOA took place at Walker's Café. The chief of the San Francisco FBI office spoke to officers of the coming of a wave of crime, spurred on mostly by the influx of organized crime. He told the local officers that California law officers, more than any others in the United States, were sent to the FBI academy for training. The result of that was that more evidence was being sent for processing to the FBI lab. California was sending twice as much evidence as the next closest state. He further advocated the withdrawal of support for inappropriate movies and radio channels, which he felt "fostered and encouraged crime in both adults and juveniles." *Salinas Californian, November 19, 1948.*

Salinas still had a police court which took care of city cases and imposed fines. During the 1949-50 fiscal year, 22,182 cases were heard by Judge Sorenson, formally a Salinas police officer. While overtime parking accounted for the bulk of the fines, cases involving disturbing the peace and drunk driving brought in over $20,000 in fines. Parking meter fines, speeding and other miscellaneous offenses brought the total amount of money brought to Salinas through fines imposed by the police court to over $40,000. Numerous reports of petty thefts, shoplifting, and burglaries were in the news daily. People left their homes and cars unlocked, and thieves made good use of the opportunities, taking everything from cameras and guns to coats, money and jewelry. Accidents continued to injure both citizens and officers. In January 1950, Traffic Officer Luther Pilcher, then twenty-eight years old, was seriously injured when his motorcycle collided with a car that turned in front of him. Officer Pilcher was in pursuit of a speeder at the time. Officer Pilcher's accident was only one of nine accidents inside the city that New Year's weekend. Police arrested drunk drivers and hit and run suspects in addition to citing dozens for speeding and other moving violations.

New officers were being added in 1949. Roland Thiesen had been a carpenter and Edward Hale was in the Army for six years before being hired as officers. Salinas officers were featured in short biographies in the newspapers. Ray McIntyre was a captain in 1949, with over eleven years on the force. Russell Hill was the "Identification Officer," specializing in fingerprint classification and filing, and early crime scene investigation work, including making plaster casts of footprints and tire marks and photography of crime scenes. After eight years in the Army, Hill had been with the department since 1945. Sgt.

Harold Duncan, nicknamed, "Dunc," was in charge of police records, citizen complaints and officer assignments. He was a member of many organizations, including the MCPOA and the International Footprinters Association. Joseph Yetter, who had been in Salinas as an officer for six years, was named Chief of Police in Gonzales in December 1949. Chosen from eight applicants, Chief Yetter had been a traffic officer with SPD before being promoted to lieutenant, a position he held until he resigned to become the chief in Gonzales. Earl Ashton was a lieutenant when he was featured in the paper. Having been a military police officer, he was now in charge of all policemen and department equipment. Willard Gilbert was a traffic officer who had been with the department for two years. A VFW member who had served in the Navy, Gilbert rode one of the motorcycles used by Salinas for traffic patrol. *Salinas Californian, December 1949.* The officers, new and old, enjoyed a family holiday party that year. With Officer Edward Hale as Santa Claus, gifts were distributed to forty-eight children.

Seven Hour Respite

The unusual quiet of a seven hour period was significant enough to warrant documentation. Late in 1949, a seven hour period during which it was raining, resulted in no traffic accidents. Not even one fender-bender was reported between 2:00 a.m. and 9:00 a.m. December 16, 1949. Officers were hoping the trend would continue.

A hit and run driver ended the 404 day safety record in Salinas, fatally injuring a pedestrian near the California Street extension in August 1950. The "Boxscore" for August 14, 1950, tragically stated, "It HAD been 404 Days since Salinas had a Traffic Death." Police investigated and an arrest was made less the forty-eight hours after the crash that killed the forty-three year old field laborer. Officers scoured the city auto repair businesses, looking for a car with front end damage. Finding a suspiciously damaged car parked on East Market Street, police were able to link the physical evidence to the crime and got a signed statement from the driver.

The education of the American public helped reduce the number of fatal accidents involving children ages five through fifteen. Chief Weight spoke of early driver education, beginning at the elementary school level when he was the guest speaker at a meeting of the Roosevelt School PTA. Coroner Elmer Machado joined the chief at the meeting, speaking about children who had been burned, suffocated, and run over. Chief Weight truly believed that education for everyone, including his officers, was of paramount importance in teaching responsibility for life.

When Chief George Weight resigned, applications were sent out for those who wished to put their names in for the chief's job which paid $450 to $653 per month. The department was authorized to have thirty-six officers at that time and the chief was responsible for reporting to the city manager.

The thirty-five candidates for chief took a three hour test covering "intelligence, aptitude and knowledge," according to the *Salinas Californian* article of January 13, 1951. While the candidates for chief and sergeant waited for the outcome of the testing procedures, police continued to battle constant car crashes, burglaries, robberies and other crimes. Officer Roland Thiesen, whose address was provided to readers in the newspaper article of January 15, 1951, had the misfortune of being involved in an accident while responding to a disturbance. Fortunately, there were no injuries. However, news articles of the time regularly listed the addresses of officers in stories about police arrests and activities. The accident came at a time when the department was launching its new Police Traffic Control Unit which consisted of one car and three motorcycles. The day after the article about Officer Thiesen's accident appeared in the *Salinas Californian,* a photo of the new unit ran on the front page. Sgt. Jack Wright, Luther Pilcher, R.J. McPeek, Richard Crocker, Harley Hayes and Andrew Cline stood proudly in front of their vehicles. Captain McIntyre announced the new unit as part of his duties as the acting chief at the time.

Sgt. Jack Wright was the commanding officer of the five man unit which would wear cap covers and white gloves. Richard Crocker, who would be Unit 5 would soon make a name for himself as he attempted to capture a loose steer on the tracks at the underpass. On his motorcycle, Officer Crocker was chasing the animal when it jumped over the wall, landing on the highway beneath the tracks. Undeterred by its injuries, the large steer shook off the fall and took off running, oblivious to a bloody nose. In an undated news article provided by Richard Crocker, a reporter made the following report; "The motorized cowcops took off in hot pursuit." Crocker, calling for assistance, was joined by numerous cowboys and was finally successful in trapping the animal in a blind canyon near the Tynan Lumber Company. With the assistance of star roper George Burns, who worked for the beef company, the animal was roped, but continued to fight, throwing Mr. Burns around a bit before being subdued and returned to its fellow inmates. Crocker would be promoted to sergeant by the time he was twenty-seven years old. He went on to become a detective, making significant drug busts. One such case would be dismissed due to his and the department's policy to protect the confidential identity of their informants. Heroin was the predominant drug at the time and Crocker played a large role in surveillance and arrests of many suspects. In the largest bust in many years, Crocker found forty-two bindles and nine caps of heroin behind a mirror at 348 California Street during a search warrant. Still living in King City, Richard Crocker provided stories and photographs of his days with SPD.

The department needed more support staff and hired Miss Dorothy Gerona as a typist-clerk in April 1950. Miss Gerona lived on Lake Street and had moved to Salinas from Los Angeles as a child, attending the local high school where she was the senior class secretary. Miss Vivian Amaya started her career with the SPD as a clerk shortly after Miss Gerona. She had attended schools in the Santa Cruz area as well as Hartnell College. Living on West Street, Miss Amaya's duties included transcribing shorthand, typing, and general office work.

Neighbors in the Maple Park area were the victims of a prowler/burglar during the summer of 1950. Multiple houses were hit by a man police searched for over a period of days and nights. Mrs. Eddie Smith, widow of the late Officer Smith, was the reporting party in the wee hours of August 19, 1950, when a man entered her home. Giving police the details over the phone as the man ran out the back door of her Maple Street house, police were able to catch a suspect, who was later identified by Mrs. Smith as the man who had been inside her home.

New traffic signals were installed downtown. Monterey and San Luis Streets, Monterey and Market Streets, and Monterey and Gabilan Streets were the first to get the synchronized light systems. Monterey and John Streets would be next on the list. A smooth flow of traffic was the goal of the lights.

The Korean War was big news, and many local men were called up to serve. Police Officer Raymond Waters had been on inactive reserve status during his duties with the SPD. As a former Air Force officer, he had served as a sergeant-pilot during the Second World War. A tail gunner and fire coordinator for B-24 bombers, he was also sent to the European theater during the war. After being discharged, he signed up for the corps of military police, where he was designated as an inactive reserve until being called up in August 1950. Married with two sons, the Salinas officer reported for Army duty to Fort Ord on September 19, 1950, as a sergeant first class with the corps of military police, leaving Salinas short yet another officer.

There were five vacancies in the department in addition to the position of chief late in 1950. Forty people submitted applications for the five positions and a dozen more had requested application forms. Testing for the new applicants took place in November, with a total of forty-four taking the police exams. By January 1951, fourteen officers were testing for the four positions as sergeants. The salary range for police sergeant was $288 to $360 per month.

January 1951, provided many photo opportunities for the police department. On January 21, 1951, another large photo and article appeared featuring those who had completed a law enforcement training school at Hartnell College. Acting Chief McIntyre, Lt. Earl Ashton, Sgt. Harold Duncan, Patrolman Woodrow Meek, and Sgt. Jack Wright were all graduates. Several days later, Acting Chief McIntyre and Sgt. Jack Wright again made the news with their presentation of a trophy to the Lincoln School children's Traffic Patrol. The same day, a comical photograph showed off the new "mechanical cop" being tested by officers in Salinas. This was the first battery operated and portable traffic signal. Weighing 250 pounds, the signal was shown off by Judge Sorenson and Sgt. Jack Wright. It had retractable wheels so officers could move it to needed locations.

Sgt. Jack Wright had been born in Hollister, but moved to Salinas to join the police department in 1942. He had served in the Army Air Corps for four years before returning to the area and becoming a police officer. As a past president of the MCPOA, he loved to golf and hunt. Still on the force, as the head of the traffic division and in charge of the school junior traffic patrols, Sgt. Wright lived on Capistrano Drive with his wife and two children. He was featured in the newspaper in a series called, "They Work For You," a series that often featured police or sheriff's officers, complete with a photograph.

A few days after Sgt. Wright was featured, the man of the day was Officer James C. Ailes, who had been with the department for only one and one-half years. Prior to coming to Salinas, Officer Ailes had worked as an officer in his native Nebraska, at the Grand Island police department. He had also served in the armed services, serving six years of duty that included the cavalry, infantry and air corps. As a former army pilot, he continued to hold certification as both a private and commercial multi-engine pilot. When not flying, he enjoyed collecting.and repairing various guns and was a member of the American Legion, the air reserve, and the Reserve Officer's Association. He lived on Archer Street with his wife and young daughter.

A pension plan versus social security was voted on by city employees in

March 1951. By a small margin, the pension plan won, paving the way for the state retirement plan. On February 19, 1951, Captain Raymond McIntryre was named chief. At a salary of $476 per month, McIntryre won the position over thirty-two other candidates. McIntryre hailed from Castroville and had attended local schools. He served in the Air Force from 1942 until 1945 and returned to the police force on January 1, 1946, as a patrolman. Promoted to lieutenant three months later and to captain just three months after that, he had been acting chief since November 1950. Chief Weight's secretary, Reba Albery had worked for him for about one year prior to his retirement. When McIntyre took over as chief, Reba was offered the job as secretary to the city manager, but, in her words, much to McIntyre's relief, she decided to stay with police department. Reba had been called upon at times to be present when women were brought in by the male officers on an on call basis. She was paid three dollars each time she was called to the station between 4:00 p.m. and midnight. She moved back into town so the police cars could pick her up when she was needed. When Reba became engaged, McIntyre worried again that he might lose his secretary, but she stayed on for another nine years, having earned the nickname, "Sergeant Major," by the officers who were so fond of her. At the top of her pay scale, Reba earned $750 per month. Her granddaughter lives locally and provided a document written by Reba, recalling her life in the police department. Reba Albery Lotten worked for three chiefs during her time with SPD. Chiefs Weight, McIntyre, and Roberson would all depend upon her assistance in their jobs. She lived in Salinas for over seventy years, and was an eighth generation birthright member of the Society of Friends, Quakers. She died in 2001, at the age of ninety-two.

Sgt. Jack Wright participated in a vocational guidance program at Washington Junior High School in November 1951. Along with fire and sheriff's representatives, Sgt. Wright discussed educational requirements for police officers and boasted of the department's ability to set up a road block covering a fifty mile radius within ten minutes. He gave a demonstration of the use of the police radio, most likely providing the precursors to the DARE programs of later years.

Woodrow, "Woody," Meek began his career as a Salinas police officer on June 10, 1948. Alive and well, Meek continues to live in Salinas and provided his memories and many photographs of his years as an officer. Meek was hired as a patrolman after returning from the war. He started work on the street the day he was hired. His training consisted of being told to go up and down Main

Street and check the doors of each business According to Meek, the probation period for new officers was simple, "Stay alive for six months, you got the job."

Newly appointed Officer Meek was on duty the night of a tragic accident involving a fellow officer. Two cars were sent to an alarm call in south Salinas. The first car contained Patrolmen Eddie Tregenza and Walter Wiechring and left from the old Salinas Street location, siren blaring and made it through the intersection of Alisal and Salinas Streets. The second car, driven by another officer came from close by, also running with lights and sirens. Two motorcyclists were on their way to the police station that afternoon, one a man with his wife seated behind him. At the corner stood a Shell Gas Station which was later moved to the city yard. The station and buildings at that intersection possibly blocked the sound of the siren and the second patrol car hit the motorcyclist who said he never heard them coming. The driver's wife was killed and the officer driving the patrol car was devastated. The driver of the motorcycle claimed to never had heard the sirens, but other witnesses working in the area told officers they clearly heard and saw both police cars with lights and sirens. Estimates of speed varied witness by witness. The officer quit that night, making promotions imminent. Meek was told to work the desk from that night on and was given thirty minutes of training. His first day on the job he fielded dozens of calls regarding the fatal accident. Officer Les Emory investigated the accident and told jurors at a coroner's jury later that the police car left skid marks of eighteen inches, the motorcycle none at all. The tragedy was further amplified by the fact that the alarm at Sears, the destination of the responding officers, had been nothing but a false alarm. The jurors heard testimony about the motorcycle having been stopped earlier that day and cited for not having a muffler. After hearing the testimony and spending forty-five minutes deliberating, the coroner's jury exonerated the former officer. A $50,000 claim was filed by the husband of the woman killed in the accident, and was denied in what everyone called, "standard procedure." A civil suit would later be filed against the city. *Salinas Californian, October-November, 1948.*

Woody Meek was sent to burglary school soon after the accident and desk sergeant training and became the resident expert in fingerprinting. He held nearly every job in the department with the exception of the juvenile officer position, which he refused to accept. He was promoted to lieutenant, and captain, a position he held until Ted Adsit, the city manager decided to reorganize the department, reducing many to a lower rank. Meek was reduced to sergeant. Adsit left town for a job as a professor in Pennsylvania and died shortly thereafter.

Commercial burglaries plagued the city, and Meek recalls repeat burglaries at El Charrito Market and Standard Furniture. Envelopes of cash seemed to disappear from the safe inside Standard Furniture on a regular basis until Meek had them put the safe right up in the front window where officers could see it. Meek had the right idea and the safe was never burgled again.

Prostitution was legal then, and the ladies registered at the police department, having their photos and fingerprints taken. Meek recalls the days when men were lined up around the corner from one of the houses, waiting to go in. Meek's vivid memories of Chinatown include an incident where a car drove into a market, breaking the glass in the windows and the shelves where liquor had been stored. The winos were there immediately, licking the wine up off the sidewalk and floor.

Chinatown in 1950s
Courtesy of Woody Meek

Inspections were unheard of until McIntyre became chief. Holding a surprise inspection, Officer Bill Hurley's weapon was found to be so corroded the cylinder wouldn't open. Another officer had no bullets in his gun, saying his religious beliefs didn't allow him to carry ammunition.

Alisal Street divided the town into two beats, north and south. Meek recalls a terrible accident where Main Street used to cross Market. Five soldiers, speeding in their car, ran into a diesel truck. Finding all five dead at the scene, Meek radioed for additional flares. Officer Kuykendall arrived at the scene with three flares, all they had at the time.

Many of us can remember exactly where we were when we heard of the assassination of President Kennedy. Meek, too, recalls that day. He had been called to the scene of a fatal traffic accident at the corner of Acacia and San Vincente. Working the accident, he saw a man running towards him, screaming. The man told him the President had been shot and killed.

Meek's favorite assignment was investigations. He liked to hunt people down and pry into things. He still keeps records of homicide and traffic fatality cases he worked and can provide the details of each case. In his time, officers typed their own reports on six by nine inch cards on three old typewriters.

Officers were required to attend certain schools, but were not paid for their time nor were they given comp time. Court was also done on the officer's own time, without compensation. Officers clocked in on a much hated time clock. Anyone not clocked in ten minutes before shift was docked pay. A class action suit later on behalf of all the officers brought a welcome check to Meek many years later in the amount of $4,343.46. His starting salary in 1948 was $264 per month. The mayor hand signed each check and officers had to track him down to get their pay each month. Meek retired after thirty-two years and continued on as a polygraph examiner for the department. Asked to name and train his successor, Meek carefully considered a number of men before choosing Paul Scott. The first Police Officer Standard Training classes for officers were initiated in the 1950s and the first use of a polygraph machine in a murder case occurred in Salinas.

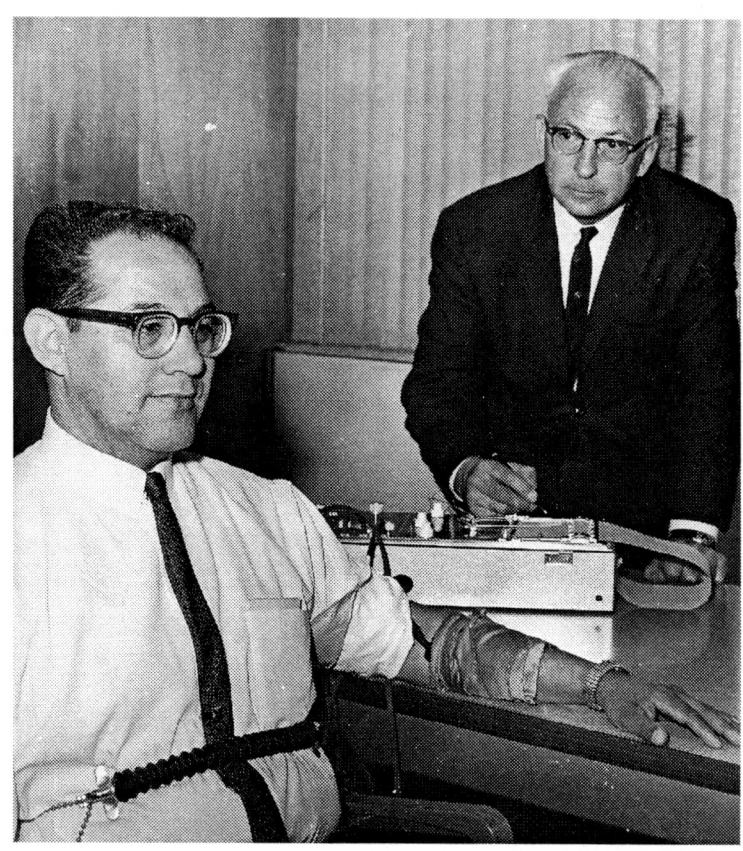
*Officer Meek uses one of the first Polygraph Machines
Courtesy of Woody Meek*

SIXTEEN

Chief Ray McIntyre

In 1950, Ray McIntyre organized the reserves for the first time.

Raymond McIntyre was formally appointed Chief of Police on February 19, 1951. He took over a very active department. Two thousand two hundred thirteen traffic citations were issued during the month of December in 1951. Two hundred seventy-one were for moving violations, but the vast majority were for meter violations. Eighty-one accidents were reported within the city that month for a total of sixteen injuries. There were twelve burglaries, fifty petty thefts, and twenty-seven arrests for drunkenness. There was one arrest for assault with a deadly weapon and numerous other police contacts, investigations and arrests.

Sergeants Robert McPeek and Jack Wright were promoted to the position of Lieutenant in January 1952. Wright was assigned as lieutenant in charge of the day traffic unit and McPeek took over the night patrol division. Wright, a past president of the Monterey County Peace Officer's Association, had been with the department since 1942. McPeek, a more recent employee, had begun his career in Salinas in 1948. With the promotion of McPeek and Wright to lieutenant, four patrolmen were named as sergeants. Homer McNabb had been with SPD since February 1949, and Herb Lasserot since April 1943. Cecil Pirtle started in January 1951, and Eugene Smith came to Salinas in June 1950. Smith had started in the service division. All four were listed as desk sergeants. The department set about testing for new applicants.

A traffic safety campaign was launched in 1952, in an attempt to lower the number of serious and fatal accidents within the city limits. Several slogans were used to promote citizen cooperation. "Go to traffic court as a visitor, not as a violator," was one such slogan. Signs showing blind justice holding the scales with the slogan boldly printed across it ran in the local newspaper. Chief McIntyre warned residents and visitors to obey all traffic laws and that ignorance was no excuse for violations.

The King of England had died and Queen Elizabeth was crowned in 1952. The cost of living was going up and local barbers infuriated residents by raising the price of a haircut to $1.50 from $1.25. The president of the barber's union pointed out that local barbers were only bringing their fees into line with the other major communities of northern California.

January 1952, proved a busy month for Salinas police. One hundred thirty-five arrests were made and 2,169 citations were issued. There were sixty-four traffic accidents and the department's training and investigation division sent many men to training in San Francisco to study narcotics. Traffic officers investigated nine injury accidents out of a total of sixty-four accidents. One hundred forty-six moving violations resulted in tickets and eighty-two animals were impounded by animal control. Local chiefs of police, including Chief McIntyre, held a meeting at which they were provided with information from a "questioned documents" expert. In-service training was required for all officers, and a two hour class each week was mandatory. These classes were held on the officer's own time, and they were not paid for attending. "When a policeman goes to work, he never knows exactly what he will be called upon to do. But he must be trained to meet any emergency that arises," Lt. Duncan told reporter LaVerne Potts. "During the course of a day's work, a patrolman may be asked to do everything from chasing a stray pig along Soledad Street to stalking a burglar through a dark building. He often finds himself flirting with death chasing a speeder along El Camino Real or speeding to the scene of an accident to give aid." *Salinas Californian, February 19, 1952.*

Four officers received vocational training credentials from the state. Lt. Earl Ashton taught subjects relating to uniform patrol and preliminary crime scene investigation. Lt. Jack Wright headed the traffic division and taught all subjects related to traffic details. Lt. Duncan was in charge of the required school for officers. He was the instructor for felonies and vice. Lastly, Sgt. Meek of San Clemente Avenue, (where he continues to reside at the age of ninety,) offered instruction in office and record procedure, care and use of radio equipment and report writing.

The Salinas Police Benefit Association had been producing a benefit show for three years in 1952. The theme for the show in 1952 was "Laugh and Live Longer." Captain Fowles, as president of the organization that year, was in charge of the annual event and expected a good response to ticket sales. Mrs. Harold Duncan was promoting advance ticket sales for the event.

Shoplifting accounted for over $100,000 per year in losses to Salinas merchants. Lt. Harold Duncan and Officer Denzil Smith photographed themselves as they stole merchandise and forged checks in local stores in an attempt to educate clerks and store owners. Chief McIntyre urged all businesses to avail themselves of the services of his officers for instruction and demonstrations of shoplifting and citizen arrest procedures.

Hartnell College was in full swing. Boasting of their 643 students, the college was proud of the fifteen veterans of the Korean War who were studying now in Salinas. The college could handle 850 students and expected enrollment to increase. One of the Korean War veterans joined the police department in 1953. Floyd Hoffman, then just twenty-one years old, had served with the Marines from 1948 until 1953. Wounded by shrapnel, the corporal was employed at a fish cannery when he made a career change. Chief McIntyre announced his hiring in February 1953.

Burglaries and thefts continued. No item was spared. During one day, a water heater was stolen right out of a house on Capitol Street, a gasoline motor was taken out of a tractor on East Market, and a pistol was taken from behind the bar of the Walker's Café. Cash, papers, microphones, and radio head sets were stolen from airplanes and hangers at the airport, and a bike was taken from a church yard. Police were busy.

Jack Wright, now a Lieutenant with SPD, attended a two week training session in Berkeley, where he honed his investigative skills. Other officers attended schools in Sacramento and Los Angeles, studying accident prevention, measurements, diagramming techniques, photography, and other crime scene procedures. The chief continued to send out tips to his citizens. Asking for assistance from witnesses, the chief listed ways to help police. He included requests such as writing down license numbers of kidnapping suspects, reminding children not to talk to strangers, and reminding people that the police officer is a friend.

Strangely enough, the parking meter situation continued to create havoc downtown. In 1953, the recommendation was made that officers carry courtesy envelopes supplied with nickels. Out of town cars would not be ticketed for overtime parking. Instead, officers would take the nickel out of the envelope and put it into the parking meter. They would then place the envelope on the windshield of the offending car, hoping the owner would be inclined to send in the nickel when they returned home.

The staggering number of traffic accidents, serious injuries and fatalities was the reason for a "Safe-Driving Day" campaign by city police. The city had formed a traffic safety commission, which discussed changes in traffic flow, the department's fleet, signage, changes in zoning and education for the public. In the first twenty-four days of December 1954, fourteen persons were injured in accidents in the city limits, sixty-four accidents were investigated and 2,656 citations were issued. There were 502 moving violations issued that month. Traffic control and arrests made daily news. Fines for traffic violations had netted over $45,000 for 1953. Chief McIntyre spoke out, saying, "Traffic accidents don't just happen-they are caused." *Salinas Californian, December 14, 1954.* The county toll for deaths due to automobile accidents in 1954 was sixty-five persons.

The city was advertising for new officers and wanted to establish an eligibility list. With a salary range of $273 to $341 per month, officers would be required to work four forty-eight hour weeks, with a fifteen day vacation period. In March, the testing procedures began with a written test taken by the fourteen applicants. The city hoped to hire at least one new officer from the list.

Virgil Smith was hired as a regular patrolman in January 1953. He had served in the Navy from 1942 through 1946. He returned home to Salinas following the war and worked as a machine operator for a local milk company before becoming a police officer. Victor Viviano also started work that week. With a college education, Viviano had worked in San Jose prior to coming to Salinas. They were joined as new members of the department by Marjorie De Wees, who began her career as a clerk.

Drugs were becoming more of a problem for police in the 1950s. Sgt. Roberson was shown in the newspaper in January 1953 with a new display case which was part of an educational program about the use of narcotics. The display was portable and available with accompanying lecture for civic groups.

The training and investigations division assisted the District Attorney's Office on the investigation and arrest of a doctor who they charged with conducting an abortion and a woman they arrested for murder. Officers continually monitored bars, discouraged prostitution, worked against narcotics and assisted on fire calls. Three hundred ninety-five warrants were processed in December alone and radio transmissions topped 3,400.

Chief McIntyre warned citizens of the dangers of winter road conditions and asked them to follow six basic rules for driving in winter.

1. Accept responsibility
2. Get the "feel" of the road
3. Keep the windshield clean
4. Use tire chains
5. Pump your brakes to slow
6. Follow at a safe distance

The Chief called attention to the campaign against winter traffic hazards. The National Safety Council slogan that year was, "Stay Alert - Stay Alive in Winter Weather."

In December 1953, Salinas police began to investigate the disappearance of an elderly man living at 244 Pajaro Street. Patrolman Dale Cheek and Chief McIntyre were active in the investigation of Winnie Freeman, a Prunedale woman who was believed to have been forging checks on the missing man's account. After thorough questioning by police and the sheriff's department, Freeman was taken to San Francisco, where she underwent several polygraph tests that showed she was not being truthful. Using the tactic of telling the suspect the victim deserved a proper burial, police were able to get her to lead them to the body. Although she continued to claim the death had been an accidental shooting, Mrs. Freeman was charged with murder after the body was found in Prunedale under bushes near her house where she had dragged it after shooting the seventy-eight year old man at the base of his skull with a rifle. She was eventually found guilty of murder and sentenced to life. At the time of the murder, Freeman was on parole out of Arkansas for the murder of her father-in-law. Mrs. Freeman would be the dubbed the "Cat Woman" for her fondness of cats and the press followed her case to the end. Pictured in the newspapers at each court appearance, Freeman was accompanied by Sheriff's Matron Mae Eisemann, who had left SPD several years earlier.

As the size of the city increased, and crime with it, the city found a need to hire more officers. Applicants were interviewed in December 1953, to fill one post and provide a list for later hirings. Grover Spotts had been the superintendent of juvenile hall before becoming a police officer that year. He had studied at the Berkeley Police School after serving in the military during WWII. He placed first in the written tests and oral interview out of seventeen applicants.

The annual report for the Salinas Police Department in 1953, showed two three-wheeled motorcycles, six four-door sedans for patrol, one four-door sedan for plain clothes work, and one panel truck for animal control work as the vehicular assets for the department. Crime was escalating as the city increased in both population and acreage. By 1954, the population had increased to 20,000 and the city was celebrating its eightieth birthday. Having annexed a number of small communities, the one square mile that had begun as Salinas City now comprised almost six and a half square miles. The dirt road known as Castroville Street until 1910 was now a paved Main Street with thriving businesses that brought customers and crime to the downtown area.

The El Charro Cafe was the scene of a stabbing early in 1954 when Pete Gonzales of 339 ½ Main Street was stabbed and taken to the county hospital. Within days, a gang war had erupted in the downtown area. Fifteen to twenty young men were involved in a street gang type fight that started in from the Cork N' Bottle on Clay Street, traveled to Mel's Drive In on Main Street and back to Lincoln Avenue, where it ended with injuries in front of the Recreation Center. The injured included two Ft. Ord soldiers who had made a remark about the color of the car the Salinas youths were driving. The soldiers were outnumbered and were beaten badly, requiring hospitalization. Chief McIntyre made a statement to the press:

"Gang fights will not be tolerated in the City of Salinas." *Salinas Californian, January 1954.* The accused included both juvenile boys and one girl. Three were arrested the following day. The defendants were residents of Kilbreth Avenue and First Avenue. One was from Chualar. Within days, another stabbing occurred at the Salinas High School gymnasium. Ill feelings between two boys resulted in one stabbing the other with a knife. One seventeen year old suspect was arrested.

The number of traffic accidents continued to worry police. One trouble spot was the Main Street Railroad under-crossing. Statistics had been kept for several years, 1951 to 1953, to show how unsafe the under-crossing was. Many suggestions for solutions to the problem were discussed over a period of years. Placement of speed limit signs in other areas of the city was an attempt to aid in reducing the number of serious injury accidents.

The Monterey County Trust and Bank sponsored an advertisement in the February 6, 1954, newspaper. It featured a photograph of all police officers, the chief, and various personnel in action. The department consisted of thirty-seven male and two female officers and two male crossing guards. Police had issued over 33,000 traffic citations the previous year and responded to four fatalities. Statistics in the advertisement included the 1953 number of detailed reports as being 11,880. 39,707 arrests were made during 1953 and there were a total of 45,969 dispatches. Lt. McPeek returned from a two week course at UCLA where he studied traffic supervision in a course taught by Northwestern University. Discussions continued on the fate of the underpass which had been the scene of so many horrible accidents.

The Chin Brothers Market opened on February 20, 1954 at the corner of North Main and what was then Carneros Street. The three brothers who owned the store also operated the Sausal Meat Market. Meanwhile, robberies at markets and small stores continued. A masked gunman robbed the Front Street Market while the female owner was counting receipts. He calmly separated the checks out and took only the cash. Removing his mask as he fled the store provided the victim a chance to furnish the description of a Filipino or Mexican male. A man was killed during a fight at the bar located at the corner of Market and Main Streets. Six to eight persons were involved in the fight which left one man with a fractured skull and brain hemorrhage which led to his death. A woman was found in her burning apartment, the victim of a gunshot wound to the head. Although Kilbreth Street was county territory at the time, the suspects were Salinas men and the victim frequented Salinas establishments. A female suspect was arrested and went to trial for the murder of her female roommate. The Deputy District Attorney, William, "Bill" Bryan claimed the case was over a boyfriend. The defendant's attorney was E.J. Leach, who later became a well-known judge.

Three administrative vehicles were converted at a small cost for use by the Salinas police department. The work cost $83.95 per car, a savings of about $250 per car, according to Thomas Dunne, the director of public services at the time. Salinas was annexing small sections to the city during the 1950s, adding to the total square footage of the city limits. Vagrancy continued to be a problem, especially around the Market Street downtown area and police tried to get them to move on. Rising unemployment was one cause of the number of vagrants.

Lt. Roberson was thought to be one of the best juvenile officers in the country during the 1950s. He spoke at various meetings of civic leaders, including a meeting of the Lincoln School PTA in January 1954. With words that ring true and are still echoed in the speeches we hear today, Roberson told parents, "little things such as an interest in the child's daily activities on the part of a parent can have a profound effect on his behavior pattern." *Salinas Californian*, January 29, 1954.

Lt. Harold Duncan teamed up with CHP Officer Mahe to capture burglars at the County Store on Alisal Street in 1955. The burglars were attempting to break into the safe at the store when confronted by officers. Back up arrived from the Sheriff's Deputies in the area, but one of the burglars pointed a gun at the officers before escaping into the attic. Numerous officers responded along with the fire department, and two tear gas canisters were fired into the store. Lt. Duncan and CHP Officer Mahe entered wearing gas masks, bringing two very sick burglars out for arrest. The two officers suddenly became very ill themselves and had to be transported to the hospital for treatment. Apparently, the tear gas was not tear gas and made a number of the officers at the scene violently ill. Later in the day, other officers were fitted with fire department issued self-breathing units to enable them to enter the building to search for the criminal's gun.

Robberies continued to escalate in the city. Service stations became targets at closing, and the Wagon Wheel Service Station at 435 East Alisal Street was only one of the places hit. Forced at gunpoint to lie down while the armed robbers yanked out telephone lines, Howard Smith was told to stay on the floor and count to one hundred while the robbers made their getaway. The two white men arrived at the station after closing, giving the attendant a story of having run out of gas. They got away with over $217 in coin and currency.

Municipal Court Judge J.A. Jeffery spoke at a meeting of the Monterey County Peace Officer's Association in January 1956. His topic concerned vagrancy and he described the crime as, "a crime of being, rather than of doing." According to the judge, a person once found to be a vagrant was thereafter presumed guilty "until he proves that he has reformed." SPD Lt. Harold Duncan was president of the organization at that time.

Fred Fowles was the Assistant Police Chief in 1957, when Salinas police displayed a number of weapons taken from suspects arrested in the city. Three large, plywood boards were required to display the knives, razors, brass knuckles, cleavers, machetes, chains, daggers, one small bomb, two grenades and a bazooka shell. The assistant chief was featured in the newspaper on January 3, 1957, as a kick off for Municipal Court Week.

Meanwhile, Chief McIntyre had a plan to reduce malicious mischief in the city, making the parents of juveniles arrested for damages responsible as a ruling of the civil code. BB guns, air rifles, air pistols, and slingshots were causing property damage and the chief wanted to crack down on the kids who were violating the curfew and causing the damage. He ordered strict enforcement by the police. In addition to cracking down on violators at home, Chief McIntyre also attended police management training at Northwestern University. By the end of January 1957, plans were well on the way for the new public safety building. Lincoln Avenue would have to be widened in order to accommodate the planned building. The department had run out of space and there were discussions about where to store old police reports. Chief McIntyre told the City Council of 153,000 case file dating back to the 1930s currently located in the old jail. Room was offered at the airport facility to store old records and it was thought the new public safety building would be able to store the most recent ten years of reports.

Salinas officers were called to round up a loose steer that had escaped from the Salinas Dressed Beef plant on John Street early in 1957. The steer was chased for some time along the railroad tracks and nearly butted one cowboy just as he attempted to capture it. This made good news as the department advertised for more officers. The five step pay salary was $330 to $406 per month for police officers who never knew what they would encounter at work was not much to offer, but some heard the call to duty.

On one February day in 1957, police took reports on whiskey stolen from a store, the recovery of silver stolen by three juveniles all under the age of seven, caught after a burglary, and multiple vehicle accidents, including a hit and run. A transient picked up for vagrancy and drunkenness kicked out the rear window of a police car and a new car was stolen out of a new car dealership. Captain Roberson was the guest speaker at the Valley Center Optimist Club meeting, discussing juvenile delinquency. Officers from several different departments suggested the names of juveniles be released to the press. It was thought that the use of offender's names would curb juvenile crime. The Chief, through the Chamber of Commerce, published a weekly "Warn-O-Gram" to businesses, giving tips on prevention of fraud and shoplifting. That was a typical day in 1957.

The City Manager, Ted Adsit, admitted the "experiment" that had placed parking meters in city owned parking lots was "a failure." Adsit chided downtown business owners for using valuable parking located behind their businesses to park their personal vehicles. He took photos of the rear of the buildings in the 200 block of Main, showing parking spaces taken up by garbage cans and woodpiles blocking access to other parking. The fight between all day parkers and shoppers continued, with Adsit wanting all-day parkers to pay to use city lots and shoppers to have free parking. Downtown merchants complained they were losing business to Sherwood Gardens, blaming the city. Adsit put the blame squarely on the backs of the downtown merchants, telling them to clean up valuable potential parking in the back of their store. The downtown parking issue of today dates back to the 1950s.

The news of the 1950s included near panic over the fear of polio and stories about the victims of the disease. These stories ran side by side with news of the fight for desegregation and equal rights, especially the movement in the southern part of the country. Traffic deaths, burglaries, and robberies made daily stories in the local papers as the citizens of Salinas felt the growing pains of increased population.

Chief McIntyre warned residents about buying BB guns, bows and arrows, and slingshots for their children at Christmas. Citing a city ordinance prohibiting possession of such weapons by persons under the age of eighteen, the chief tried to avert a repeat of the previous year's damage to homes and businesses. Assistant Chief Fred Fowles reported the arrest of two men who had stolen checks from the Salinas Steel Mill Supply Company and the Valley Hotel Supply. The two were driving on West Market Street when they noticed a Salinas Police vehicle behind them. Watching the police car in the mirror, the driver ran into a parked car, continuing on until police were able to make the stop and arrest. The men admitted to the thefts and to having cashed the checks in San Francisco and Fresno.

November 1957 had been a very busy month for police. Sixty-one car crashes were investigated, with eight injuries. Over 2,230 citations were issued. In December, working on an anonymous tip, Captain Harold Duncan, with the assistance of the FBI and other officers, closed in on an inmate who had escaped from Soledad Prison. Located at a Chinatown hotel, the escapee was tricked into capture by being told he had a phone call. Captain Duncan made the arrest and the dangerous escaped convict was returned to prison.

Women took over traffic control duties for the department on December 26, 1957. Having replaced the old three-wheeled motorcycle originally used by Barney Abel for marking cars, the Chief was photographed showing Mrs. Edith Chappell and Mrs. Alice Foster how to operate the new dual-control electric carts. The chief reported this would free up the male officers for "other duties." The new carts had a top speed of twelve miles per hour and were operated by six batteries.

Bob's Shooting Gallery at 134 Main Street was the scene of an unusual event in December 1957. A man went to the shooting gallery, telling the owner he wanted to shoot. Taking the .22 caliber gun from the attendant, he put it in his mouth and pulled the trigger. He was dead by the time police arrived.

The third annual employee service recognition dinner was held in December 1957. Helen Krieg was awarded a five year pin for her service as a police clerk as was Don Moss for his work as police officer. William Rabesa also received a five year pin as a police officer.

First Home Invasion Robbery
395 San Miguel Avenue

Robberies of businesses and individuals continued in the city, but a 1958 event appears to be the first major home invasion robbery in Salinas. A drug addict with a one hundred dollar a day habit, forced his way into the old Bingham mansion at gunpoint, robbing the couple of jewels, money and furs worth over $30,000. Chief McIntyre sent Herb Roberson to investigate and interview the suspect in San Mateo where the suspect confessed not only to the Salinas robbery, but to several others. The beautiful old Bingham property was considered one of the finest homes in Salinas. Later purchased by the Gheen family, the home sat on three lots and stood majestically. In recent years, the property was tragically parceled off and modern houses were built on each side of the mansion. Today, it stands squeezed between symbols of "progress," shivering in the shadow of the looming structures where once lush lawns and gardens stood.

Fort Ord was the site of a firearms training program by the FBI for local law enforcement agencies early in 1958. Officers practiced using handguns at seven, fifteen and twenty-five yards, shooting from the hip and at high level. The were taught "defensive shooting," and were expected to shoot ten rounds in twenty-five seconds, including reloading time necessary for the weapons they carried at that time. "Speed in getting the weapon out of the holster and accuracy in shooting is the difference between life and death in a gun fight," reported the newspaper. *Salinas Californian, January 6, 1958.* In addition to the revolvers, officers practiced with the shotgun. Improvements were shown by all the officers who were allowed only 125 rounds per man for the shooting school. The newest members of the department, Dale Beaman, and Paul Diaz were shown in photos that day, as was Officer Lee Graham, who shot a ninety-eight out of a possible one hundred points while shooting with his "wrong arm," better than he did with his dominant arm.

Construction of the new public services building was under way and controversy surrounded each step. A lone redwood tree stood on the building site and city administrators could not agree whether to remove it to provide much need parking spaces or leave it standing. After much investigation, discussion and political waggling, it was announced the city would try to keep the tree adjacent to the building. The $290,000 building was dedicated on February 24, 1958, with Judge Stanley Lawson speaking and the Ft. Ord Band playing.

The chief was on a campaign to upgrade the standards for his officers. Chief McIntyre was the president of the California League of Cities and proposed standards for education, training, and physical requirements. He claimed it would guarantee more qualified applicants and said it had nothing to do with setting pay scales. With the rise of drug abuse, the need for highly trained officers was crucial. Captain Harold Duncan spoke at local clubs on the history of training for the local police department, pointing out that although the national police academy training started in 1937, Salinas did not begin their own training program until 1950.

In spite of the training, accidents did happen. The reserve officer's unit received firearms training on December 8, 1958. Ten days later, while walking through the main hall in the public safety building, Reserve Officers Gene Amaral, Robert Black, Roy Guerraro, and John Spencer were discussing their holsters. Reserve Officer Amaral was handling Officer Spencer's weapon when it went off, sending a round into the wall three feet away where it hit a steel beam before ricocheting across the hall and landing some thirty feet away. Fortunately, no one was injured and Chief McIntyre ordered an investigation.

Crime took no break in the 1950s as three officers broke a big check fraud case involving checks stolen from the R & S Packing Company. Chief McIntyre praised the work of Captain Herb Roberson, Lt. Harry Wilson and Detective Eugene Paul Jones for their untiring work on solving the case and arresting the criminals. Officer Les Rodman worked with fire department officials to solve the New Year's Eve bombing of Palma High School. Seven boys were eventually arrested for the incident in which over twenty windows were broken, damaging curtains and the interior of the building at a total cost of $1,500. The seven were lodged at juvenile hall charged with being "in danger of leading an idle life." Names, ages, and addresses were listed in the local paper, where it stated the boys were said to have been playing a prank on the school. The FBI was called in to assist, as the explosion was much larger than probably anticipated, sending debris and metal fragments over 150 feet away from the school.

The boys set the bomb up and then drove to the dead end of Romie Lane to watch the blast.

Policewoman Rosalie Nunez had been with the department since 1951, when she was featured in the newspaper as she discussed her job. While juvenile work was her primary duty, she also worked as a plainclothes detective, carrying a .38 snub nose revolver. She started her police career as a clerk-typist in 1951 and was assigned to the juvenile division in 1954.

Changes were in store for the department in the late 1950s. Detective Eugene Jones was promoted to Sergeant when Harry Wilson left to become chief in Placentia. Jones had been with the SPD since 1951. Officer Dale Cheek, second in the testing procedure, was transferred to the detective division to replace Jones. Sgt. Lasserot, who moved to administrative sergeant, had started with SPD in 1943, but left for a brief time to become a district attorney investigator. He returned to the department in 1958. Nancy Edmunson was a desk clerk who had begun working for the SPD in 1956. She also left briefly, returning in 1959. The addition of several new patrolmen was announced by the chief. Charles Walker, Jr., Gregory Perez and Tom Brooks all began work in Salinas in February 1959.

A POACHER IN THE FISH POND

Salinas police were called to the county courthouse on the night of February 4, 1959. Custodians had caught a suspect poaching goldfish in the courthouse pond. The masked bandit had been chased up a tree by the custodians who waited for police to arrive. "Mister Coon", a raccoon, was eventually caged by the Salinas police officers but didn't like the accommodations. He quickly tore the cage apart after being placed in the back seat of the patrol car. Loose in the back seat, but separated from officers by the most fortunate placement of wire mesh, the suspect was "plenty angry." Donning heavy duty gloves, officers went in and recaptured the suspect before he could tear the police car apart. *Salinas Californian, February 5, 1959.*

In October 1959, a Soledad Prison officer picked up a hitchhiker who talked him into helping him rob the Bank of America in North Salinas. The proceeds of the robbery were $2,900, and the two men were in custody within a very short time. Both men were given twenty year sentences.

Officers were receiving better training, and the department was growing. William Nelson, cited in two separate instances for outstanding police work, was promoted to detective in December 1959. The same month Cal's Liquors was robbed, and the El Serana Motel was the scene of an attempted robbery, with threats made to kill the clerk. Harris' Food Market was robbed by two youths with a sawed off rifle, and a local man shot his wife three times in the back in an attempt to kill her. Robberies were daily events and patrol officers and detectives investigated every one.

Fifteen year pins were awarded to Captain E. Fowles and Policeman Arthur Barnes at the annual employee recognition dinner in January 1960. Policemen Richard Crocker and Roland Thiesen and Mrs. Reba Lotten received ten year pins, and five year pins were given to Policeman E.R. Belgard, Mrs. Marjorie DeWees, and Policeman Clarence Graham. Chief McIntyre and Detective William Nelson, along with Officer Leslie Rodman, were recognized for their outstanding sick leave records.

While fire fighters wanted a reduction in shift hours, Salinas police continued to fight crime and accidents. The population in Salinas had grown to 26,875 and the Monterey County Peace Officer's Association held a meeting to discuss the Monterey Peninsula College police school and the merits of police work. Lt. Earl Ashton received a revolver during that meeting.

That year, Robert Stroud, the, "Bird Man of Alcatraz," was denied parole after spending fifty years in prison for the 1909 murder of a bartender in Alaska. While Salinas didn't have as notorious a felon as Stroud, juvenile crime continued to escalate. In one weekend, youths were arrested trying to break into coin boxes in the laundry room at 10 Front Street, and 210 Riker Street was burglarized, the thief getting a piggy bank with five cents. Appling's Used Car lot was vandalized and the offices ransacked. Payroll checks were stolen from the Soilserv offices in another burglary and cigarettes and change were taken from a break in at the Rodeo Driving Range. Numerous other burglaries were reported that weekend. Salinas officers, following up the burglaries and an escapee from juvenile hall, arrested a local youth trying to get out of town at the Greyhound Bus Station. He admitted to seven of the burglaries, telling officers he was trying to get enough cash to get to Missouri.

The city council was discussing the budget for the 1960-1961 fiscal year. The total budget for the city was $2,685,772, with the police department receiving $350,407 of that. Markets and restaurants were popular with burglars, especially those with an appetite. Seeing a person standing at the bar of the Pub after closing and in the dark, an officer called for backup. After surrounding the Pub officers were able to arrest two men who told them the Pub heist was their second of the night. Earlier, they had sawed through the roof of the

Central Market on Cabrillo Avenue and tried to break into the safe. Failing, they settled for a few coins they found in the cash register. Hungry, they helped themselves to a large quantity of salami, rolls, and cherries before leaving through the roof. Not satisfied with their night's take they decided to try the Pub where they pried open a skylight with one of several flashlights found on them. Their take for the evening was a total of $41.47 in change found in their pockets when they were searched after being arrested. *Salinas Californian, May 25, 1960.*

The Monterey-Market underpass continued to be the scene of roll over and other serious accidents. Intoxicated tramps and trains were a deadly combination, as officers cleaned up after a drunk tried to board a fast moving train, fell under and suffered massive limb loss, dying several hours later. Free safety checks for cars and safe bicycle riding citations were some of the ways officers tried to make the city safer for its citizens.

SEVENTEEN

THE RED LIGHT BANDIT AND OTHER STORIES OF THE 1960s

Someone was masquerading as a police officer in Salinas. Stopping motorists by flashing a red light, he caused the unsuspecting drivers to pull over. The bandit would assault and rob the occupants who thought a police officer was stopping them. Chief McIntyre warned citizens of the danger, telling them real police officers used both their siren and red light when stopping any vehicle in Salinas. The red lights on the tops of police cars at that time included one blinking red and one constant red light. He also warned drivers and passengers to keep their doors locked at all times. The chief warned that several years earlier a Salinas police officer had been kidnapped by a man with a gun because he had failed to lock the right side of his car. The chief told motorists who might be the victim of the fake officer to drive to the police station and "lean on the horn." The Red Light Bandit not only operated from cars but sometimes would simply climb into unlocked vehicles when they stopped at lights or stop signs. *Salinas Californian, May 26, 1960.*

The census report was released in May 1960, and showed Salinas had a population of 28,639. It had more than doubled since the 1950 census, and continued to be the largest city in Monterey County. Salinas officers were working a forty-two hour week and wanted a reduction. Robert Taylor joined the force that year after working in the painting business with his family for some time. Taylor would spend nine years with SPD before moving on to become the chief investigator for the prosecutor's office. A man of strength and integrity, Taylor had served in the Army from 1951 to 1953, before returning to Salinas. He attended the FBI Academy in Quantico, graduating in 1979. Robert Taylor died July 10, 2005, leaving his wife, children, and grandchildren, along with his many friends and fellow officers to remember him.

Elton Conner, the man who had shot his wife three times in the back pled guilty to attempted murder. Judge Brazil was asked by both the defense and prosecuting attorneys to allow Mr. Conner out on bail so he could tend to his bedridden wife. Judge Brazil denied that request and placed Conner in the jail to await trial in spite of the fact that he was told of the couple's intent to reconcile. The same day, another man pled guilty to involuntary manslaughter in a case where he was accused of, while intoxicated, striking another man with a coffee cup, killing him.

Captain Duncan was busy setting up anti-crime clinics to teach merchants and clerks how to spot bad checks and help them recognize criminals in their stores. Other Salinas detectives were successful in tracking down the husband and wife team who had robbed the Purity Store in August 1959. The two had held the store manager at gunpoint, making off with bags of money. Both would later admit their part in that and other robberies. Juvenile Officer Janice Saxton, a new member of the SPD, worked on a program to educate young children about the "Dangerous Stranger."

Chief Ray J. McIntyre was now in charge of a department that included fifty-one total personnel, including ten women. Two thousand five hundred ninety-eight arrests were made in 1960 and 350,000 miles were logged on police vehicles. SPD had its own radio station, KMA 925, and the phone number to the police department was HA4-6464. Police advertised in the local paper, saying they were willing to watch the homes of people going out of town.

SALINAS SAM

Maple Park awoke one morning in June to find an unwelcome prowler in the neighborhood. A man on Grove Street found a two hundred fifty pound male black bear in his garage. The bear was later seen on Santa Ana Street, but it fled when police arrived. Two hours later, sleeping soundly in an airport hanger, the bear required some discussion before a livestock dealer was called. Armed with a syringe containing a potion that would keep the bear asleep until officials could decide what to do with him, the bear was shot with the syringe. The animal became sick and groggy from the injection, but stayed awake and had to be lassoed. After being trussed up, an effort that took additional officers and the livestock dealer, another injection of sodium pentothal finally put the bear to sleep. The department pickup was used for delivery of the wild bear to the city jail where he resided in Cell No. 1. Offering a home to the bear, the El Camino Real Trail House Club intended to keep the bear in a six-foot square cage. They wanted to use the bear to "lay a trail," so their dogs could be trained to follow the scent.

Salinas Sam in holding cell
Courtesy of Woody Meek

The bear was held at the police department for two days until an offer came from a zoo needing a bear and arrangements were made to transport it to San Francisco. Accepted by the Fleishacker Zoo, the bear was tranquilized for the trip to the city. Officers Gerald Schmidt and William Horton were assigned to drive the bear to the zoo in the department pickup. When they reached Morgan Hill, the bear awoke and began tearing up the car, trying to get out of the chains used to restrain him. The officers stopped and received assistance from a local veterinarian. Given a second dose of tranquilizers, the bear died, ending the sad story of the bear that had come to be known as "Salinas Sam" to the officers of the department.

Horse Thieves

By the 1960s there were not many horses seen downtown, making officers suspicious when two men riding one horse and leading a second horse, were seen just after noon on South Main Street near the high school. The riders fled when police approached leaving the horses behind and jumping over fences, escaping from the pursuing officers. The horses were stolen from W.J. Culligan of San Benancio Road, who told officers the two horses had been kept at 468 ½ Main Street. *Salinas Californian, July 23, 1960.*

Hartnell was offering the third year of courses for aspiring police officers. General education requirements were in addition to the special classes required for peace officer candidates and included a class in "Mechanics of Arrest," taught by Lt. Herb Roberson. Other courses included those taught by a CHP captain, Bill Bryan, and Sgt. Lasserot.

Chief McIntyre provided some new and interesting statistics in the fall of 1960. The department had begun to assign consecutive numbers to police reports in 1933. On June 27, 1952, the first 100,000 reports had been taken during the nineteen year period. Between June 27, 1952, and September 1, 1960, a period of only eight years, the second 100,000 reports had been filed using the letter "A" to designate the second 100,000. The letter "B" would designate the third 100,000 reports. The chief estimated that, at the present rate of reports in the city, there were more than 1,000 per month with everything from informational reports to murder cases being recorded. Today, officers take seventy to eighty reports per day, often reaching well over two thousand reports in one month.

The Resignations

Officers were leaving the department for other jobs at an alarming rate late in 1960. Six resigned in less than thirty days, leaving for mostly unrelated jobs. William Horten left to work in San Francisco as a trainee in a chain store. Sgt. Eugene Jones, Patrolmen Roland Thiesen, Robert Wayman, and Richard Crocker left for jobs in completely unrelated fields. Recruiting was still not easy. At a starting salary of only $405-$493 per month, officers were given a bonus of $12.50 as a uniform allowance. The resignations came at a bad time for Salinas as officers were investigating the murder of a woman by her husband and the apparent kidnapping of the couple's baby boy. Shot three times with a .22 caliber weapon after an argument at their Lunsford Avenue home, the woman died less than two hours later. Juvenile gang fights had reached "epidemic proportions" and Chief McIntyre said, "We won't tolerate one more instance of this dangerous foolishness" after one teen was booked for possession of a deadly weapon and another was stabbed in the arm during a fight. Officers were instructed to stop giving warnings and start making arrests. Halloween was days away and the chief told gangsters, "No one is going to play handy-panky with juvenile trouble makers." There had been six gang fights during the week leading up to Halloween but only one arrest. Rumors were flying about gangs from Paso Robles coming to Salinas. All dances were canceled at local schools and the recreation center. *Salinas Californian, October 28, 1960.*

It was the end of a busy year and statistics for the department showed 1,250 complaints investigated in October, an "unusually high number," according to the chief. With the six resignations several new officers had been hired and others were promoted. Vern Ricky was promoted to sergeant and William Brown to detective after a three hour written exam and an oral interview. The new detective would quickly go to work arresting a robbery suspect after seeing seeing him driving away from the area in a reckless manner. The teenage robber had just left the Thrifty Market on Abbott Street where he had robbed the clerk using a revolver. Detectives Brown and Nelson followed the car to Abbott Street and flagged him down two miles out of town. The suspect admitted the robbery, and told the lawman his mother was not working and he needed the money to run the house. No gun was found in the car and the suspect told the detectives he had used a cap pistol, throwing it away in an alley after the robbery. *Salinas Californian, December 21, 1960.*

Leading the news in 1961, were stories about thefts and robberies. The thieves seemed to have no particular items in mind as the reports of stolen items included undergarments, sun visors, hubcaps, radios, and keys. Juveniles were being arrested for strong arm robberies. One subject walking on East Lake Street, was beaten and knocked unconscious before being robbed of the two dollars he had in his pocket. With a black eye and bruised nose he was able to describe the green and white vehicle the robbers had been in. Police arrested three juveniles. Thefts from stores and parked cars were also a big problem around town. Window smashings in the Station Place area as well as multiple thefts from the East Market Street area plagued shoppers and business owners alike. Even the airport was hit, with go carts being stolen from a warehouse, along with a number of tires. A North Main television shop was hit the same night with radios and televisions being taken.

Officer Ray Belgard, a detective with SPD, testified in a murder trial about the clothing and knife found at the suspect's residence in the Merrill labor camp, then located on Moon Street. The victim had been found in the burned out Suey Sing organization headquarters at Pajaro and Lake Streets. The knife, found in the suspect's locker, was the type used for cutting vegetables in the field and blood, along with charcoal had been found on his boots.

The Frontier Inn was robbed and the desk clerk threatened with being shot by a bandit who also took the clerk's wallet. The Thrifty Market on Abbott street was also the scene of the second armed robbery in two days, when the owner was robbed of $445. Two nervous men had entered the store, pretending to be shoppers before both pulled revolvers out and demanded money.

One Gabilan Street business was burglarized four times before a juvenile was finally caught. Deane's Tire Shop, located at 31 East Gabilan Street, had been the victim of burglars repeatedly until a passerby saw someone on the roof one night and called police. Calling for a fire department ladder truck, officers went up on the roof and captured the thief. He admitted to having taken forty boxes of shotgun shells, two cartons of .22 shells, a pistol, eight cartons of ammunition. At another location he took five cartons and a hunting knife, along with another pistol during the earlier burglaries.

Another juvenile was arrested inside a store after he burned records and telephone books on a new desk. Police felt they had the suspect responsible for three burglaries, all of which had included serious vandalism to the properties. When the suspect was searched at the police department, cigars belonging to a title company manager were found, a strong indication he had also been in another burgled business.

Drunk driving and automobile accidents were also a continuing problem. Over the New Year's weekend in 1961, seven people were injured in crashes within the city limits and twelve arrests were made, ten of which were for drunk driving. Monterey and John Streets, Carmel and Acacia Streets and South Main and Romie were the scenes of three of those accidents. The power pole on East Laurel was seriously damaged, and hit and run drivers sped around the city causing damage and injuries.

Plans were in the works for a central communications system that would come under the direct supervision of the police department. The need to separate police and fire radio frequencies stemmed from the need for a dedicated line on the city switchboard for police only. The upgrades were included in the fiscal budget for the year.

The Monterey County Peace Officer's Association heard how devastating a loss in West Berlin would be to America when Col. Howard Salisbury, Provost Marshal of Fort Ord, spoke during the January meeting in 1961. The association voted that evening to associate with the California Peace Officer's Association. Luther Pilcher, formally an officer for SPD, voted in his capacity as an officer of the organization. He was now the chief of the Seaside Police Department.

"Narcotics in California" was the subject of a one hour lecture given by Sgt. Eugene Smith of the SPD. Part of a driver education course given to North Salinas High School students, the speech covered the use of marijuana, opium and heroin, morphine and codeine. February had only twenty-eight days in 1961, but that did not stop the officers in Salinas from setting a record of four hundred forty-four arrests for drunkenness. That was in addition to the one hundred thirteen arrests made for felonies and misdemeanors.

Escape from Custody

The police department had moved into their new, modernized headquarters in 1958. A fight promoter, in town to discuss supplying boxers for entertainment, was picked up and taken to the department for questioning about some bad checks. He was escorted to the detective's offices where one detective was making a phone call when the suspect ran down the hallway and out the back door. He fled across Lincoln onto Main Street and was lost. Detectives received word the suspect might be in the valley and Merced police were alerted to a particular motel. They arrested the suspect the next night. He was held on five felony counts.

Drive-by vandalism was rampant in the city. Six businesses and several private homes in the South Salinas area were damaged in one night. Stores on Park Row, in the Valley Center Shopping Center, and on Salinas and John Streets had their windows shot out by what Chief McIntyre believed to be a pellet gun fired from a moving vehicle. San Luis and Abbott Street residents also had damage to windows. A forty-five minute chase later that week led to the arrest of a juvenile burglary suspect. Seen entering Roosevelt School, officers surrounded the area. The sixteen year old boy momentarily escaped by throwing his socks in the face of one of the officers. He fled to the campus of Hartnell College, and officers were able to follow his footprints to a garage on Cypress Street. One resourceful officer climbed a tree and spotted the suspect lying on a roof. Caught, he told officers he entered the school to get warm and took only band aids. However, a record player was found outside the school, and the suspect's shoes were there as well.

The population in Salinas was growing by leaps and bounds. The total population in 1960 was 28,957 people, up a staggering 108% from the 1950 census bureau statistics. Chief McIntyre, recognizing the need to promote and recruit officers, announced the promotion of Detective William S. Nelson to sergeant. Nelson, with the department since 1956, had been promoted to detective in 1959. Taking his place in the detective bureau was Michael J. Rodriguez. Rodriguez had joined SPD in 1951. Sgt. Eugene Smith was retiring, making the promotions necessary.

New hats were given to the department by the Salinas Chamber of Commerce. The white cowboy hats were presented by the merchant's committee, as a gesture of the Big Week spirit. Officers would wear the cowboy hats during the entire week. Salinas had its own "Annie Oakley" that year. Policewoman Nancy Bottero, featured in the newspaper in July 1961 in her rodeo finery, carried a vintage rifle and long braids. The .25-.35 caliber weapon was inscribed with the words, "This weapon was manufactured for the use of smokeless powder." It was said that Bottero was an expert horseman and a good shot at the range.

When George Weight left the police department after many years as chief in 1951, he opened a photography shop in King City. Weight was a pilot and had flown the planes used for many training exercises with the department and the FBI during his time at SPD. Weight took over the job of loading and dispatching for the Forest Service in 1961. The former chief had worked for five years as a dispatcher and two years as an assistant patrolman for the U.S. Forest Service before taking over the duties that included supervising the loading of the chemicals to be dropped on forest fires. George Weight hoped to be able to get in some flying time with his new assignment.

The Salinas Fairways golf course asked for an increase in rates as they prepared to open the second nine hole course. Adult rates of $1.50 were to be increased to $2.00 or $2.50-$3.00 for weekends and holidays. Youths under twenty-one, who had previously paid only $.75, would now pay $1.00 for weekdays. The angry citizens complained about the rise in fees, but continued to play.

Elsewhere, small fights broke out at the carnival late one night. Within minutes, a riot had police cornered and outnumbered. Calling for assistance from all neighboring departments, Salinas officers were battered. Officer Les

Rodman was struck with a shuffleboard puck with such force that he required ten stitches to close the wound to his head. He credited his big hat with saving him from even worse damage. Hospitalized briefly, Rodman returned to duty later that night. Other officers received less serious, but painful injuries. Officer Tom Quinn was hit by a bottle, but refused to leave the scene. Eleven juveniles were arrested, their names, ages and addresses published in the paper the next morning. Lt. Herb Roberson told reporters how good it felt to all the men to see the Sheriff's and Highway Patrol units roll in to assist, saying fellow law enforcement had provided the, "best of cooperation" to Salinas. Watsonville and other adjoining departments stood ready to come to Salinas as the rioters, who outnumbered police greatly, attacked. Unable to use tear gas to subdue the crowd due to the presence of many children, one officer reported that if the riot had become any worse, they would have been forced to gas the crowd, regardless of the families present. Chief McIntyre praised his men, both regular and reserve officers, who had worked during the rodeo week, crediting them with a job well done and praising the assistance from the other agencies.

Captain Harold Duncan had started his career with SPD on June 4, 1943. Only his Navy service had taken him from his job. He had attended the FBI academy in Washington in 1951 at his own expense and had been in charge of the detective and services divisions and the patrol and traffic divisions as a captain. For unexplained personal reasons, Captain Duncan requested he be reassigned as a sergeant, making three lieutenants eligible for promotion to captain and three sergeants eligible for promotion to lieutenant. Herb Roberson, with the department for over ten years, was promoted to Captain. Herb Lasserot, who had served the department for over eighteen years, since 1943, was promoted to Lieutenant.

The new leaders of the department had their hands full immediately as the burglary of a sporting goods store netted the criminal nine weapons, including three .38 caliber revolvers, one magnum, five .22 caliber pistols and one .32 caliber pistol. The burglar had cut himself on the window glass broken to achieve entry. Thirteen people were injured in traffic accidents that first weekend the new captain and lieutenants took over. One police officer, Gerald Thomas, was not injured when his police car was hit by a man whose brake line had broken. In another major accident, a hit and run driver completely destroyed the new addition to the Drive n' Eat restaurant on East Alisal Street. Officers measured one hundred eighty-seven feet of skid marks leading into the restaurant. A new radio room was installed in the public safety building and would be used for all police, fire and city hall communications. The new center opened in December, with Operator Clara Borrego in charge of the new system.

FBI agent Quinn came to Salinas to teach "print dusting" technique to Salinas officers and deputies in the fall of 1961. Salinas Officer Jerry Schmidt was one of over fifty officers from various agencies to attend classes for five weeks. The focus of the FBI class was evidence collection and fingerprinting. Salinas would initiate its own training program soon after. By November 1961, Salinas had implemented a program thought by Chief McIntyre to be the first of its kind in California. Supervisory level acting sergeants were assigned as "Instructors," and would wear identifying chevrons under the shoulder patch on the left sleeve of their uniform shirts. Each instructor worked a different shift and was responsible for training new officers. Two hundred forty hours of instruction would be given during the thirty day period to new officers, who would then have another sixty hours of training with other sergeants and lieutenants before being allowed out on their own. The first instructors to take over this training program were, Charles Walker, Tom Brooks and Les Rodman. They earned no extra money for their new positions.

The FBI classes and training would pay off immediately as officers investigated a slashing at a labor camp. The victim had near fatal injuries and Officer James Siedel was photographed next to a big pool of blood at the scene. A suspect was arrested and gave a statement. *Salinas Californian, December 1961.*

There were so many drunks on the street later that week officers simply could not arrest or book them all. In one eight hour period, thirty-four men were rounded up and sent to jail. In the twenty-four hour period, fifty-one were charged. The chief told reporters there were many more candidates for arrest but he did not have the manpower to bring them in. The chief ordered a crack down on places selling liquor to obviously intoxicated men. Within days an employee of the Palace Liquor store was arrested, sending a message to owners. Instead of arresting the drunks and letting them out when they sobered up, the chief was sending them all to court in an attempt to get them to move on to another area.

THE RAT HOLE GANG

Seven burglaries in one night in downtown businesses were the work of organized burglars. Gadsby's Music, Virginia's Draperies, Daley's Bootery, Carmen's Gifts and Brown's Department Store were some of the victims. All stores were found to have been entered through the roof. Thieves had cut small holes in the walls giving them access to safes and tills. The safe at Daley's was torn open but the burglars found it completely empty. More property damage was done than actual goods stolen, although Gadsby's did lose $500 in cash. Salinas police appropriately named the burglars the, "Rat Hole Gang." *Salinas Californian, December 1961.*

The Greyhound Bus depot was a hotbed of criminal activities. Federal agents busted a man as he removed a travel bag from a locker. Inspection of the bag netted a pound of marijuana. Salvadore Casteneda and George Valdez were arrested for shooting at a car at the corner of Gabilan and Salinas Streets. The intended victims were from Castroville and the confiscated .22 caliber pistol turned out to have been taken in a recent burglary of the Deane Tire Shop on East Gabilan. Both men had extensive prior records. Casteneda had just been released from California Youth Authority, where he served four months on a burglary charge. Both men admitted their part in the burglaries and the shooting.

Salinas was awarded a certificate of safe driving for its record of safety over a twelve month period. The two motorcycles and two electric powered parking control vehicles were in service for twelve months during 1960-1961, without interruption or accident. Captain Roberson, then in charge of the unit, accepted the award on behalf of the department.

EIGHTEEN

THE ANNEXATION OF THE ALISAL AND STORIES OF THE 1960s

Talk of annexing the Alisal district was nothing new. In 1962, the city began looking at the effects the annexation of the Alisal district would have on the various city services and departments. The expected requirements for city police taking over from the sheriff's office and CHP patrols, was to establish two 24-hour per day patrols in the Alisal area. In addition, it was expected that there would be some need for detective and juvenile services, and parking, traffic, and animal control officers. In all, twenty additional police personnel were thought to be sufficient. The department also expected to need four additional radio equipped patrol cars and one motorcycle. Plans for the annexation included the hiring of new officers as well as the need for new equipment. In 1963, John Carr and Larry Irwin were part of the hiring of more than a dozen new officers. While the purpose of hiring those officers was the expected rise in needs for services to the Alisal area, many of those officers were also put to work in other parts of the city. Their skills would be immediately put to use in the days to come.

The children of City Manager Thomas Dunne were sleeping in the front room of their home at 48 Talbot Street when shots were fired into the house. Hitting just above the heads of the two boys, the .380 slugs struck books and drapes and broke windows, causing concern throughout the city. Police initiated an intense investigation and tried to calm the public outcry.

Police were often in harm's way when they were on the job. Officer Robert Taylor was twenty-eight years old when he was hit by one car being pushed by another. The drivers of both vehicles were cited for speeding. Traffic crashes were still a major concern and police arrested thirty-one people over the New Year's weekend in 1962 in an effort to get the public to slow down and drive safely.

Driving citations were given out in 1962 for "courteous" drivers as the city council voted to reduce the police forty-two hour work week to a forty hour week. This reduction created a need for additional officers to cover the gaps in coverage that resulted. One of the last remaining "services" provided by the department was that of checking houses while people were out of town. That program, considered by Chief McIntyre as one of the best the department ever had was slated for elimination in order to free up officer time for other calls. At that time officers made over fifteen thousand house checks each year.

Six officers faced an angry crowd on Soledad Street in March 1962 when they tried to arrest two men fighting with knives. Two hundred people faced off with the officers, having emptied out the bars to watch the fight. One man kicked officers and had to be placed in a padded cell when he continued kicking. It was the largest crowd in many months to be found in the old Chinatown area. Police activity was up from the prior year by over twenty percent, with juvenile crime topping the statistics for 1961. Two murders in 1960 and three in 1961, joined four fatal car accidents in the staggering statistics. Over sixteen thousand reports were made that required investigation in 1961. Three sets each of 2,234 fingerprint cards were made by Salinas officers, and there were 88,793 radio transmissions.

The top television shows in the early 1960s were Father Knows Best, Ben Casey, and The Danny Thomas Show. John Glenn made his historic space flight on February 20, 1962. The Marine was photographed in his space suit and made this statement to the press, "This is the new ocean, (space), and I believe the United States must sail on it and be in a position second to none." *John Glenn, Salinas Californian, February 20, 1962.*

Sgt. Woodrow Meek investigated a grave found in the 300 block of North Main Street just after the New Year's celebrations in 1962. Bones were exhumed and were determined to belong to a dog that had died in 1954. The dog was thought to have been the pet of the former blacksmith, Jim Lively, who had moved to Gonzales some time ago. The property on North Main was being prepared for development, and the grave, with a marker inscribed with the words, "Cherta.....1940-1954," had puzzled the builder until police unraveled the mystery.

The largest number of prisoners in years, 109 total, was marched to municipal court by Salinas police on a morning in February, 1962. Chief McIntyre reported that this high number of prisoners had not been seen since the days of the Saturday night street dances during Rodeo week in years past. One hundred six men were charged with disturbing the peace and drunk charges. One woman was also charged with being drunk. The remaining two had miscellaneous charges. Most of the 109 were given five day sentences, which were suspended for one year.

Transients were bothering people on downtown streets and the city council was told that the police department would be delighted to address the problem if they would hire an additional officer to patrol the area. The laws regarding vagrancy had been changed in 1961, ruled unconstitutional. Officers now had to witness the offense or have a person willing to sign a complaint for offenses like begging. Sixty-eight persons were in court on April 15, 1962, the result of arrests for drunkenness. *Salinas Californian, April 16, 1962.*

THE COP AND THE OCELOT

Officer Ernest Brown was confronted by a large field jaguar, or ocelot and was forced to use a stick with a loop of rope to contain the animal after trying to pick it up. It had escaped for the second time in two months from a house on Chaparral Street. The house pet fought with a dog and had become very frightened during its time out on the loose. Following its capture the animal was taken to a downtown pet shop. The officer was photographed holding the animal by the loop as far away from himself as his arms would allow. *Salinas Californian, May 9, 1962.*

The following day, Officer Gerald Schmidt was shown in the newspaper helping a little five year old girl across a busy city street. The accompanying article discussed an ongoing program called "Operation Safety" which had been in place for several years. There were different phases of the safety program highlighting one particular segment of the population each month. The safe driving citations, safe routes to and from schools, bicycle safety, fraud and bad check writing classes, were only part of what Salinas officers were offering to educate the public. A bicycle "rodeo" was an opportunity for bike riders to show their skills and local clubs and the employee's association sponsored some events.

Former officer Robert Wayman shot and wounded a prowler outside his Shasta Drive home. Another transient was run over by a train while attempting to jump on and Green's Camera store was the victim of the latest commercial burglary downtown. It was June 1962 before the city council approved a reduction in the work week of officers from forty-two hours to forty hours. A two and one-half percent pay increase would be effective soon. Officer Tony Rodriguez was on patrol one night when he saw a car, the driver's side door open and facing an open garage door. There had been a series of garage burglaries and the alert officer, stopped to investigate. Putting his spotlight on the garage the officer saw two men immediately run out the back door, knocking over a garbage can. More officers and a detective unit soon arrived and searched the area of the home on Capistrano Street. One man was soon found hiding in the bushes at Palma High School pretending to be asleep. The other was found on Sierra Madre Drive. Both were drunk and in their car officers found the loot from five other garage burglaries, solving the string of thefts. *Salinas Californian, June 29, 1962.*

Eight accidents on one Sunday left five people injured, one fire hydrant destroyed, and electric and telephone communications out of service around town, including service to the Monterey County Communications station and the county hospital. Emergency lines had to be installed while workers repaired the main lines. A toy poodle suffering from a broken leg sustained in one of the eight accidents, was taken to Hafen and Campbell Veterinarians for treatment.

When city manager Tom Dunne delivered his annual budget speech, one of the major upcoming projects for the year was the constructions of a new city hall. $278,500 was allocated for the building, with the rest of $475,000 needed for the project being in the budget for the following year. The tax rate of $1.55 was expected to raise enough to fund the city for the next year. The reduction from a forty-two to forty hour week meant additional officers would be needed, and three more were budgeted for the upcoming year. The police department's budget for 1962-1963 increased from the prior year to $431,043. *Salinas Californian, July 9, 1962.*

THE RIOT SQUAD

Eleven American soldiers were reported killed or missing in Viet Nam the day the department announced the formation of the "Riot Squad." Shown in a newspaper photo in the "Flying-wedge formation," the members of the Riot Squat were: Lester Robinson, Joe Klis, Phil Tull, Larry Sterling, Jim Seidel, Bob Taylor, Sgt. Harold Duncan, Dave Gaber, Tom Brooks and Vern Parker.

Other members included Ernie Brown and Bill Olea The men had been hand picked by the chief for the special training necessary to handle crowds and riot control. Headed by Officer Tom Brooks most squad members had prior experience in the military. Started because of the riot at the carnival the previous year where several officers were badly injured, the squad had special equipment, including helmet liners, and all had special training in jujitsu and karate. *Salinas Californian, July 16, 1962.*

CAPTURED IN FIFTEEN MINUTES

Sgt. Harold Duncan was on duty one night when he heard the broadcast of a suspect wanted for the robbery of a Safeway Store. Stan's Department Store on East Alisal had been robbed at 8:50 p.m., followed by a second robbery at the Safeway at 9:39 p.m. Driving in West Market Street area Duncan noticed a car matching the description parked at a liquor store at 555 West Market Street. Leaving a second unit with the car, Sgt. Duncan went into the bar. When a man came towards the sergeant, out of the men's room, Duncan questioned him because he fit the description of the robbery suspect. He also had a plastic gun in his pocket. While Duncan questioned the suspect, a detective unit looked in the car and found $700 under the floor mat and clothing resembling that taken from Stan's. The suspect denied being involved saying the evidence, including groceries bought at the Safeway store must have been put their by his wife.

Officer Jim Seidel was credited with solving two school burglary cases late in 1962. Following the investigation of extensive damage to Washington Jr. High and Roosevelt Schools, Seidel acted on a hunch. Police had arrested one boy for several malicious mischief cases in the area and knew his friend to also be familiar with the area and the two schools. Officer Seidel, accompanied by Detective George Garwood, went to the suspect's home, where they found him changing clothes. The clothes he was changing out of were marked with telltale red and black ink stains. The boys confessed saying they had been on their paper route when they decided to detour to vandalize the first Roosevelt, and then Washington because they did not like some of the teachers. *Salinas Californian, November 24, 1962.*

Bill Lippert came to the Salinas department in 1963, after eight years as an officer in Ohio. He had also spent three years in the Army during the Korean War. Lippert had already been through the academy in Albuquerque and found himself unpopular in Salinas due to his age and training. The younger officers were afraid he would get the much desired promotions. Lippert, however, had other interests and spent his time becoming an expert in fingerprint identification. At that time, forensic science, as we know it today, did not exist. In fact, Lippert made one of the first fingerprint identification cases with a match in a robbery case here in Salinas. Rather than seek promotion, Lippert took the job as Bailiff, giving him access to, and time to review and work with physical evidence. He moved the evidence room to the basement and reorganized the fingerprint files by the classification system, removing the alphabetical system that had been used until then. Lippert's best memories of police work involved his many cases with Joe Gunter and Andy Enni. According to Lippert, who wrote a book about his experiences as a crime scene investigator, he, Gunter, and Enni were a successful team because the detectives let him do his job without interference. There was a mutual respect among the three men that led to many cases being solved. While other officers and detectives would contaminate a scene, or try to tell him what to do, Gunter and Enni went about their jobs as detectives and allowed Lippert to process the scene undisturbed.

Even in the 1960s, crime scene work was limited to fingerprint and blood examination. Fingerprints, if found, had to be compared by a human eye and could only be compared to what the department and the sheriff's office had on file. Blood work entailed simply determining whether a stain was blood, or not. There was no DNA. When the state put in the automated latent print identification system, it was not an instant success. In fact, it was a case worked by Detectives Joe Gunter, Andy Enni and Officer Bill Lippert that saved the program from the scrapheap. A subject had been paroled from another county to Monterey County on a murder charge, without any notification to local authorities. A murder took place at the Pink Ribbon Shop on Gabilan Street and Lippert found prints. While the detectives searched the Field Interrogation cards for suspects, Lippert sent the prints off to Sacramento, marked for a rush search. Within days, a match was found and Gunter contacted the parole agent. Gunter, Enni, Lippert and the parole agent found the suspect at a downtown hotel and made the arrest. The powers in Sacramento used that case, along with several others like it, to make the decision to continue with the automated print program. Lippert continues to live in Salinas with his wife and now spends his time caring for his great-grandchildren.

Television in the 1960s became a regular household appliance and shows were produced that brought new interests to many homes. *Dragnet* starred Jack Webb, and while somewhat dry, it gave audiences a glimpse of the life of a detective. Other shows like *Adam 12* shared the prime time spots with *Rawhide* and *Alfred Hitchcock* and brought the dream of becoming a police officer or cowboy to many American children. Here in Salinas, the police department had nine cars and one pickup. Vehicles were automatically replaced after twelve months or thirty thousand miles, whichever came first. Replacement costs for the fiscal year 1963-1964 amounted to $9757. The budget for overtime during that year was $2140 for investigations and $6710 for patrol, a total overtime budget of $8850.

The dream often became a nightmare for the few who took the challenge of police work. On August 31, 1963, Lt. Robert McPeek was stabbed in the back breaking up a fight while on duty at a rock and roll dance at the Armory. His lung was punctured and he was seriously injured. Lt. McPeek asked Officer Orville Bronson to walk outside with him, away from the dance. In front of the armory building McPeek told Bronson he had been stabbed. It was impossible to identify the assailant in the crowd of over twelve hundred and McPeek had delayed sounding the alarm. McPeek lost a lung because of the attack but returned to work and was promoted to Captain when Earl Ashton left the department. As a result of McPeek's injuries, all dances were banned in Salinas. Saying the dances attracted a less than desirable group from all over California, the chief told the city council he could not police such large functions with the force he had at the time. City Manager Tom Dunne agreed and the new policy was voted into place. Juvenile crime was the reason Chief McIntyre asked the community to return to the morals it once knew in earlier years as he spoke at a convention. Quoting statistics that showed a doubling in crime since 1946, the chief told the audience that forty-three percent of the crime in the United States involved people under the age of eighteen. His point was well made when days later, a seventeen year old boy was shot at Main and Avenue B after a football game.

Local armed robbers were becoming bolder in their tactics. When the clerk at a liquor and deli store at 64 West Market was held up by two men, they pointed a gun at him without any evidence of nervousness. The two robbers had been drinking at Maida's Bamboo Village next door. The infamous Maida's, torn down to build new county offices, was a notorious strip joint, where the girls inside bird cages would dance topless. Parents, with children in their cars would cover their eyes as they drove past.

As the postal rate was increased from four cents to five cents for first class letters, city councilmen argued over the length of the probationary period for both firemen and police officers. Chief McIntyre, speaking for the entire police department, agreed to an eighteen month probationary period for incoming officers saying the extra time was needed to fully train recruits. Addressing once again the increase in juvenile crime, the chief also listed the top three reasons leading youth into a life of crime: "1) Lack of religious training and moral training; 2) Lack of respect; 3) Lack of Parental supervision." *Chief McIntyre, Salinas Californian, February 1963.*

Police had a steady number of burglaries, robberies and assaults to investigate. The December 1962 murder of a man who had been beaten to death on Gabilan street resulted in a jury verdict of manslaughter in March, 1963. Accidents were still taking much of the time of investigators and safe crackers were at work in the city. Officer Bill Olea was photographed while taking fingerprints off a broken safe at the American Laundry Company on Abbott Street.

Thefts and burglaries were commonplace, but the theft of policeman's uniforms from the cleaner on East Alisal was cause for concern. SPD and prison uniforms had been stolen in a nighttime burglary. Officers had no chance to slow down as they investigated accidents, drug trafficking, robberies, and stolen vehicles. Reserve Officer Richard Gourley was badly cut when he was thrown through a window at Loretta's Café at 36 Soledad Street during a fight. Another Reserve Officer, Emil Morello, received lacerations and bruising when he fought with a subject at the carnival. It was rodeo time.

When Captain Earl Ashton pinned a Lieutenant's badge on Detective George Garwood it was because Lt. Bill Brown had asked to be reduced in rank to Detective for health reasons. Brown had a stomach ailment and felt the detective position would mean less stress. Garwood had been the juvenile officer for some time and was thirty-two years old. Brown, a former army first sergeant, had joined the department on January 1, 1958, and was promoted to detective December 5, 1960 making lieutenant in 1962. The upcoming months were busy ones for everyone at SPD, with the sixty officers writing 3,793 traffic citations in the month of May and taking 464 persons into custody. *Salinas Californian, June 18, 1963.* Enid Hartman was appointed Supervising Clerk for the department in June that year. With the department since 1959, the Kansas native had started as a radio operator. Her new duties would include being in charge of the radios, telephones, files, and records and she would supervise a staff of eleven women, six clerk-matrons and five operators.

It was November 23, 1963, when America was shocked by the assassination of President Kennedy. Kennedy, who had taken office in 1960 as the first

Catholic President, was not the first President to be assassinated, but was the first since television made access to the news instantaneous. A controversial but popular man, Kennedy's death would be a challenge to the role of America in the world. Conventional weapons had given way to the potential of nuclear war and Kennedy had sought in his words, "a more perfect union with our European friends."

By 1964, former police officer Luther Pilcher had become the chief of the Seaside department. Indicted on charges of felony wiretapping, along with a sergeant in Seaside, it was believed to be the first time two law officers had been charged with such a crime. Both remained on active duty and eventually pled guilty to misdemeanor wire tapping. They were sentenced to a fine of $11 each, with no probation.

Salinas police replaced sheriff's officers and highway patrolmen early in 1964 in East Salinas. Two cars cruised the East side at all times. Photographed handing over the patrol to Salinas officers, deputies shook hands with the first Salinas police officers to take over patrol duties for the former Alisal now to be known as East Salinas. Those first officers were Lt. Herb Lasserot and Officers George Garwood and Bob McCullom. Their first morning on patrol brought only one call, to a domestic disturbance on Cross Avenue at 2:21 a.m.

As his officers took over patrol duties in the Alisal district, Chief McIntyre left for Illinois to attend a twelve week course in police management. Herb Roberson, then a captain, took over as acting chief, with the assistance of Captain Earl Ashton. Crime took no holiday while the chief was gone to school. Burglars smashed windows and stole cigars, dropping some boxes as they ran away. An alert officer, Joe Coito, suspicious of two men in the area, gave chase and captured one while another officer nabbed the second. Other victimized businesses that night included Harry's Garage on California, Valley Feed on East Market, Domestic Cleaners on East San Luis, La Gloria Club on East Market, and numerous private residences.

Sgt. Duncan and Captain Roberson reported to the Chamber of Commerce several weeks after taking over the Alisal. Calling the transition smooth, Roberson reported that eighteen men had been sworn in and uniformed for the duties and had access to a multitude of vehicles. Citing a total of eighty-three men in the department, some uniformed and others detectives, he quoted the FBI suggestion that cities have one officer for every five hundred residents. The department proudly featured seventeen of the newly hired officers, providing biographies of each late in 1963. Ralph Bohn was a former prison guard,

John Carr a graduate of Hartnell. Donald Cobleigh was from Los Angeles and Joseph Coito was a San Francisco police reserve. Don Davis had been with the Tulsa Police Department, Joe Fitzpatrick was a Navy veteran, James Frenzi, and William Gilmore had worked at Soledad prison. Randy Grooms was an Air Force veteran, and Larry Irwin was a member of the SPD reserve unit. Russ Dubree had been a military policeman, Russell Newby was a Navy veteran, John Prather had four years experience as a police officer in Yuma and Ed Sznaper was a former Marine and Los Angeles County Reserve Officer. Curtis Weir was a Navy veteran and Conrad Wynter was an Army veteran. *Salinas Californian, November 23, 1963.*

The new officers would eventually receive copies of the 273 page manual it had taken six years to write. With chapters on various aspects of police work in Salinas, the book would be given to each officer, who would have to sign a statement after thirty days saying he read and understood the contents. Several members of the department helped write the book, but it was Reba Lotten, the chief's secretary, who typed, planned and indexed the extensive document.

Seventy-three SPD officers stood at attention on December 21, 1963 as they were inspected by the city council. An annual event, the inspection took place in the parking lot behind the police station. Photos taken from atop the department that day show the old home that sat on the space now occupied by the north wing of the modern courthouse.

Congress was debating whether to continue the Bracero program in 1965. Public Law 78, which brought thousands of Mexican farm workers into California to work in the fields, was the issue of hot discussions locally and nationally. The minimum wage for field workers in 1965 was $1.40, up thirty-five cents from the 1964 rate of $1.05 per hour. Charged $1.75 per day for their meals, the braceros came to pick crops like strawberries. Local growers and their representatives were concerned about who would be responsible for the housing, medical care, and education of the workers. A Border Patrol officer spoke of the MCPOA meeting the same month the Bracero program was being debated. The Border Patrol, originating in 1924, had formerly been a group of men who checked alien Chinese. That group was given the added responsibility of the United States borders in 1924 and the Gulf Coast in 1925.

Officers in pursuit of a stolen car watched in horror as the suspect turned too fast and drove into a house on Rosarita Drive. Fortunately, the car sped into the garage and no one inside the home was injured. Two hours later a police car backed into a pole on West Laurel Drive as the officer, John Davison, tried to turn around to pursue a speeding driver. Traffic accidents escalated in 1964, with nineteen accidents within the city in just over twenty-four hours. Most of the accidents were in the South Salinas area and included one man's car that was struck by a train while he tried to push it across the tracks, jumping out of the way just in time to watch as his car was demolished. Other accidents included cars running into houses, garages and each other. From Main and Gabilan to Market and Villa, in parking lots and on the streets, the eighteen accidents resulted in mostly minor injuries. Within two days, nine more accidents would injure two more citizens. The police department was not spared as a chain reaction fender bender caused damage to several vehicles parked directly in front of the station.

Police officers gave great service to their citizens, even recovering a stolen vehicle just as it was being reported to police. Officer Lee Farmer noticed a car that had driven around the same block two times. Finding it suspicious, he stopped it. The driver told the officer he had just purchased the car which had Alabama plates, but he had no license. The officer noticed empty beer bottles in the car and radioed in the license number. The victim was inside the police department reporting that he had been choked and robbed of his wallet and his car. He heard the license number over the radio broadcast and told officers that it was his car. The crime which had taken place out in the county area, was solved before the report could be made. The suspect was turned over to the sheriff's department.

The alley behind 45½ Soledad Street was the scene of a stabbing in January 1964. Police took statements from witnesses who had seen the victim talking with a man after walking a woman to her car. The man had pulled a knife from his belt and stuck it into the victim's abdomen. The Caravan Bar at 17 West Gabilan was the scene of a violent slashing within weeks of the earlier stabbing. A woman was charged with cutting a bartender with a broken beer bottle. Trying to calm the woman the bartender was slapped by her, causing a nosebleed. While in the restroom tending to his nose, he was advised the woman was breaking things in the bar. The bartender removed the woman from the bar because she was throwing bottles and glasses inside. After he dragged her out of the bar she hit him, slashing his neck and face. The suspect's husband had tried to get her to leave earlier, knowing she had been drinking heavily, but the woman bit him.

National Peace Officer's Memorial Day, signed into law by President Kennedy, fell during National Police Week in 1964. Chief McIntyre wanted to change attitudes towards police officers and planned an open house, tours, and events for his officers. McIntrye wrote an article for the newspaper asking citizens to reflect on the job of police, to be more careful in following laws, especially traffic laws and explaining that the "Obverse side of the badge," the one you see when you look at a police officer, indicates authority, and "law and order." But, he continued the reverse side of the badge, is "pinned to a man," who the chief wanted citizens to get to know better. Chief McIntyre told readers that law enforcement's duty was "to help to maintain the delicate balance between the rights of the individual and the rights of society." *Salinas Californian, May 9, 1963.*

Crime continued with murders, fatal traffic accidents, thefts, burglaries, and a series of rapes. By October 1964, fourteen officers had resigned or had been fired. In an attempt to strengthen the top level administration of the department, the position of deputy chief was created and Captain Roberson was reassigned to head investigations. Back at work after losing one lung, Lt. Robert McPeek was appointed acting captain of patrol and traffic. The resignations continued with Detective John Weimer resigning one day, then asking for it to be withdrawn the next. Earl Ashton, demoted from Detective Captain to Sergeant, had had enough. The newly created Deputy Chief's position would handle many of the administrative matters formerly the chief's responsibilities. *Salinas Californian, November 6, 1964.*

Conrad Wynter resigned two days after a fatal accident in which he was driving and killed his best friend, a passenger in his car. The judge called him "a disgrace to the police department of Salinas," before sentencing him to one year in county jail and three years probation for the misdemeanor manslaughter charge. The judge suspended nine months of the sentence because he felt the man suffered enough from having killed his best friend. *Salinas Californian, December 7, 1964.*

In Tennessee, Jimmy Hoffa was sentenced to eight years in prison and fined in 1964 for his part in an attempt to rig a federal grand jury. Jack Ruby was sentenced to death for the murder of Lee Harvey Oswald, the man thought to have assassinated President Kennedy. Here at home, the Salinas police with help from the Rotary Club, formed the first Explorer Post with twenty-four local boys selected out of fifty-five applicants. Police officers who would lead the program included Capt. Earl Ashton, Capt. Herb Roberson, Sgt. Vern Ricky, Sgt. Tom Brooks, Sgt. Bill Nelson, Det. John Wimer, and Det. Charles Walker and Officers Arthur Barnes, Gerald Thomas, and Robert Taylor.

Robert Taylor's daughter, Terri, then four years old, dressed up in her father's police uniform and sat in a small rocking chair in the spring garden of her home to watch the flowers in March 1964. The darling photo of the child in her father's uniform and holding his nightstick, was great public relations for the already popular department.

Terri Taylor guards her flower garden
Courtesy of Mrs. Taylor

In 1965, the department included Chief of Police McIntyre, Deputy Chief Roberson, and a secretary to the chief, Miss Todd. The patrol division was headed by Captain McPeek. Three lieutenants, Lasserot, Ricky, and Nelson and five sergeants, Wiechring, Brooks, Moss, Parker, and Tull presided over forty-four patrol officers and two "meter maids." Harold Duncan was also promoted to sergeant, having been with the department since 1943.

The officers of the SPD were a generous group and often contributed to community fundraisers. In 1965, it was reported that contributions by Salinas officers to the Community Chest fund were the highest of any city department.

Salinas officers had a donation rate of 97.8%, only two of eighty-nine had refrained from donating. The next closest department was the firemen with only a 75.6 % rate. Not only did officers have the highest participation rate, they also gave the most, donating a total of $1,243. *Salinas Californian, 1965.*

NINETEEN

IN THE LINE OF DUTY

The department was plagued by injuries that year, costing taxpayers more than $20,000 in 1964. Twelve officers were on leave due to being stabbed or cut or for receiving puncture wounds. Eleven officers were off with back injuries and three had serious eye injuries in the line of the duty during the 1964 year. Between May and July 1965, seventeen officers were injured in the line of duty. These statistics were staggering for the small department. Traffic accidents, along with wounds suffered during fights and arrests happened in spite of the self-defense training officers now received. McPeek's stab wounds to his back cost him eleven weeks off as he recovered. Officer Bob Russell's hand was infected after he was bitten by a suspect and a tendon was cut. Detective Mike Rodriguez had to have surgery after fighting with a prisoner, and Detective Vern Parker dislocated a shoulder scuffling with a suspect. Officer Roy Hanna was hurt during an arrest, and Art Barnes' big toe was broken. Officer Ray Mallow was off for thirteen weeks following a traffic accident at Pajaro and John and was saved more serious injury by the helmet he was wearing for the first time that night. But, even with the credit going to the helmet for saving the life of Officer Mallow, the helmets were hated by the officers who were forced to wear them all the time, both inside and outside their patrol vehicles. Resourceful officers soon found a way to rig the helmets using seatbelts, thus making it appear that the helmets were on their heads at all times.

Officer Edward Naldoza was twenty-three years old in 1965 when he was attacked while attempting to arrest a subject on Monterey Street. Hit in the head with a tire iron as he tried to handcuff the suspect, he was taken to Salinas Valley Memorial Hospital, (SVMH) for treatment. Days later, Patrolman Robert Russell was bitten, struck, and kicked in the groin while trying to arrest a battery suspect on Hebbron Street. The annexation of the Alisal District was blamed for an eighty-one percent increase in major crime. The number of traffic collisions increased by a huge ninety-two percent. The annexation, which increased the size of the city from 34,000 to 52,000, created a steady demand for city services. Six murders were reported in 1964, while in 1963 there had been none. Burglaries doubled, as did grand thefts.

Detectives Mike Rodriguez and Phil Chlopek were partners one night when they were called to Dick Bruhn's. Joined by other officers, they surrounded the store after a radio alarm sounded, and found all doors locked tight. The burglar had gone in through the roof, gathering up a variety of goods. Caught, he confessed he had also burgled the Vogue Dress Shop, getting in the same way.

The department was reorganized when Captain Roberson was appointed to the newly created position of Deputy Chief of Police. This attempt to strengthen the administrative division of the department placed Roberson in operational control of the department, answerable only to the chief of police and city manager. With his promotion, Harold Duncan, with the department since 1943, became a lieutenant. Roberson said of Duncan, "He is a loyal and dependable policeman and is my choice to head the detective division." Duncan had been number one on the eligibility list. Sgt. Vern Ricky, with SPD since 1965, was promoted to acting lieutenant and would take Duncan's place in the traffic division. Detectives Don Moss and Charlie Walker, with the department since 1952 and 1959 respectively, were promoted to sergeants and assigned to patrol. Replacing them as detectives were Phil Tull and Orville Bronson, both relative newcomers to the Salinas department. Lt. George Garwood was transferred to head the newly created services division.

An officer on duty and stopped at a red light at Sanborn and East Market Streets was hit by a citizen. Officer Robert Hagy was twenty-five years old and hired Bill Bryan, filing a civil suit against the driver for $25,000. Officer Ed Sznapper, was kicked in the chest by an angry man, and was taken to the hospital and treated. Six police officers were needed to subdue the man, who had attacked the officer in front of 16 East Market Street. The offender was placed in a padded cell for his own protection.

The traffic meter madness was not to be put to rest. The city, wanting to avoid the scandal in San Jose where the parking money had been embezzled by city employees, turned the task of counting the money over to the Wells Fargo Bank in Salinas. A clever city clerk noticed an increase in the number of citations and a decrease in the amount of deposits and initiated an investigation. It was learned that two bank employees, independent of one another and each without knowledge of the other, were skimming cash out of the traffic meter and citation fund. The investigation was taken over the FBI as losses appeared to exceed $2,000. Months later, the two now former bank clerks were arraigned on charges of embezzlement.

The Salinas Police Reserves celebrated the fifteenth anniversary of their organization in 1965. President Walter Perry and Secretary-Treasurer G. Darwin Peevy were elected officers of the organization when it held its first meeting in 1950 and continued in their capacities as officers for the entire fifteen years. All reserve officers wore badges numbered above one hundred. In May 1965, there were seven openings for men having the requirements of "good moral character, good physical condition," and having achieved the age of twenty-one.

The Salinas Police Wives Association was going to be assisting with an Open House at the department. With the observation of Peace Officer's Memorial Day, the department would host an open house, inviting the public in to see the behind the scenes operations. More than three hundred attended and were treated to homemade cookies during their tour. Officers helping with the tour were on their own time as they explained how things worked in the busy department. Mrs. Robert McCullom was in charge of the refreshments that day. It was the highest attendance of all open houses to date.

A transient sleeping with his head on the rails, was partially decapitated and killed when a train hit him. The same night Officers Don Davis and John McKinney investigated bullet marks left on the metal door of a company warehouse on Lake Street. Numerous bullets had been fired, causing indentations on the door. The shots were aimed at a Japanese laborer who had been badly beaten before being shot three times by unknown assailants.

Two men were shot during a barroom brawl at the Frontier Club at 455 E. Alisal Street. Officer John McKinney, answered a call to the area and was able to arrest one suspect as he ran from the scene. Drawing his service revolver and holding the suspect at gunpoint, Officer McKinney asked the man if he was the one he wanted. The suspect replied, "Yep, I'm the guy you want." One of the victims had been shot in the eye and was in serious condition. The second was hit in the chest. The argument had started when the men disagreed about the winner of the dice rolling game they were playing. A third man was involved and began using foul language in front of women when officers placed handcuffs on him inside the bar. He was arrested for disturbing the peace. The shooter, interviewed by Detective Sergeant Woody Meek, told him he hoped the two men would die. He was later released after posting $1,100 bail and was arraigned on two counts of attempted murder.

Salinas administrators and officers were considering the purchase of a radar unit which would cost $1,200. Using the Alisal Street corridor in front of Hartnell College, an experiment showed that most cars exceeded the twenty-five mile per hour speed limit. In fact only two cars, one of them a patrol unit, traveled at the posted speed limit during a thirty minute period. Citing increased enforcement with fewer officers needed, Deputy Chief Roberson saw the radar unit as a much needed tool that would aid officers and benefit the citizens of a city where police officers' responsibilities had been steadily climbing. The new system would be in the 1965-1966 budget, in spite of one city councilman who considered it a "peeping Tom." *Salinas Californian, June 1965.*

Chief McIntyre announced his intention to retire after twenty-nine years of service. He had already been hired by U.C. Santa Cruz to direct their security department.

*Chief Ray McIntyre
Courtesy of the Salinas
Police Department*

On February 10, 1965, it was announced that Herb Roberson would become the new chief in Salinas. Chosen from fifty-one candidates, Roberson had extensive administrative and operational experience and had been with SPD since 1951. The change in chiefs had little effect on the crime rate and accidents in the city. Major accidents continued to cost lives, money and time. Officers still faced drunks and belligerent suspects who chose to fight rather than be arrested, injuring officers and resulting in many being charged with battery on a police officer.

Harry D. Treager, twenty-nine years old, was an outstanding police officer who joined the department on June 1, 1964. He was named Officer of the Year in 1966. Gary Edwards rode with him as a Reserve Officer. Treager moved first to Santa Barbara Police Department, then moved up to Alaska where he worked for the office of the Alaska Attorney General, and later died of a brain tumor. He was featured in a "Warning" issued to residents in the October 8, 1965, edition of the *Salinas Californian* in an attempt to get citizens to slow down.

Officers Roy Hanna and Glenn Parks were honored by the Jeweler's Alliance of the United States for their investigation of a smash and grab at the Carlyle's Jewelry Store at 362 Main Street. The thief, arrested and tried, was sentenced to six months in county jail. The two officers were presented with a check for $200 which they donated to the Police Benefit Association. The Jeweler's Alliance association, formed in 1883, had the sole purpose of promoting crime detection and prevention in crimes against jewelry stores. It was the oldest organization of its kind at the time.

Three unnamed officers investigating a disturbance in Chinatown were injured by a laborer who had to be locked in a padded cell. All three officers were injured and one had his uniform pants and shirt torn off him during the altercation. Judge Stewart ordered the man to serve eighty days in jail and to reimburse the officer $26.50 for the shirt and trousers. *Salinas Californian, May 1965.*

It was May 1965, when the city purchased the fist transistorized polygraph machine. Operated by Woody Meek, who had completed a very intensive course in Pasadena, the machine made by Keeler came in a metal box two feet long and ten inches wide and cost $1,325. The original machine recorded the breathing rate and perspiration, along with monitoring blood pressure. While the test results would not be allowed in court officers could use "the box," as it was called for gaining information from suspects.

Officer Bob Graham was saved from serious injury when he was struck in the head by a bottle during Big Week. His helmet sustained a dent and the officer knew who had hit him, but was uninjured. Other than backed up traffic, a domestic "misunderstanding" where a man was shot in the head, and other minor incidents, Big Week in 1965 had less major crime than previous years. Salinas officers, with information about the potential civil disobedience, had called on both the Sheriffs and California Highway Patrol to be available. With the exception of one large burglary of equestrian equipment, several accidents and the fight in which Officer Graham was hit, it was a quiet week.

William Settrini was on duty one night when he discovered a man lying in the weeds at 25 Soledad Street. Wanting to question the man, Officer Settrini spoke to him and was quickly charged by the man who had a knife and tried to slice at the officer. Drawing his service weapon Officer Settrini was able to hold the man at gunpoint until he could be disarmed.

Roy Hanna was busy gardening during the hot summer months in 1965. A citizen waiting for a backyard plant to bloom and finding it was marijuana, asked for the police to remove it from his yard. The plant, almost six feet tall, was given to state narcotics officers to be destroyed. Narcotics, while not new to Salinas, were becoming more and more prevalent. Sgt. Vern Parker, with information gleaned from an informant, was instrumental in leading the largest raid on narcotic users to date. For his outstanding work, he was awarded the Monterey County Peace Officer's Association's Officer of the Month plaque in September 1965.

The Salinas Police Officer's Wives Club was planning its first luau, complete with food, entertainment, dancing and more. Dressed in their island finery, the wives of Paul Diaz, Phillip Tull, Roy Hanna and James Rochester, along with the wives of Lester Robinson and John Weimar, invited the public to enjoy the event. The dinner-dance was held at Portuguese Hall and featured Eddie Malie and His Islanders band, who would also put on a floor show during the evening. Shortly after the luau event, the ladies were planning for a Halloween "Hobo" party for the entire police department. They also planned a children's Christmas party later in the year.

Meanwhile, officers were working on plans for the police auction. Thirty bicycles, a meat cleaver, two wheels, a garden hose, ten hubcaps, a Christmas tree stand, and clothing were all to be sold. The sale would eventually net $421.75, with Stingray bicycles bringing in the highest bids of $35 to $40 each.

It was October 1965, and officers arrested fifty-one drunks in one day, expecting to find a total of over 10,000 booked by the end of the year. Officers, familiar with some of the drunks who were habitual "guests," booked a pair of brothers with the unusual name of, "Shot-With-Two-Arrows." It was of sufficient interest to be noted in the local newspaper. *Salinas Californian, October 14, 1965.*

Officers were also asking parents to watch their children and not allow them to wander in the streets. South Salinas had been the scene of several exposure and molestation cases, and the description of the white male, about thirty years of age and with brown hair, was circulated.

The much anticipated radar unit arrived in August 1965. Deputy Chief Roberson told citizens there would be a grace period during which officers would be issuing courtesy citations, with no fines. Warning signs would be posted at the entrances to the city.

The case which would be responsible for a new policy in the department involved a California Highway Patrol, (CHP) officer. CHP Officer William Brennan was on temporary assignment to Salinas to help with race traffic when he shot and killed a Salinas man outside the Hyatt House Hotel on Sanborn Road. CHP officers were staying at the hotel during their temporary assignment to the area. The circumstances of the shooting were sketchy, with the main witness being the wife of the victim. Brennan left the scene and traveled to Gilroy, where he told officers there he had been the victim of a robber and claimed injury to his ear from the firing of a weapon inside his car. These were statements he would later recant. The victim, shot twice by a .38 caliber weapon which was being sought by Salinas police, died at the hospital. The shirt worn by the CHP officer and discarded en route to Gilroy was found by officers soon after the incident. Chief Roberson, enraged by the behavior of newsmen who had broken into the department disrupting the investigation, even "bursting into – and listening in on – interrogation of witnesses," issued a new policy. "Henceforth, on major cases, the news will have to come from the division commanders or myself," Roberson stated. Citing the former policy of allowing newsmen access to all police reports, the new requirement would force them to acquire such reports only from ranking officers. The number of people coming and going from the department during a major investigation would be curtailed. The *Salinas Californian* was quick to note that it was not one of their reporters who had acted with such impropriety. *Salinas Californian October, 19, 1965.*

A local man driving a 1959 salmon colored Cadillac led Salinas officers on a merry chase up and down Market, Alisal, Lincoln, Church, Capitol, San Luis, Riker, West, California, and Pajaro Streets and up Natividad Road before he lost control and ended up in a field. Two officers were in close pursuit. Stanley Edwards, then thirty years old, put his patrol unit into a controlled broadside skid. As he tried to extricate himself from his seatbelt in order to chase the fleeing suspect, Officer Edwin Bradshaw, only twenty-two years old, "came barreling up the road." The young officer tried to fit his fast moving unit between the other patrol car and a fence but failed, striking the first patrol unit in the left rear end. Officer Edwards suffered minor injuries as did the suspect, who was eventually arrested for reckless driving. *Salinas Californian, October 25, 1965.*

As expected, the number of arrests for drunkenness climbed during 1965. With Salinas officers making 8,819 arrests by November that year, Deputy Chief Roberson discussed the problems faced during the rainy season. Because the county jail was located in Salinas all arrestees, when released, were released into the city area. Belligerent, and usually without any money, those released from the jail would simply stay in Salinas causing problems and injuries to officers here. The panhandling problem was an offshoot of the drunk arrests, and while officers tried to keep the panhandlers away from the central area of town, there was a certain "geographical proximity" to the red light and bar district. *Salinas Californian, November 10, 1965.*

Chief McIntyre had reason to be proud of his men and women. The Community Chest Drive benefited in 1965 from one hundred percent participation from Salinas officers, who pledged $1,435 to the local charity, up from a ninety-nine percent participation rate the year before.

The First Savings and Loan located at Main and Romie Lane was robbed for the first time on December 5, 1965. The suspect, who had worn a white stocking cap, left the scene in a car described by witnesses who were able to get the license number. Road blocks were set up by officers of many agencies. A CHP officer setting up a road block, spotted the suspect's car and followed it into Hollister. The suspect ran a roadblock in Hollister and made it through the city before being arrested on the outskirts of town by CHP and San Benito County Sheriff's Deputies. The FBI was called in to transport the man back to Salinas.

The Salinas Police Benefit Association held an important meeting in December 1965, to elect new officers. Max Thomasson was elected president following a barbecue at the posse grounds. Don Thomas would serve as vice-president, Enid Hartman as secretary, Dolores Ivey as treasurer; and Tom Quinn and Charles Walker would fill out the board for the upcoming term. Herb Lasserot would continue as a board member for another term.

Speed processing was a term used by Captain Jewel Ross of the Berkeley Police Department when he spoke to the graduating class of the, Peace Officer Standard Training, (POST) program at Gavilan College on December 17, 1965.

Three Salinas officers heard the speech that day. Captain Ross speculated about the future probability that officers would someday be equipped with individual and portable radios and that computers would play a big role in policing. The three Salinas officers graduating that day were: Jim Rochester, Bill Settrini, and Tony Bogacz.

THE "JUNGLE CONTROL" OFFICER

By early December 1965, officers had arrested 10,548 people on drunk charges. A lack of facilities to accommodate this large number of arrests was the principle reason for release after arrest, causing widespread criticism of the department by the law abiding citizens. Deputy Chief Roberson explained that the police were simply trying to harass the offenders to encourage them to move to other cities. A paddy wagon would soon aid officers by providing mass transportation to jail. Roberson had deployed a "Jungle Control" officer to roam the areas where hobos camped, disrupting their lives and arresting them for trespassing. He asked property owners to prominently display "No Trespassing" signs which would give police the legal authority to make arrests on private property. Officer Curt Weir was the "Jungle Control" officer assigned to the task. A sensitive man who had felt sorry at first for those he found he eventually became accustomed to the repetitious nature of his work. Often, he had to roust the same hobos or campsites several times in one day.

Salinas Police Officer Bob Russell received the Officer of the Month award for July 1966, from the MCPOA for undercover work done in Seaside which resulted in the break up of a gambling business. Lt. George Garwood and Deputy Chief Roberson, were considered two of the best juvenile officers in the country. Retiring officers were recognized along with other city employees at the annual dinner held at the Elk's Lodge in December 1966. Sgt. Walter Weichring received a standing ovation when he was presented with his twenty-five year pin. Retiring Chief McIntrye and Art Barnes were also commended for their service to the city. Fifteen year pins were presented to Mike Rodriguez and the new chief, Herb Roberson. William Nelson and Leslie Rodman received ten year pins and Clara Engle, Florence Hansen, Guillermo Olea, Lester Robinson and Phil Tull received their five year pins.

Walter Perry, the first and only Commander of the Reserves Unit retired. His retirement badge was presented by Chief Herb Roberson. Of his original reserve unit only two others remained, Darwin Peevy and Andy Snyder. Perry started as a reservist, making only $.50 per hour. Upon his retirement, the pay had increased to $3.41 per hour for special events. Gary Edwards' stepfather, Al Stalter, took over the duties of Commander of the Reserves until his retirement.

Joe Callahan worked burglary cases with Gary Edwards until he moved to Fresno. Edwards believes Callahan made Captain and still lives and works in Fresno. Mr. Peevy would make a name for himself after being attacked by diving birds in the employee parking lot one day. Arriving at the office with a bloody head, the result of an early morning and vicious bird attack, Peevy seemed very calm to everyone. The next day, getting out of his car in the same spot, he was once again attacked, but this time he was ready. Peevy raised a tennis racket and with a single swing eliminated the offender, never missing a step as he walked into the department.

TWENTY

CHIEF HERB ROBERSON

Chief Herb Roberson Courtesy of Chief Roberson

On January 1, 1967, Herb Roberson became the police chief for Salinas. Having held "operational command" of the department since 1965, he had joined the SPD in 1951, after spending three years with the department in Watsonville. He worked as a sergeant, detective, lieutenant, captain and division commander of traffic and patrol. He was the division commander of the investigation unit when he was promoted to deputy chief. Chief Herb W. Roberson took over a department with ninety-one members, including twenty women and twenty vehicles that traveled over 1,255,202 miles that year. Of those numbers, thirty-eight officers had a basic POST credential, five had intermediate level credentials, and ten were qualified for, or had already received, their advanced credential. Thirty-one officers were attending night school classes in law enforcement, and Roberson believed in the education of his men. During his career, Roberson, who was one of the ten men to hold the advanced credential, was known as one of the best juvenile officers in the country and also worked very successfully in the narcotics division. He investigated the "prank" bombing of Palma High School in 1955, participated in drug raids, and was instrumental in bringing radar devices to the traffic division. Roberson was a Deputy Chief when Chief McIntyre announced his intention to retire after using up accumulated vacation time. He still remembers many of the cases he worked and felt the best job in his career was as an investigator. Chief Roberson lives in Northern California, but returns to Salinas to visit his family here.

FIRST DAY AS CHIEF

On 2:00 a.m. on January 1, 1967, the first murder of the year took place at 50 Willow Street. Two women, coming home from a New Year's party, walked up the driveway together and were gunned down by a male friend who had made multiple threats to one of the women. The intended victim was badly hurt, but crawled into the house to phone police. Her less fortunate friend lay dead in the driveway, her rabbit fur trimmed beige coat soaked in blood. The suspect also went into the house, where he got sick after looking at the dead woman in the driveway. He shot himself in the lower chest before police arrived. The previous threats were well documented. The last threat by the gunman, made on New Year's Eve, was that the woman should, "Be home by midnight – on peril of your life." The suspect would later die from his self-inflicted wound.

The next day police made an unusual arrest after responding to a domestic disturbance at 150 W. Gabilan Street. Investigating the reason for the call, officers noted a slot machine. The man of the house told them he had found it at the dump and repaired it. He offered the officers an opportunity to, "risk a coin" if they liked. Instead, they arrested the man for possession of a slot machine. Such an arrest had not been heard of for over twenty years.

For the first time, POST fees for new officers were reimbursed to the city through a program that was financed by assessments on criminal fines. POST training, which had begun in 1960, established minimum standards for police officers. Salinas was one of the first cities to voluntarily adhere to the program, hiring and training many new officers in 1964 because of the annexation of the Alisal District.

But, Alisal was not the main source of police enforcement problems. Officers were spending precious hours arresting and booking drunks on "skid row," better known as Chinatown or the Soledad Street area. Between January 1, 1965 and March 11, 1965, officers arrested 1,171 persons for drunk and disorderly conduct. For the sixty-nine officer force, that was an average of sixteen arrests per officer. At the time, according to Chief Roberson, it took twenty to thirty minutes to arrest, book, and jail a disorderly drunk; however, that did not take into account the amount of extra time spent picking the drunks up and trying to control their behavior. Improved lighting in the Soledad Street area was planned in hopes that it would deter the activities of the district. In one four day period, police made 247 arrests in the skid row area. One man had been arrested nineteen times in the past few years. Crime was climbing throughout the city and statistics for the first three months of 1965 showed a sharp increase in felony arrests. Two hundred eighty-eight felony arrests at the end of February 1965 accounted for more than a ten percent increase over the same period of one year earlier.

The number of burglaries was staggering, with few being solved. One victim, a reverend, heard a burglar in his house and became frightened, opened his bedroom window and fired several shots off from his handgun. The burglar, already having helped himself to several one hundred dollar bills, fled out a window, cutting himself in the process. In the Alisal, a woman admitted firing a shot into the head of the man she lived with, killing him. The man, who the woman claimed had "been mean" to her, had told her to go ahead and kill him. He dared the woman to shoot him several times. She finally accepted. With a history of domestic issues in their past, the couple had both armed themselves, the man with a knife and the woman with a gun. During an argument on the street, the woman fired one shot which entered the man's head through his left ear. Officer Dick Hack and Reserve Officer Gary Jones made the arrest. The editorial the following day discussed how much easier it was to purchase a gun than to get a driver's license.

While police searched for two young girls suspected of cutting the face of a thirteen year old girl on John Street, Officer Harry Treager saw a man being beaten in an alley off Market Street. Treager was able to break up the robbery and beating and arrest the suspect. John Carr was considered one of the best of forty-five officers learning defensive tactics. Carr, along with Detective Vern Parker and Officers Dick Canas and Les Robinson, put on a demonstration of

Judo and Karate defensive tactics. All officers participating in the training program were doing so on their own time, taking classes three nights per week.

Officer Larry Sterling was featured in an article about the policeman's day off. Sterling, along with several other Salinas officers, had purchased reloading equipment due to the high cost of ammunition. Once each week, on his day off, he went to the Fort Ord pistol range and practiced a variety of different types of shooting. He was quoted in the *Salinas Californian* as saying, "An officer must train constantly to become proficient in using a gun-someone's life may depend on his ability." Sterling would soon be one of the best shots in Salinas. Along with Darrel Booth, Don Watkins and John Dawson, a team from the SPD won the Class B top honors at the Central Coast Counties Police Pistol Shoot. Class C was also won by Salinas officers Sgt. Vern Parker, Dick Canas, Henry Casolari and Jim Berwanger.

Burglaries were second only to injury accidents in challenging the limits of the police force. Five injury accidents in one weekend in January 1967, resulted in eleven hurt. Locations were familiar to the officers; Sanborn and E. Laurel, E. Alisal and Monterey, and Garner and Mae. Some involved drunk drivers and one was a man testing out a motorcycle offered for sale who found himself in the hospital with broken bones and scrapes. Robberies were common as well. Cal's Alisal Liquor Store was robbed of $271. The bandit told the clerk, "Don't make any funny moves, the last guy that did, I had to shoot." *Salinas Californian February 1967.*

In January 1967, three astronauts, trapped on the Apollo I spaceship, were killed in a flash fire. With televisions in many American homes, the tragedy struck hard. The Viet Nam war was also in full swing. Joe Gunter was in Viet Nam in 1967, serving in the Marine Corps, when eight Marines were killed by "friendly fire." The army had just announced the establishment of a permanent American camp in the Mekong Delta. Locally, North Salinas High School was selected as a pilot school for West Point. The cost to attend West Point at that time exceeded $50,000.

Chief Roberson was out to protect the children and pedestrians of the city. Sending officers to teach traffic safety at schools, he ordered a crack down on jaywalking. Forty-three pedestrians had been injured in 1966, with one fatality. Verbal warnings would be followed by courtesy citations. The final phase of his program would include issuance of citations that would require court appearances by offenders. The chief sent out police photographers to catch jaywalkers in the act. Published in the newspaper, were photos taken during the holiday season of various people crossing Main Street surrounded by passing vehicles.

Jim Backus was named peace Officer of the Year by the MCPOA in February 1967. He had saved a small child by using mouth-to-mouth breathing after the child stopped breathing twice. Roy Hanna was the runner-up. Hanna had disarmed a knife wielding man on Soledad Street who was threatening a parole officer. Hanna's hand was cut during the rescue.

Officer Richard Canas was hurt while breaking up a domestic disturbance. Spotting an argument while on patrol, Officer Canas stopped his car to investigate. Tripped by one man while pursuing another, he was then punched in the face, a blow which resulted in his helmet and glasses being knocked off. The wife of one of the men, weighing 110 pounds, was also arrested and charged with battery on a police officer after interfering with the arrest and becoming violent and profane. The husband was arrested the next day.

Chief Roberson Congratulates IAS Graduates

The Salinas Police Department made the pages of the February 7, 1967 edition of *FingerPrint and Identification Magazine*. Detective Roy Hanna received his IAS diploma, presented by Chief Roberson. Also pictured in the photograph taken that day were other Salinas officers working towards proficiency in fingerprint identification. Along with William Lippert, who had already graduated and begun to work within the department, were Officers Treager, Olea, Davison, Casolari, Backus, Dewey, and McKinney.

Harry Treager was selected as officer of the year for the SPD based on his overall performance as a police officer, rather than any one outstanding act that year. Treager had been with the department since 1964.

Officer Bob Russell had been with SPD for three years when he was asked to accept an assignment that included, "great personal risk." The Seaside department was having a difficult time infiltrating a gaming establishment. Wanting an unknown officer, they requested SPD provide them with someone the crooks would not be familiar with. Bob Russell accepted the risky assignment and talked his way into the game. He was unarmed and no assistance was available to him if things went bad. Cooperation between the two departments led to the successful raid and arrests of those involved. Bob Russell was commended with the Officer of the Month award, presented in July 1966 during the MCPOA meeting. *Salinas Californian, July 28, 1966.*

When John Wiemer resigned to start working for the U.S. Customs Service in San Francisco, it was a blow to the department. Weimer had been to several police schools and had been with the department since 1960. A detective for three of those years, his experience would be missed. Weimer had worked both juvenile and adult cases before leaving the Salinas force. An increase in glue-sniffing cases had officers and detectives searching for ways to stop the dangerous habit. While there had been no deaths reported in Salinas from glue-sniffing, youngsters eleven and twelve years of age had been found with the harmful chemicals. The city council publicly complimented Deputy Chief Roberson and the department on their efforts to make the city safer. The use of radar, the paddy wagon and the polygraph were mentioned as some ways in which the department was using modern technology to fight crime. *Salinas Californian, May 24, 1966.* Burglary was still one of the hardest crimes to prevent in Salinas, but officers were doing their best. When they cornered a suspected burglar at 7 East Gabilan Street early one morning, the man yelled, "I want to hurt one cop before you arrest me!" He also told them he wanted them to shoot him. Pelted by a fire ax, shovel and sickle, the officers tried to figure out a way to arrest the man without being injured themselves. Phil Tull, one of the officers at the scene, found some garden hose and made a lasso. He was able to get the lasso around the shoulders of the suspect and force him to the ground while other officers took him into custody.

Sid Gadsby was mayor of Salinas during the summer of 1966. Needing to attend a meeting at the courthouse, and finding limited parking available, Mayor Gadsby parked in a limited time zone. He was not worried, however, since he saw a meter maid. Telling the meter maid to, "Keep an eye on my car, would you please," the mayor went on his merry way. The meter maid, only too happy to comply with the instructions from the mayor, did keep an eye on his car, placing a ticket for overtime parking on it when his time limit was reached. *Salinas Californian, June 24, 1966.*

In the fall of 1966, the "Implied Consent" law went into effect. Simply stated, it required drivers to take a test if they were suspected of drunk driving. Giving drivers the choice of blood, breath or urine tests, it would give law officers the ability to better enforce the drunk driving laws of California. Drunk drivers and drunk citizens continued to be problems within the city. When Officer Chris Jimenez tried to arrest a drunk in a café on Soledad Street, the fight was on. The officer asked for assistance from nearby citizens, but no one came to his aid. By the time help arrived, the officer was badly injured and could not use his arms. Pulled muscles caused a brief hospitalization and the officer was going to be off duty for some days.

A series of kidnappings had taken place in Salinas during the summer months of 1966. Police had arrested several people they believed involved and the children had all been rescued quickly. When another child was abducted from her own room, the mother was able to give officers a description of a suspicious vehicle she had seen earlier. Officer Fred Rau was on patrol when he spotted a pickup matching the description. The driver refused to stop at first, but finally pulled over and the child was found lying on the seat. He was charged with kidnapping, having taken the child by reaching through an open window of the house. *Salinas Californian, October 6, 1966.*

A football jamboree at Salinas High ended with officers responding to post-game fights. Nine arrests were made and one officer was injured. Numerous fights were happening all around the school lawn and the intersections of Avenue B and Lincoln and Clay and South Main streets. Mace was used to control the "mob." Officer Larry Sterling was hit and injured during the brawl after the Salinas High School jamboree on September 15, 1967. Assisted in trying to calm things down by Detective Bacolas at the Clay and South Main Street location, Sterling was hit in the shoulder. Fights and hostility towards officers during high school sporting events was becoming more of a problem each week and meetings with school principals were being held with police department administrators.

Detective Tony Rodriguez was congratulated in an article in the local newspaper for receiving a certificate for a thirty day course in narcotics investigation. Along with Detective Mike Rodriguez and Sgt. Les Rodman, the officers went to local high schools with a display about narcotics. Many young people were being arrested on drug charges and the classes were part of an ongoing attempt to educate the youth of Salinas about the danger of drug use.

DOWNTOWN REVITALIZATION

The city was in the planning stages of a downtown revitalization project. There was a drive to rejuvenate the central business district and plans for a 2,500 seat auditorium, an elevated plaza, and a, "super block" bordered by Lincoln, Market, Gabilan and Monterey Streets were in the works. A downtown mall was sketched out, with shops, parking, restaurants and a huge auditorium. Commissioner George Kuska called it a "ridiculous plan." The Mayor at the time was Sid Gadsby, and he, along with the city council and planning commission, determined the main points for Salinas: "1) Blight in Central Salinas can only expand if no steps are taken toward correction. 2) Redevelopment having been considered along alternatives, seems to be the most feasible means of correction." The date was January 26, 1967. *Salinas Californian, January 26, 1967.*

The city council authorized the revitalization plan and instituted the GNRP, (General Neighborhood Renewal Plan.) Many questioned the ability of the city to make good on this grand scale plan for the one hundred block. It was February 1967, and citizens parking in the downtown area were being asked questions by Wilbur Smith and Associates. The city had hired the firm to do a parking survey. They were paid $18,000 to develop a long-range parking improvement plan. The city would engage in decades of planning for the downtown area, reaching the nexus of their plan when the earthquake of 1989 provided them with the opportunity to tear down the old Cominos Hotel. The grand old hotel did not go down easily and the city promised a new downtown center featuring a hotel and businesses that would revive the ever struggling Old Town area. The ghost of the grand Cominos Hotel can still be heard laughing in 2005 as the site remains empty except for a parking lot of black tar, a hideous reminder of the old hotel taken down in a moment of opportunity. Many grandiose plans were promised and planned over the years for the old Cominos site. Most recently, after three years of negotiations with a foreign-born master of smooth talk, the city council finally broke off negotiations and reopened the bids for what is now promised to be a less grandiose, but more reasonable project. The plan for a fourteen story luxury hotel with condominiums at the top and a parking lot located at the Greyhound Bus Station site was supposed to put Salinas on a par with Monterey as a convention destination. Salinas natives were skeptical, and with good cause. Politics in Salinas, payments to out of town experts for "studies," and a lack of common sense have long plagued the city.

HANDIE-TALKIES

Up until 1967, officers relied solely upon their patrol car for radio communications with dispatch. An officer having to leave his vehicle for pursuit or investigation was without contact with others who could come to his aid, or that of an injured victim. Only twenty-five portable units arrived in the first shipment. Assisted by federal funding, the department paid only $350 each for the $1500 radios. Chief Roberson was assigned the first call sign, "3300," in his police vehicle. The Chief immediately began serious recruitment for reserve officers. Capt. Harold Duncan, head of the detective division, headed up the reserves, who were paid one dollar per hour for eight hours per month.

BOL for a Masked Bandit

Bob Ellis was hired in 1968, and recalls how the city had only five beats with one man per car when he started as a Salinas officer. Those sharing patrol duties with him were Dick Canas, who later went to the FBI; Don Watkins, now retired in Florida; Mike Gibbons, who has passed away; and Eddie Naldoza. McPeek told Ellis who was then twenty-one years old, that his hiring was the first one of an officer at SPD who had not yet been born when McPeek began his career.

Ellis was on patrol by Roosevelt School one morning just as children were walking to school. He noticed a very large sewer rat running down the middle of the street, right at his headlights. He got out and tried to hit it with his nightstick but it lunged right at him and he only hit his own foot, causing a lot of pain. Eventually, he was able to kill the oversized rodent. Lt. Tom Brooks had him put in for an injury claim on his foot. Ellis seemed to attract animals and soon after the rat incident was called to take custody of a pet raccoon in a cage. There were no animal control officers at that time and Officer Ellis put the cage in the trunk of his patrol car. When he opened the trunk the animal was loose. His backup, Officer Stirling Collins, arrived and the two men tried to get a noose around the raccoon's neck, but it escaped and ran up and down the road. The two officers ran after it and Ellis threw his nightstick at it, but missed. The nightstick split in half as the raccoon disappeared into the night. Officer Collins left the area leaving Ellis to contemplate the loss of his prisoner. Returning to his car Ellis realized he had lost his keys which had been tucked into his waistband during the chase. He had to call headquarters and have another set brought out. Later that night, a BOL, (Be on the lookout broadcast,) went out over the radio for a suspect wearing a fur coat and mask in the area of John and Abbott Streets, possibly with keys in his mouth.

Officers were pranksters and always looking for some fun. When a rabbit that had been dyed pink by some citizen was found roaming around the downtown area, officers took the animal to the station. Someone unknown to this day, put the rabbit in a box on the chief's desk, where it was found the next morning. When the chief arrived to the stench of urine, he found his desk had been ruined by the acidic urine. The department had to have the top of the desk completely replaced.

Not all the stories from the Ellis period were funny. Officer Snodgrass, having purchased a brand new six-inch, clamshell holster, put a four-inch weapon into his new pride and joy. Looking in a mirror to admire himself, and asking the question, "Does your appearance command respect?" he tried to draw his weapon and shot himself in the foot.

When the call came in of an armed robbery at the Wal Mart Store with a description of a male suspect dressed as a woman, all patrol units responded, eventually chasing a suspect vehicle out to the area of the airport. Pulling over into the high grass while they made the stop, officers left their patrol units running and the catalytic converters caught the grass on fire, destroying the patrol cars.

A woman seeking commitment papers for her abusive and drunken husband was killed by the man who had just been released from Agnews State Hospital. Carrying a rifle, the man entered the couple's home on Alma Avenue and shot her multiple times while their son played outside. The woman had previously received fractured ribs and other injuries from the man she feared. Concerned about what he might do to her family while intoxicated, she had tried to have him committed. Judge Brazil ordered the man sent to Agnews for two years but he was released after only six months because the assistant superintendent of the hospital felt he was doing well. *Salinas Californian, April 17, 1967.*

By July 1967, the city was discussing the budget for the upcoming year. The police department was to have eleven percent of the total budget, what amounted to $868,000. They were earning it as they investigated murders and dope cases. Seizing over seven ounces of cocaine with a street value of over $67,000, they made numerous arrests. They continued to fight an escalating burglary rate and were often injured in confrontations with suspects. When Detectives Bacolis and Sterling were working vice they tried to arrest a transient. The man rushed out of a hotel room with a big knife, cutting both men who had to be taken to the hospital. The football jamborees were also the scene of fights between juveniles and often resulted in charges of battery on police officers. Stabbings in the Chinatown area, domestic assaults, murders, and shotgun wielding juveniles were only some of the calls officers were answering on a daily basis.

Officers were honored along with other city employees at the annual dinner. Rosalie Nunez received two special pins in honor of her twenty years of service. Don Moss, Robert Cash, Robert Bacolas, Richard Hack, Roy Hanna,

Larry Manalo, Earlinor Odom, Tony Rodriguez, Paul Scott, and Jack Wilson were also honored.

The newspaper called 1967, "an extraordinary year" as they recounted the dozen murders the county saw that year. From the man who lay in wait to shoot his wife in the driveway of their home, killing her friend by accident, to the husband released from Agnew Hospital early who returned and shot his wife inside their home, the news was grim. A step-father had taken an eleven year old girl from her home in Salinas, raped and killed her, then buried her near San Lucas. A barmaid was strangled, a man beaten to death, and a young woman shopping downtown was found dead, stabbed to death off San Juan Grade Road. It had been a violent year, with females the victims in many cases. *Salinas Californian, December 30, 1967.*

The traffic news was not much better since it was reported that one person had died every three days on the streets and roads of Monterey County. The number of fatal accidents had increased twenty-one percent from 1966 and excessive speed and alcohol were pointed out as the two most often contributing factors. The total number of people who died violent deaths in Monterey County in 1967 included both victims of traffic accidents and homicides. The staggering figure stood at one hundred ninety-two deaths and was thought to be the highest in the history of the county. Sixteen homicides, one hundred thirty-six traffic deaths, and forty suicides accounted for the statistics.

Former police officer Al Storm died early in 1968. With SPD for four years between 1945 and 1949, he chose to leave Salinas to work in the Sheriff's Department for many years. He was bailiff for Judge Machado and had retired in 1963. He was an honorary life member of the MCPOA and had served in Troop C, going to the Mexican border during the 1916 incident. Bill Ward, a former Sheriff's Deputy well known to local Salinas officers, died the same day. Ward had been chairman of the Big Hat Barbecue and was a member of the posse.

SPD badge during the Roberson years
Courtesy of Chief Roberson

Salinas continued to send officers to available training programs. In March 1968, three Salinas officers graduated as part of the eleventh POST academy held in Hollister. Officers Robert Kammeyer, Donald Thompson, and James Wilson proudly accepted the congratulations of Captain Harold Duncan who had been one of their instructors during the two hundred forty hour course. *Salinas Californian, March 16, 1968.* The new officers were able to put their training to use quickly as multiple burglaries, robberies and murders happened in the city. Former Officer Merwin Wayman was only forty-two years old when he died from injuries received in a motorcycle accident. Wayman left the department to purchase the Harley Davidson Motorcycle Agency located on North Main Street. A veteran of World War II, he had lived in Salinas for fifteen years at the time of his death. He was given a funeral with full military honors. *Salinas Californian, March 25, 1968.*

When Chief Roberson's car was stolen, it made the newspapers. The chief's car, driven by his wife, had been parked on Main Street and was taken while she was attending a movie. The theft was only one of many that day. In another incident, a man stopped for speeding ended up in jail for battery on a police officer. The man was upset about the traffic stop and refused to sign the ticket.

He became more and more angry and grabbed at the officer, demanding his badge number. He had ample opportunity to memorize the badge number as he was transported to the jail. Officers were always looking for things out of place. When an officer noticed a man getting into a Great Western Laundry truck at 1:20 a.m. he thought something was not right. The theft of the truck, and the recovery thereof, was thought to be one of the "shortest lived vehicle thefts on record." The man told the officer he was headed to Alaska. *Salinas Californian, April 8, 1968.*

Larry Myers, Ron Scott and Joe Gunter were all hired in 1969. Myers, Gary Edwards and James Snodgrass graduated in the sixteenth Peace Officers and Training Class on December 12, 1969, at Gavilan College along with the first female to graduate from the program and who had been hired by the Carmel Police Department. Myers, who left for several years to work for the Los Angeles County Sheriff's Department, returned to Salinas and spent twenty-five years in various positions, retiring as a captain. Myers attended the sixteenth academy at Gabilan and worked in patrol and as a detective before making sergeant. A lieutenant and acting captain for twelve years, he was promoted to captain, a position he held for the ten years leading up to his retirement. Myers recalls spending one year arresting prostitutes on Soledad Street. After arresting over one hundred that year, he received a letter of commendation. He never made another arrest for prostitution.

Myers was, in his own words, "a very outspoken" member of the department. Other officers who worked with Myers recalled how the captain's car smelled and was always full of hay and horse manure. The captain drove out to the posse grounds in his police car on a daily basis to feed his horses, often taking other employees or officers with him, carrying supplies in the back seat. Myers himself recalled being called into the chief's office one day with Captain Tom Brooks. Knocking before entering, the two found the chief standing behind his desk in Speedos swim trunks and wearing a diving mask. The chief was trying on gear he would use in an upcoming trip to Hawaii. Unable to contain their laughter at the sight, the two captains backed out of the office.

TWENTY-ONE

LEGENDS IN THEIR OWN TIME

Ron Scott began his career in Salinas after a short time working in Probation. It had taken him three tries before he was hired because Harold Duncan had known him most of his life and had some reservations about his maturity level. His first shift was on July 19, 1969, the day of the first moon landing. That night on patrol with Eddie Naldoza as his training officer, Scott experienced the Saturday night parade held during Big Week. Naldoza told the new officer not to touch any of the buttons in the police car and to keep his weapon in his holster. The first call of the night was to a bar in Chinatown and Scott was told to "Stay here and watch the car" while Naldoza went in. Naldoza soon returned, dragging a guy out and throwing him on top of the patrol car. He told Scott to watch the guy so Scott got out of the patrol unit, picked the guy up, dusted him off and told him to go on his way. He received some training on the handling of prisoners when Naldoza returned and found the man gone. His second year at the rodeo, Scott was driven to Acacia and Main Streets and told not to let any traffic through during the parade. One of about twenty officers on duty that night, he was instructed not to leave his post unless someone was being murdered. During the parade, several people came over to Scott, who was standing in the middle of the intersection, telling him a woman was trying to kill people. After the third report, Scott decided that murder was the only reason to leave his post, so he went to investigate. He was directed to a woman with a four-pronged wrench who was hitting people in the back of their heads. He went after her, with the crowd yelling, "Get her, get her!" in support of the officer. He had to tackle the woman on the Salinas

High School lawn and the fight was on. After a brief escape, the woman was handcuffed. By then, the crowd was yelling, "Get him, get him!" He made it over to the staging area for the parade by Valley Center, but the crowd grew more hostile. Fortunately, a color guard of Coast Guard personnel, finished with their part in the parade, and armed with M-1 rifles with chrome bayonets, escorted the officer and his prisoner to Valley Center and waited with them until the paddy wagon came to collect the woman. Trying to keep a low profile and standing behind a building, Scott was unsuccessful. Pelted by bottles thrown by drunks in a flatbed truck, Scott saw an MG Midget with its top down driving by. He jumped into the passenger seat, telling the driver he was commandeering his vehicle and was driven back to the department.

Ron Scott spent eighteen years working the Saturday night parade and still remembers the challenges of the night parade and the carnival violence. With a police car at the end of the parade, all the officers on duty there would walk behind that last car back to the department. He recalled one such night when they received a request for mutual aid at the carnival because of a large crowd and fight. The officers jumped onto a labor bus, going code three to assist. The fight was on and the officers were outnumbered once again.

When Ron Scott started working at SPD, there were no radios and officers were still using call boxes and whistles to call for assistance. Officers were issued eighteen rounds of .38 caliber ammunition, two uniforms, a Sam Brown gun belt and a department weapon. A whistle and helmet were required and useful to the officers. The whistle was used when officers needed help and worked quite well, especially during foot chases. One night as Sgt. Harold Duncan checked the alley behind the bus station, he saw a suspicious man. The man ran from the officer, who began blowing his whistle to call for aid from other officers. In those days, many citizens were willing to come to the aid of the law officers in town. Hearing the whistle from his office in the Army recruiter's building, a recruiter fired one .45 caliber round into the fleeing suspect, killing him instantly.

Scott's training lasted a full thirty days, after which he was on his own. At that time the department sent officers to the academy only after they had completed their eighteen month probationary period. Near death incidents were quite common and Reserve Officer Peevy was almost electrocuted one night when he tried to get out of a patrol car after lightening had struck and downed some power lines on top of the car. His life was saved when Ron Scott, the driver of the car, yanked the man back to safety.

Harold Duncan gave the Ethics classes to students at the academy on a regular basis. One of the examples he used for training the officers was his own experience as a new recruit. According to stories told by "old-timers" who worked with Duncan, when he was hired older officers took him to the Gabilan Streets bars where they met with a bartender. The bartender handed over the money the officer would need to purchase his uniforms.

Sgt. Woody Meek was in charge of sighting in the department's vintage four inch, .38 caliber weapons that had fixed sights and lanyard strap rings. Watching Meek one night as a new recruit, Scott saw how this was done. Meek would shoot at the target, see which way the gun needed to be sighted, then bang the gun on the table to "adjust" the sights. Scott went out and bought his own gun after that. Range stories were legend then. The department's new range was only one week old when it became the scene of its first accident. Tony Sollecito, "dry-firing" his weapon fortunately downrange, shot out the new range window. Annual firearms range practice was held in a cow pasture off Highway 68 in an area that is now Toro Park. For this, officers were given a fifty round box of ammunition which included the eighteen rounds issued for the upcoming year.

Quickly moving up within the department, Scott was a sergeant when the city faced major problems connected to the produce farm labor strikes of the late 1970s and early 1980s. When Don Watkins was seriously injured in an incident on Abbott Street, the department realized they could not handle the strike situation with beat officers only. Sgt. Scott was put in command of a twenty-five member "Strike Team," that worked long, hard hours closely allied with the Sheriff's Department where Scott's father, Captain Walter Scott, was in charge. The Strike Team started at 4:00 a.m., often working until all field workers were bussed back to their respective companies, sometimes as late at 6:00 p.m. Sgt. Scott shared command duties with Sgt. Sam Tashiro and recalled one frightening event where United Farm Workers had lined the street in front of the old county jail where Caesar Chavez was being held, holding vigil during his incarceration. On the other side of the street were members of the Farmers of America and the two groups were ready to battle. The Strike Team members dressed at the department and walked through the courthouse to get between the two groups. Joe Pezzini recalls being a young boy that night. He carried an American flag and stood on the side of the street with the farmers. The officers made the walk up the street between the two groups, placing one Strike Team member approximately every thirty feet along the route. When things appeared to being headed for disaster they sent word to headquarters, requesting the gas masks and tear gas. It arrived in the form of World War II Navy surplus equipment, unfamiliar to the officers who had never been trained for the use of the masks. Fortunately, Captain Walter Scott was able to reason with both groups, avoiding any violence.

The Strike Team did have some sense of humor in spite of the seriousness of their work. When the Sheriff's Department, waiting to escort a labor bus to the highway in the East Market Street area called for code three backup requesting Salinas officers to respond, SPD arrived quickly at the scene where VFW workers were throwing bottles and rocks at officers. As the Salinas officers contacted deputies, their radios could be heard playing the cavalry charge!

Another request for mutual aid by deputies outside the city area had SPD officers responding code three to Old Stage Road. One hundred people were close to rioting and deputies needed help fast. Gary Edwards was driving with Bob Benson in the passenger seat as the two responded. Gary, then a chain smoker, decided to throw the cigarette out the window as they flew at over one hundred miles per hour out to the scene. Patrol cars had only manually operated windows at that time, so Gary rolled the window down with his left hand, while he steered the car with his knees and continued smoking with his right hand. Reaching across himself to throw the cigarette out with his right hand, he quickly rolled the window up with his left hand, trapping one finger of his right hand as he did so. As the unit sped out to Old Stage Road, Gary struggled to control the car with his knees yelling at Benson, "Hey Benson help me out here." Benson eventually took the wheel until Edwards could roll the window down far enough to retrieve his finger.

Old Stage Road and the fields there saw its share of problems during the strike days. In one incident, the United Farm Workers, (UFW) showed up en masse, greatly outnumbering both the two hundred officers present and the Filipino field workers. Rushing out into the fields to fight, the UFW workers were later taken to the hospital, many of them with stab wounds. All the officers could do was to try to keep them apart. The Sheriff's Department tried to ease the burden of the long hours of all the Strike Team members by providing lunches to everyone on duty, wherever they were. The lunches came to be known as the "M-1 Lunches." M-1 was the call sign of the unit that delivered the lunches to the officers in the field. Made by inmates at the jail, they were dry bread sandwiches with suspicious baloney and a piece of cheese accompanied by one piece of fruit. The officers would sometimes get so hungry at their remote duty locations, they actually ate part of the lunches.

The Strike Team members were working long hours and were often worn out. When the sergeant saw one of his patrol cars pass by with an obviously sleeping passenger, he waved the car over. Telling the driver to take his own car, the sergeant got in and drove away with the sleeping officer beside him. When the officer started to wake up, he said, "Well, what did the sarge want?" He got a little surprise when the sergeant answered, "Oh, nothing much." It was during this same time period that the sergeant found Gary Edwards asleep in his patrol car behind the library in East Salinas, his junior officer seated beside him. The sergeant had the junior officer get out of the patrol unit and into the sergeant's vehicle, calling all the other units over to the area. According to Edwards, the entire team had surrounded his patrol unit and waited until he woke up, with all his team members staring at him.

Ron Scott recalled the first gang homicide he worked with Joe Gunter. According to Scott, it was the first recognized gang-related homicide in Salinas. Scott and Gunter heard the details of the murder from a terrified witness. The two detectives located the body buried in the Salinas River bottom. The suspect was a Mexican Mafia member who had been driving with two juveniles in the back seat. When one made a comment about the Nuestra Familia the suspect got upset, turned around and shot the victim five times. With no idea where the suspect was the detectives searched the city for the car described by the witness and found it in a motel parking lot. They went into the room of the suspect on a "No–Knock Warrant." When four officers burst into the room the suspect reached for his gun, but thought better of it and surrendered. The suspect was eventually convicted of the murder.

Scott stayed with the department and worked in various assignments before choosing to leave on the same date he had started, twenty-one years later on July 19, 1990. His career was far from over as his skills were put to use when he became the Chief of Police for Livermore. Ron Scott retired in July 2002 and continues to live in Livermore, where he enjoys golfing, traveling and spending time with his grandchildren.

Larry Manalo was well known by all the officers and many of the citizens of Salinas for his antics. Rick Moore received a call from Manalo one night, telling him to meet him at the golf course. When Moore arrived, Manalo was in a ditch, digging golf balls out, then hitting the balls out onto the airport runway. Manalo, who never used a sick day during his career, expected everyone to follow his lead in that regard. Officers on his shift soon learned that calling in sick to Manalo was simply not worth the trouble they would get. They would wait until they knew someone else was at the phone before calling in, but even that did not stop Manalo from inquiring as to their illness. Known to go to an officer's house and knock on the door, demanding an explanation, Manalo made it known that a simple cold or fever was not enough to keep an officer from work. Manalo also liked to save things and was found one night, standing on top of his patrol car at the old Lacey Auto building. Scheduled for demolition, the old building had some florescent lights Larry thought would look good in his garage workshop. He was busy taking the lights down and putting them in his car. When the Cominos Hotel suffered minor damage in the 1989 earthquake, the city ordered the demolition the beautiful old hotel. Larry Manalo and another officer went through the building just before it was torn down, taking old menus and sets of plates to keep for their historical value.

Manalo was a pyromaniac, a fact that was well known. He would make bottle rocket launchers, using them to frighten young officers. A young officer gassing up his unit would be startled to find a bottle rocket flying over his car, exploding as he tried to start his shift. Manalo also made a cannon to launch projectiles he made by stuffing tennis balls with wicks and gunpowder. He would launch the incendiary devices and watch as they exploded in the air.

With public apathy given as one of the reasons for the increase in crime, Chief Roberson tried to instruct the public on ways in which they could help their officers. Many crimes were not even reported, in spite of the fact that there were witnesses to the crimes. In one recent incident, several adults had watched as juveniles entered a store and looted it, doing nothing to intercede. Telling citizens they needed to be forthcoming with information, he also asked them to refuse to become involved in any illegal activities and gave this advice. "Law enforcement, in general, realizes its responsibility and is attempting in every way possible to curb our mounting crime problems, but without full citizen participation in OUR MUTUAL PROBLEM, we are fighting a losing battle." *Salinas Californian, January 30, 1968.*

Officer Tom McDonald was awarded Officer of the Year by the MCPOA in 1968 for his efforts in saving a young child from choking. The child was blue when the officer arrived on scene, a piece of candy stuck in his throat. The officer was able to get the candy ejected and gave mouth to mouth resuscitation to the young boy, saving his life. The winter was wet that season and flooding was causing disaster both in town and in the fields surrounding Salinas. When a group of east side teens, part of "The Warlords" organization stepped in to help fill sandbags, they did not have much fondness for the police officers of the city. Chief Roberson called the group, asking for their help and they responded with over one hundred young people willing to help. They did not ask to be paid, but Chief Roberson delivered a check for $198.97, representing the eighty-three hours of hard labor the young men and women had done to help the city in its time of need.

Joseph Gunter
The Legend of "David-1"

On December 10, 1969, Joe Gunter was hired. As a new officer in a department trying to improve public relations, he received a big lecture about what was then called, "public relations." There had been a rash of complaints about officers being rude to members of the public and Sgt. Richard Hack, the Watch Commander for the midnight shift, carefully instructed the new officers about polite behavior during a lengthy lecture. Wanting to impress his superior, Officer Gunter went out to patrol his beat and came upon a citizen with a stranded vehicle at Pearl and East Alisal Street in the wee hours of the morning. Asking the man if he required assistance Gunter politely jumped out of his car, placed his hands on the citizen's trunk, and helped push the car until it started. The satisfied citizen went on his way. An hour later a smirking Officer Gunter told the story of his good deed at coffee. Thirty minutes after that, the car was reported stolen by the owner who told police he had thousands of dollars worth of tools in the trunk. Gunter figured he would get fired when they recovered the car and found his fingerprints all over the trunk. The nightshift worked all night, trying to locate the stolen car. Finally, they found it and all held their collective breath as they opened the trunk. Gunter breathed a sigh of relief when he saw that all the tools were still there.

In June 1970, Officer Gunter received the standard letter from the city manager stating he had passed his initial six month probationary period, giving him an increase in salary to $671 per month. Officer Gunter made a name for himself immediately, receiving numerous commendations for his investigative work. Gunter was praised for his work on a theft at the Crocker Citizen's Bank within months of completing his probation period. He received further commendations from Sgt. Roy Hanna, Captain Garwood, Chief Roberson, Lt Lasserot, Instructor Don Thompson, and others for his work on burglary, indecent exposure and drug cases. He was also praised for his cooperation and assistance to other officers by Lt. Nelson in a series of memorandums and letters placed in his file.

He was surprised, then, to see his name in the paper, listed as having been arrested in a stolen car case. Appearing in the *Salinas Californian*, the "Pair Booked in Car Theft" article stated Joseph Gunter of 222 Lincoln Avenue, along with a juvenile female, was arrested as a joy rider and found to be in possession of marijuana. Gunter received a letter of apology from reporter Paul Kessinger, who claimed he was "in a hurry" and didn't check the names. The retraction article ran in the November 3, 1973, newspaper, correctly listing Gunter as the victim of car thieves. The reporter thanked Gunter for being, "so good-natured about the mix-up." A copy of the letter of apology was sent to Chief Roberson.

By 1975, Gunter was taking exams for both Detective and Instructor. On September 28, 1975, he became a Detective, a position he held until his retirement in 2002. Commendations continued and were warranted for the work the detective did. In 1978, during one thirty-nine day period, Gunter participated in eighty-four arrests resulting in one hundred thirty-six crimes being charged. He confiscated over $17,800 worth of heroin in addition to thousands of dollars worth of cocaine, LSD, marijuana, mushrooms and other drugs. Chief Ferguson commended Gunter for his promotion of team work effort, both with SPD officers and others.

By the mid 1970s, Gunter hooked up with Andy Enni to form the most effective detective team the city had ever seen. From 1976-1983, there were no unsolved murder cases. The credit was given to their ability to talk to people and get information on the street with their success. The detectives got out into the community, patrolling their "territory." The two solved eleven homicides in 1981 that had occurred during an eleven day period, and both said they wouldn't trade their jobs for anything.

The details of one murder investigation were featured in the March 1985 edition of *Official Detective Magazine*. Wendy Prender, a prostitute involved in drugs, had been shot in the back of the head in her apartment on Maple Street. Gunter and Enni caught the case and worked it through a series of leads and informants. The suspect finally confessed after realizing the two detectives were close to arresting him for the murder. Later, he would retract his confession, but Gunter had tape recorded it and the suspect was eventually sentenced to thirty-three years to life for the murder.

Many of the detective team's cases were memorialized in print over the years. The 1984 murder of a young girl in a mobile home was featured in *True Detective* in March 1985 and showed the importance of I.D. Technician Lippert in helping solve the case. Gunter and Enni were again assisted by Lippert in the murder investigation detailed in the August 1985, *Official Detective Magazine.* All three men were meticulous about crime scene investigation and the two detectives were insistent about proper evidence collection. The victim, deaf and elderly, had been awakened in her bed and senselessly murdered. Developing information about a similar crime in Santa Rosa, the detectives traveled to interview potential witnesses while Lippert worked the evidence. Months later, an anonymous tip would lead to the suspect. Finally, good old-fashioned leg work would provide the necessary evidence for a charge of murder. Patience paid off and the suspect was arrested in Greenfield after returning from Mexico where he fled following the initial investigation.

Enni was National Police Officer of the Month in the September 1985 edition of *Master Detective.* He and Gunter had solved seventy-two homicides by that year. Enni had first worked with the Monterey County Sheriff's Department, working undercover as a "hippie" before becoming a bail bondsman. Then he began a career with SPD at the age of thirty-five.

In February 1986, Gunter was the National Police Officer of the Month in *Master Detective.* Gunter was quoted in words that ring as true today as in 1986, "Sometimes an hour or two can make all the difference. Evidence won't wait. Witnesses won't wait. The sooner you get the facts, the better chance there is you'll solve the murder." The article featured a number of the detective's cases. The head of the Detective Division at the time was Captain Les Rodman who had this to say about Detective Joe Gunter. "In seventeen years of police work, Detective Joe Gunter has earned the reputation for being one of the most successful homicide sleuths in the business. Over a six-year period, he and his partner, Andy Enni, have cleared every murder case they were assigned to investigate. Almost everything they do is perfect. They are excellent investigators."

Joe Gunter was the last of the designated "Detectives" in the Salinas Police Department. Changes within the department made the experienced detectives like Gunter extinct, replacing them with others assigned for only two years. While that provided more slots for officers to work as investigators, it eliminated those with long years of experience and the valuable street contacts detectives like Gunter, Enni and Edwards had benefited from over the years. Detectives are called "David" units and "David 1" was the senior or supervising detective in the unit. As "David 1," Joe Gunter personified the tradition of excellence and integrity in law enforcement until his retirement in 2002. Even after retirement, he continues to serve his department as one of three Background Investigators looking for those who will follow in his footsteps. Amazingly, he still runs into many paroled felons he once put in prison. They always inquire as to his health and status and seem to genuinely respect him, often wanting to tell him about their lives and crediting him for getting them straight. He also continues to receive tips on cases from informants and citizens more comfortable speaking with him and unwilling to seek out the new generation of investigators.

MCPOA

Chuck Foster was the Vice-President of the Monterey County Peace Officer's Association, (MCPOA) in 1973 when he wrote a letter to John Wayne, inviting him to be the guest speaker at the annual dinner-dance to be held in February the following year. In documents provided by Chuck Foster of the Sheriff's Department, a response was found. On letterhead simply engraved with "John Wayne," the famous actor sent his regrets. He was working on a sequel to "True Grit" at the time and would not be able to make it to the event in Monterey County. Offering his regrets and compliments to the members of the organization, the actor signed his name. The original letter and envelope also bearing his name is certainly a gem in the history of the MCPOA.

1973 was a very busy year for the officers and board members of the MCPOA. They were in the process of designing and constructing the Toro Park Range, for use by all the law enforcement agencies in Monterey County. The original documents relating to the progress of the range are also in the files supplied by Chuck Foster. Salinas Reserve Officer Gary Waller donated $800 in blueprint work to help with the project. Those records include a questionnaire asking MCPOA members to provide information about their estimated use of the range and requesting their input on the plans. Copies of the maps and plans for the buildings and range area were included in the packets sent to all members. *The Monterey County Lawmen* was in its thirty-eighth issue in November 1973, when the cost of mailing each newsletter was eight cents.

In April 1974, the MCPOA wished Salinas Officer Lee Farmer the best of luck in his retirement. Farmer had been with the department twelve years when he was injured in a car accident during a robbery investigation. It was during that time that Larry Oliver was promoted to detective and Jim Foster became an instructor, receiving congratulations in the newsletter. One hundred thirty-one police officers had been killed in the line of duty in 1973, a record the organization published in the same newsletter alongside photographs of Clint Eastwood, who was honored by the organization for his shooting abilities shown in the "Magnum Force" movie.

Officer Ken Brown received the Peace Officer of the Month award in August 1974 for saving a woman from drowning in the pool at her home. Responding to a call of a woman drowning, he found her face down in the pool. Pulling her out and finding she was not breathing, he began artificial resuscitation, turning treatment over to paramedics when they arrived, and was credited with saving her life.

It was in 1974 that the Department of Justice opened a criminalistics lab in Salinas to serve the Central Coast Counties. Staffed with five ciminalists, one technician and two clerks, the lab was located on Airport Boulevard. Available services included trace analysis, ballistics, blood grouping, (the three enzyme system) arson evidence examination and analysis of blood taken for ethyl alcohol content. *The Monterey County Lawman, Issue No. 61, November 1975.*

In early 1975, Monterey County was set to begin operations in the new county communication centers located in both Salinas and Monterey. The 911 system was the geographically largest system in the country and the only county-wide system in the west. This meant calls for all emergencies including fire, crime, accident, and medical calls would go through the new system.

SKEETER INNOCENTI

Skeeter Innocenti was a Municipal Court clerk in 1974 when she heard about an opening at the police department. The deadline for submitting applications was noon that day and she scurried to fill out the application and get it in on time. Her oral interview with McPeek, Roberson, and Dellfous focused on her father's work. Henry Garcia owned Garcia Sadlery, located directly across Gabilan Street from the old City Hall where the department was located at one time. Garcia's work was top notch and Skeeter had often delivered specially ordered belts and other leather work to officers at the department. All the officers talked about during her interview was her dad and his saddles. Thrilled with getting the job which paid much better than the court job, Skeeter started work at SPD as a clerk on the graveyard shift. She had only been on the job a few nights when she was standing at the copy machine one night. She was startled by a loud gunshot and felt something running down her body. Thinking she had been shot, she realized shortly thereafter that it was foam from the ceiling falling down on her. The foam was also covering Sgt. John Carr and was all over his uniform. Carr had been cleaning his gun when it fired a round into the floor and ricocheted up into the ceiling. Skeeter, Carr, and others spent the rest of the night cleaning up and searching the basement for a tile to replace the one on the floor before the Captain came in the following morning.

Skeeter was also there when someone put a chicken in Captain Rodman's office one night. When he arrived the next morning everyone was watching as he opened the door to the stench and mess of chicken shit and feathers. There were no windows in the office. The graveyard shift was always exciting. One night, Innocenti was in the coffee room downstairs with Larry Waller and several other clerks and officers when an earthquake hit, knocking out all electricity and plunging the room into complete darkness. Everyone scrambled to get to a door jamb but Larry Waller, petrified of earthquakes, would not allow anyone else to stand with him in one of the two doorjambs in that room. The other five people had to huddle together in one doorway while Waller held fast to the other. They found their way by using their cigarette lighters. Smoking was still being allowed in the department at that time.

Skeeter Innocenti was promoted to Senior Police Clerk and supervised various shifts for many years. She spent seven years in the chief's office before moving to Records and later worked as the secretary for Investigations. Rick Moore was the sergeant in Investigations at the time and Skeeter was happy to get the Monday to Friday job with weekends off. Skeeter recalls knowing all the bad habits of each detective, something which kept her from ever getting involved with anyone in her division. She spent over fourteen years in Investigations and retired out of that division with intimate knowledge of everything that went on there. She recalled when the captains got televisions in their offices so they could watch developing news or stories about the department. One was set on the western channel where John Wayne movies played more often than the news. The other was set on the golf channel. As part of her job in Investigations, Skeeter kept track of the PC 290 registrants, those required to register as sex offenders, devising a filing system that allowed her to access information very quickly when detectives asked specific questions. She also issued card room and gun dealer permits.

Now retired, Skeeter lives in a beautiful area fourteen miles outside of Paso Robles where she in enjoying every minute of her leisurely life.

On May 31, 1975, Bob Ellis, while on patrol and on a traffic stop, was hit by a speeding vehicle with such force that the resulting impact sent him one hundred thirty-five feet from the point of impact. The skidding of his body actually ground his pistol down through the chamber and into the bullet. He woke up two weeks later and was told his right knee was badly damaged. He was eventually retired with a seventy-nine percent disability and a pension of six hundred fifteen dollars per month. He has had seven surgeries since that night and one more is planned. He still comes to all the retirement parties and currently has a successful real estate business in Jackson.

THE TEN PLAN

Chief Roberson found support for the "Ten Plan" where officers would have four, ten hour days followed by three days off. This allowed for overlapping shifts, putting more officers on the streets at one time. More officers were needed as there was a phantom in town. New officers sitting in their cars writing reports would sometimes see a unit go by them "code three". Calling into communications, to ask where the code three traffic was going, they would be told there was no such traffic at the time. Puzzled, the young officers now in pursuit of the code three unit, would invariably lose sight of the car. One such officer was sitting in his patrol unit one night when another Salinas unit went by him. Inquiring of radio what the code three traffic was, and following that unit, he could see the unit number. The sergeant on duty responded that the unit number he was referring to was sitting in the back lot. The officer, obsessed with finding the phantom car, sat in the back lot all night as cars came in from their watch hoping to find a car with the same number. Apparently, the phantom had used black tape to change his vehicle number, torturing new officers with the code three drive-bys. Warned at briefing the next night that the phantom would lose his job if it ever happened again, the phantom never rode again, and no one ever really was able to figure out exactly who it was. The officer later called his watch commander, Sgt. Rocha, and quit. When Rocha asked him to come in to the department to talk about it, he refused, telling the sergeant he could send somebody to pick up his equipment. He left all his equipment in the phone booth at a service station then located at the corner of Nissen and Main Streets.

Jim Wilson, known to all who worked with him as "J.W.," came to SPD in 1967. Recalling Joe Gunter's rookie days, J.W. told the story of Raymond Gamboa with no little amount of enjoyment. J.W. and Larry Sterling received an alarm call at a doctor's officer behind Salinas Valley Memorial Hospital

(SVMH). With Gunter watching the side of the building, J.W. and Sterling went in to investigate and found Raymond Gamboa inside. The fight was on. Sterling, his gun drawn, jumped on top of Gamboa during the fight. Not realizing his finger was on the trigger, he hit Gamboa over the head and the weapon fired. Gunter was outside waiting, heard the shot and reacted. Gamboa, beaten up and frightened thought he had been shot, and followed by the pursuing Sterling, crashed through a window to where Gunter was waiting and was arrested. He was screaming that he had been shot but was uninjured except for bruises received during his fight with the officers. The bullets had destroyed the medicine cabinet in the doctor's office and the officers put a band aid on a bottle of cough syrup they found dripping when they cleared the building. Gamboa would later be arrested for a drug related robbery homicide.

In a chase following a domestic incident on West Acacia Street, Wilson stayed to speak with the victim's wife, sending his rookie to run after the fleeing husband. As the chase progressed, the suspect, running at top speed turned to hit the rookie and ran straight into a telephone pole, knocking himself out cold. They had to call an ambulance and transported the unconscious man to the hospital.

THE HIT MAN

Steve Perryman had a source who gave the story about a man who wanted to have his wife killed. The source even had a folder about the habits of the wife which he gave to Perryman when they met. Perryman sought out Gunter and Scott, then working as night detectives, and showed it to them. They suggested Perryman act as a "contract killer," giving him the idea of taking on the persona of a deranged Viet Nam veteran willing to kill the wife for money. Perryman changed into street clothes and stuck his .45 caliber weapon in his waistband. Going out to the meet the "client," Perryman worried he might not be able to carry off the act. He started acting deranged right off and became more confident as he learned he easily fit into the role the detectives had given him. In fact, he played the part so well, that when they arrested the man later that same night, the man said he was grateful to the detectives because he was actually really afraid of the hit man. He pled out at arraignment. Perryman was given the Award of Merit at the March 1976 meeting of the MCPOA for his role in playing the hit man. *The Monterey County Lawman, Issue 66, April 1976.*

TWENTY-TWO

A SUNROOF FOR GARY EDWARDS' PATROL CAR AND OTHER QUICK DRAW STORIES OF THE 1970S PERIOD

Gary Edwards had a new trainee riding with him the night John Carr provided shotgun training during briefing. Carr had made it clear that the safety was to be on at all times on the shotguns, unless they were being taken out of the car for use at a scene. Gary sent his trainee out to the car to check things out and put the shotgun away. The officers were on assignment in the Commission Street area where picketers would come at 4:00 a.m. to protest and police were to keep the laborers safe. Larry Waller was driving a second patrol unit and pulled up alongside Edwards and his trainee. Edwards, in the passenger seat at the time, was talking across the car to Waller, who was reading a book.

The officers were talking and laughing and Edwards was scratching his left leg as they watched the laborers entering the manpower area. Suddenly, the shotgun went off. Waller, not realizing what had happened, accused Edwards of throwing a firecracker into his unit, but it soon became apparent that there was a hole in the top of Edwards' unit. The laborers, hearing gunshots ran away quickly, and Edwards returned to the office to make a report on the incident to Sergeant John Carr. Carr, who had just given the safety lecture, chastised Edwards for not having checked up on the trainee's procedures. The trainee had reversed the entire safety procedure, putting a round in the chamber and leaving the safety off as he placed the shotgun in the car. The trainee, who remained silent during the entire evening, was told by Edwards that he had requested a sunroof and since the police department wasn't going to give him one, he made one of his own.

OFFICER SNODGRASS AND THE QUICK DRAW INCIDENTS

According to stories told by now retired officers, there were several accidental discharges over the years. Fortunately, no one was injured and the stories remain part of the legend of the department.

Officer Snodgrass was practicing his drawing technique in the locker room one day with his "unloaded" weapon. He managed to shoot himself in the leg. Larry Irwin was removing his Derringer while in the locker room when it went off, shooting him.

SHOOT OUT AT THE T.V.

Ray Jackson was practicing his quick draw while watching old westerns at home. Aiming at the television set and pulling his weapon out, Jackson shot and wounded his television.

WITNESS INTERVIEW TECHNIQUES

John Carr, while working with the victim of a 417 case in the glass office at the station, was asking her if the clicking sound she had heard the weapon make in the incident on Homestead Avenue sounded like his gun as he pulled the trigger of his unloaded weapon. The gun went off, sending a round into the floor of the station.

Gunter was in the office and saw smoke billowing around Carr and the woman and walked out of the area just as Chief Ferguson ran into the office. Carr was calmly continuing to ask the woman if that was, in fact, the way it had sounded earlier that evening.

HOW TO TEST FIRE YOUR NEW WEAPON

The department had issued new automatics and Jerry Maricle was testing his out in the detective offices at the police department. He test fired the empty gun, which fired a live round into the ceiling. Maricle, and his partner, Claude Sparks, spent the rest of the night trying to cover up the hole so no one would find out what had happened.

Officers Injured in Carnival Brawl

In July 1972, Officers Charles N. Jancich and Mike Duval were injured in a fight at the carnival, then located at Abbott and Harkins Roads. Jancich was hit by a hammer and injured seriously. Thirty Salinas Police officers, along with Monterey County Deputies, arrested six people after a hostile crowd attacked. The incident began when Officers Richard Hack and Donald Watkins tried to arrest fifteen year old Ramon Acosta for public intoxication. Family members of Acosta interfered with officers and the crowd became hostile. Carnival employees shot at the fleeing assailants after the officers were injured, but they escaped on foot. Duval lost his gun to his assailant who actually was able to point the gun at Duval. Duval eventually regained control of his weapon, but his police baton and two officers' helmets were missing by the end of the incident. The crowd continued to throw bottles and rocks at arriving police. Two police cars were damaged and a third car, driven by Joe Gunter had a window smashed.

Shooting Board Clears Detective

Detective Donald Thompson was found to have been acting in self-defense when he killed Bobby Bachart during a raid on 203 W. Alisal Street in October 1972. A coroner's jury decided the detective had fired in self-defense. After entering the house and seeing guns in a closet area, Detective Thompson heard the toilet flushing. Believing drugs evidence was being destroyed, he pulled his weapon and demanded the bathroom door be opened, identifying himself as a police officer.

Fearing complete destruction of the evidence and getting no response from the bathroom, Detective Thompson broke in the door and saw a male subject on his knees near the sink. Another person was behind the door and a third subject, Mr. Bachart, was holding what the detective believed to be a knife. Bachart spun around and advanced toward the detective, who fired his revolver, hitting Bachart in the head.

Knife-wielding Man Shot by Detectives

On November 30, 1972, Detectives John Carr and Ray Jackson shot and killed Reginald A. Mintz on Pearl Street. Carr and Jackson saw a man with a large knife walking in the Pearl Street area and attempted to speak with him. The man was stabbing cars before entering a house. Both detectives went to the house, identified themselves, and tried to talk to Mintz who came out brandishing the knife. A full can of mace was used in an attempt to stop Mintz, but it was unsuccessful. Detectives moved back as Mintz advanced on them, finally getting one up against a fence. One detective fired a warning shot before both fired, hitting Mintz in the chest. On December 8, 1972, Carr and Jackson were cleared in the shooting of Reginald Mintz.

Hartnell College began an internship program with SPD in June 1973. Interns included Terry Davis and James Culligan, who later became an officer with Salinas before moving on to become a sergeant in San Diego. The class instructor was Robert W. Cash. While some went to college, others received on-the-job training. Detective Paul Scott showed James Culligan and others the polygraph machine.

On November 14, 1973, Salinas opened a 24-hour "Tip Line". Cost for the installation of the line was $354. Offices were desperately trying to get citizens to provide information in difficult cases. Public relations in the late 1960s and early 1970s was the responsibility of the Watch Commander. Lt. Vern Ricky had a singularly efficient way of handling most of the citizen complaints that would come to him on his watch. Suffice it to say that an officer had to do something "really bad," according to Gunter, to get a complaint in his file. A tall man with a husky build, Lt. Ricky's office was painted green and was in the area designated for officers to write their reports. One evening, as Gunter and others wrote reports, they heard a huge crash from the W.C.'s office and ran in to see what had happened. Lt. Ricky's feet could be seen atop his desk, clad in the standard issue pull on uniform boots. The Lieutenant himself was on the floor, his floppy cowboy hat still atop his head, making quite a sight for the young officers. Inquiring if their supervisor was all right, the officers were told to, "Get the hell out of here." He had clearly fallen off his chair!

"MOTHER MOSS"

Don Moss was the sergeant in charge of the swing shift in those days and kept a close eye on his men in the field. Known to hide out around town, Sgt. Moss would watch his officers as they responded to calls, often calling them on the radio telling them to, "Slow down, you're going too fast, you'll get there." His "mothering" became the subject of many conversations among the younger officers. One Mother's Day, a woman came to the front counter with several cakes left over from parties during the day that she wanted to give to the policemen. The cakes, all inscribed with the words "Happy Mother's Day," were the perfect opportunity for the sergeant's men. They took the cakes to his office and thereafter, Sgt. Moss was known affectionately as "Mother Moss."

GARY EDWARDS USES HIS RADIO

Most patrol officers still did not have portable radios. When making a stop or getting out of the car, officers would radio in their location and hang the car radio out the window. That way, if they needed help in a hurry, they could get to the radio to request assistance. Gary Edwards had one of the first portable radios, a cumbersome and heavy instrument attached to the uniform by a long leather strap. Edwards made a car stop on a stolen Corvette driven by Ronnie Dugger somewhere around Wood Street and ended up in a foot chase. While running after the suspect, Edwards wound up the leather strap and flung the radio at the fleeing man, hitting him in the head, knocking him out cold and making the arrest. Called into Lt. Bill Nelson's office and chastised for his actions, Officer Edwards listened to the lieutenant as he asked why the officer, who had been given a radio costing $2,500, didn't use it to call for assistance instead of using it to knock out the fleeing suspect. Suggesting the use of the two dollar baton for such activities, the fact that he had knocked out and arrested the car thief wasn't mentioned.

Gary Edwards spent more than the average amount of time in the offices of his supervisors. All patrol officers were detailed to the "3-5 duty" at least one day each week. From 3:00 a.m. to 5:00 a.m., cars could be cited if they obstructed the path of the street sweepers. Diligent officers could write twenty to thirty tickets a night. Edwards, out on Santa Rita Street and anxious to begin writing his share of tickets one night, got out of his car quickly and then watched as it continued on the downhill street, hitting parked cars as it went. Running after it, Edwards jumped half way in the window as the car crossed the street and crashed into another parked vehicle. It was 4:00 a.m. and kids were coming home from partying and screamed epitaphs at the officer who finally succeeded in getting the police car into park. Reluctantly calling in his "problem," Edwards greeted Instructor Mike Gibbons and his trainee, Ron Scott when they arrived at the scene of the devastation. Telling Gibbons that a Mexican kid had jumped into his police car, then jumped out, leaving it in drive and causing the crash, Edwards watched as young Officer Scott was sent by himself to make an area check for the described hoodlum. Alone, Gibbons told Edwards the story just didn't sound right, and the embarrassed officer confessed the true story.

TWENTY-THREE

RED JACKETS, WRECKS AND RESERVES, AND THE 1970S

Late in 1973, Deputy Chief McPeek's title was changed to Assistant Chief of Police. McPeek was the "King" of accident investigation. He put himself through a traffic investigation course and taught the Salinas officers how to diagram scenes. At the time, there were no computer assisted drawing programs and all diagrams had to be done by hand, taking hours. McPeek would "grade" the diagrams turned in by the younger officers, marking them with red ink, forcing them to spend hours remaking diagrams to his satisfaction. Gunter had his first fatal scene to document within three weeks of being out on patrol alone. A double fatal, single car accident at Market and Sun, the car had run into a pole with such force that it flung both occupants into the back seat. The front seat was occupied by the engine. When medical crews arrived, they pulled the two young men from the car and thought one had a pulse. Trying to revive him with early CPR techniques, the medics and police faced an angry crowd of onlookers who thought they were beating up the victim.

Chief H.W. Roberson now had a staff of over one hundred, eighty-six of whom were sworn officers. Marjori DeWees became the first female detective at the department. Gary Edwards remembers her as a "very good lady" assigned mostly to juvenile or family matters. She died of cancer. Everett Mudersbach, an officer for only a short time, later became a private investigator.

On January 1, 1974, the department began to recruit reserve officers. Seventy-one applications were processed, and the department had twenty-nine reserves. Reserve Officers worked at least eight hours per month, were paid one dollar per hour, and had to be eighteen years old. They had to be 5'9" tall with at least 20-100 correctable vision to 20-30. A high school diploma was needed.

POLICE UNIONIZE

In mid-1974, Salinas officers joined the AFL-CIO Operating Engineer's Union Local 3. The President of the Salinas Police Benefit Association was Len Shuette, and the Association's Vice-President was Jerry Joseph. Dispute over pay for officers was constantly in the news. City Manager Bob Cristofferson claimed officers made $17,759 per year, including their uniform allowance, costs for physicals, disability insurance, etc.

LULAC made claims against police for harassment of young Salinas Chicanos. Cpt. Roy Hanna cited weekend problems at West Acacia and Main Street parking area saying racial tensions between young people in cars, vandalism, and other crimes were affecting merchants. Merchants placed signs in the parking area so officers could cite offenders and paid the price for their efforts.

In late 1974, Larry Irwin and Frank Bernardasci received a commendation from the Monterey County Police Officer's Association, (MCPOA) for making one hundred ninety-nine arrests in a twenty-one day period of assignment to the one hundred block of Main Street. Their arrest record was outstanding with 111 felony arrests, 119 arrests for drunk and more than $10,000 worth of heroin seized.

Leonard Shuette was the Outstanding Police Officer of the Year. He had joined the department six years earlier, and taught at Hartnell and Gavilan Colleges. He held both basic and intermediate POST, (Police Officer's Standard Training) certifications.

THE CASE OF THE CHANNEL LOCK BURGLARS

In February 1975, Detectives Frank Bernardasci and Ron Scott were assisted by Mike Gibbons and Larry Oliver in breaking "The Case of the Channel-Lock Burglars." Arrested were John Luna, Robert Castenada, Juan Niablis and Juan Molena. They used channel lock pliers to break into two to three houses per day, selling the stolen property to unsuspecting people, then going back to those same people and stealing the property from them.

THE RED JACKETS

Promoted to Detective at the same time were Andy Enni, Jerry Shuck, Gary Edwards, Leonard Shuette and Joe Gunter. This was a group of detectives that would soon earn a reputation for hard work and integrity. Detectives then, as now, worked a number of different assignments. Gunter remembers the years as an undercover narcotics officer where a grungy appearance and beards sometimes made officers indistinguishable from the crooks. The narcs were getting ready for a big raid one night when they heard a request for all available officers to assist at the Sundowner Club on East Alisal Street where a fight was escalating. John Gates was supposed to be doing a simple walk-through. Sgt. Scott, hearing him dispatched, paid for the coffee he had just ordered and walked with a heavy heart to his unit. Meanwhile, hearing a call for help from fellow officers, the undercover officers raced to the scene. Some made it through the door before Reserve Officer Kenny Wynne, not recognizing Gary Edwards, who was trying to pull an assailant off a fellow officer, walloped him in the stomach with his nightstick, doubling him over and forcing him up against the wall. As Sgt. Springer went through the door and tried to pull a man off Sgt. Scott, who had arrived seconds earlier, Sgt. Duval grabbed him by the head and was about to smack him when Scott yelled out not to hit him. Scott had entered the building to find a haze of mace covering some people who were still dancing and the others who were fighting. The group included some bikers and some dopers and many arrests were made. The paddy wagon was called and mutual aid had been requested from both the California Highway Patrol and the Sheriff's Office. Telling officers in charge of the paddy wagon not to put anyone in unless they knew who had arrested each subject, supervisors wanted to make sure they could document each arrest. Other experiences had taught them that mutual aid stopped after the fight, with some Salinas officers unable to identify some suspects in custody because outside agencies had made the arrests. Scott finally made it out of the club that night and witnessed Leonard Shuette with a suspect in custody whose shirt had been removed, writing his name across the man's chest to claim him as his arrest because the paddy wagon officers would not take him in without proper 'identification' of the arresting officer. When the arrested subjects arrived in court several days later, some were banged up and bandaged. One man, a bandage wrapped around his head, was told by Judge Machado, "I don't care what religion you are. You will take your hat off in my court!"

Officers were injured and were lucky more serious injuries had not occurred because of the lack of identification when they entered the club that night. That incident led to the purchase of the famous, "Red Raid Jackets." The red jackets with a gold star on the front and "Police" written on the back were used for many years to identify officers on the site of a raid. Many years later the red jackets would be replaced by the black ones worn today.

RENT-A-WRECK

The undercover narcotics team needed cars for their surveillance and buy work. With a clear understanding of who they were investigating, a deal was struck with Rent-A-Wreck for six months. Sgt. Springer, then head of the division, got the pick of the litter of the first cars, choosing a Buick special four-door car that was so ugly it fit right into the drug scene of the time. After an officer had a minor accident in one of the rented wrecks, Sgt. Springer lectured his squad about driver safety and the high cost of repairs to the rented cars. He emphasized his desire for the officers to be more careful with their driving. Later that night, while working a sting operation with a female decoy, one car lost sight of the decoy and called for the sergeant to pick the car up from the other direction. Sgt. Springer, responding to that, pulled out of an alley without looking and was hit by a drunk driver, who fled the scene before other officers could arrive. Gunter and the other officers arrived to find Sgt. Springer sitting in the Buick, the front end of which had been completely torn off the car, totaling it. The officers wisely left their sergeant there with his wrecked Buick to continue their work that night. Needless to say, all the rented wrecks had to be turned in after that, and a deal was made with Richardson Chevrolet to provide bottom end used cars for the squad. The used cars often had major problems when they were picked up. Flat tires, dead batteries, and burned out transmissions were only some of the problems with the old cars. The officers turned the cars in and got replacements every thirty days and considered themselves lucky if they had radios and windows.

Proud of their new, fancy, high-tech bug, the undercover officers tried it out on George King Garcia, giving him $80 to make a buy. They thought things were going well, the reception was clear as a bell as Garcia went from house to house in North Salinas talking about dope. At one house, he went up to the door and the officers could hear a short discussion about drugs, but then it went completely silent. They waited and waited, hoping to hear something until, fearing the worst for their informant, the officers raced to the house. They began to hear feedback as they approached and after an extensive search found their brand new bug up on the roof. Two weeks later, they arrested Mr. Garcia, charging him with the theft of the $80 they had given to him for the buy.

The Salinas Police Benefit Association had eighty-one members. Salary negotiations took center stage again as bargaining continued and officers wanted better benefits. Steve Perryman started at SPD in 1974, during a time when the hot topic of conversation was the need for a new police building. With sixty-three officers at that time, it was felt the department had outgrown the existing building. There was a five-year plan to build new quarters for the growing police department, which continues to occupy the same space today with one hundred and sixty-seven officers and many more non-sworn personnel.

Perryman, now a lieutenant, recalls the early days of his career when the Lion's Club sponsored citations for safe drivers. Almost all drivers stopped and presented with safe driving certificates were angry and ready to fight. Some didn't understand that they weren't getting a ticket, others accused officers of wasting their time with the stop. Public relations was still drilled into the heads of the new officers and this was the reason Perryman stopped a man who had allowed a pedestrian to cross the street, giving him a good driving certificate. Five minutes later, when the car was reported stolen, an embarrassed Perryman went back to try to find the car, but both the model citizen and the car were gone.

Pat Duval was an FTO (Field Training Officer,) training Steve Fausbinder one night when officers were called to the Olympus Market, a well-known and often problem area where partying groups would hang out. Duval, as the senior officer at the scene, tried to calm the large crowd, but one man kept driving by, up and down the street, yelling obscenities at the officers and trying to incite the crowd. After several slow passes Duval saw the car coming by again, crawling at less than two miles per hour. He walked up to the driver asking if he was directing his words to the officers. Duval grabbed the man by the collar and dragged him out of the car through the window as officers watched the car slowly continue down the street. Fausbinder had to chase the car and jump in the window to prevent it from colliding with other cars or people.

It was during the mid-1970s that the department started the first motorcycle club. Called the "Blue Knights," Salinas had the first call sign for the group and was designated "California 1." Mike and Pat Duval, along with Rodman and Ellis participated in club activities. The Duval twins often played jokes on unsuspecting citizens. When one would stop a driver who would then insist on seeing a supervisor, the other would respond.

The Big Week Carnival was another source of history for the officers in Salinas. It was in 1975 that Henry Yoneyama and Steve Perryman tried to arrest David Trejo, a large man with a violent history of drug use. He started fighting and grabbed onto a chain link fence. Perryman, using his baton, tried to control the suspect who literally grabbed hold of the baton through the fence holes and lifted Perryman off his feet. Yoneyama, thinking he would assist the officer, tried to hit Trejo to get him to release Perryman but missed, striking Perryman in the right shin. Perryman recalled the incredible pain and still carries a scar associated with that incident. Trejo later nearly ripped the holster off Jim Toft's side at a fight at the Del Monte Market. He was also arrested for injuring an officer in a fight, forcing the officer to retire.

The officers got to know some of the regular crooks around town. When Nick Palofax was stopped for drunk driving while driving his car without headlights, (there weren't any on the car) one night he decided he didn't want to be handcuffed. Passively resisting, Palofax simply held his arm straight out to his side and Perryman couldn't budge it to place the other hand in the cuffs. He called for back up and Jerry Lambert arrived. At the jury trial, Perryman told his side of the story before the D.A. called Lambert to the stand. Lambert, asked what he saw when he arrived at the scene said, "I saw Mr. Palofax shaking Officer Perryman like a little puppy dog."

Judge Ray Simmons determined that male customers, along with female prostitutes, should be charged with crimes. This led to an evaluation of the statistics of arrests for prostitution. Police, ordered to arrest the male customers due to claims of discrimination against females, began to do so. Detective Michael Gibbons testified that Detective Sgt. James Backus ordered the arrests, but after only six arrests, he was told by Detective Captain Les Rodman that the District Attorney's Office was "upset." Then Assistant District Attorney John Phillips gave an order to stop arresting the men. District Attorney William Curtis testified there was no discrimination against females using Bobby Lauser, who often solicited while dressed as female, as an example of the males that had been arrested. Reserve Officer Jackson was in the station one evening when he felt the urge to use the restroom. The public restroom in the lobby was the easiest to access and he went into the men's room and found an attractive and busty lady in a tight red sweater about to avail herself of the facilities. Jackson was shocked when the lady walked up to the urinal, hiked up her skirt, pulled down her pantyhose and proceeded to use male equipment to urinate. Jackson had just met Bobby Lauser, an articulate and intelligent person in spite of an unusual lifestyle. Lauser had once taken a young and unsuspecting army sergeant up to a room in the old Cominos Hotel. When the military man discovered Bobby's secret, he beat him up before throwing him out a second floor window.

There was not much training for reserves on the department during these years. Larry Waller first worked in the department as a reserve officer and was out on his first night of training with Bill Jackson when they needed to take someone into custody. Jackson told Waller to put the cuffs on the man. Waller took out his cuffs, took out his handcuff key, and proceeded to unlock his handcuffs so he could put them on the suspect.

Jackson and the other reserve officers recalled many incidents that took place during their early years with the department during one of their regular reserve meetings. At the scene of a motorcycle accident, Jackson found the victim torn up and tangled in the wreckage of the bike. He called for fire and ambulance and the man was taken away, the motorcycle hauled off, and final measurements were being taken when a small boy tried to speak to the officer in Spanish. Seeing Jackson did not understand, the boy took the officer by the hand and led him to a house across the street. Lying in a planter box behind some flowers was a passenger who was badly injured. The ambulance was called a second time, forty-five minutes after the first victim had been transported.

Jackson with was Henry Yoneyama when they saw a man staggering in the street near the overpass on North Main and 101. Stopping to help the man, Yoneyama was in front of the patrol unit when it was rear-ended by a large car that ran over the officer. At that time, reserves were not allowed to carry radios and Yoneyama had the radio on him underneath the car, only his head sticking out. Jackson could not fit under to reach the radio to ask for help, but a young man came along and used the jack in his car to jack the patrol unit up until Jackson could reach the radio. Calling for a 940-A, the code for "officer needs help," Jackson waited for assistance. Deputies, CHP, Salinas officers and even Fish and Game showed up to help. There was no sign of the driver that had hit the patrol unit. Yoneyama was taken to the ambulance and wreckers towed away the two vehicles. Jackson rode back to the police department with Sgt. Jancich to write his report. The sergeant wanted to return to the scene because he wondered what had happened to the staggering man who had been the reason for the patrol unit stopping in the first place. Jackson had forgotten all about the man in his panic and concern for his partner. They looked around and were ready to leave when they heard moaning and saw the poor man had gone over the side of the bridge and was laying in ice plant. They called for fire and ambulance and the medical team had to get to the man from the freeway. With the second victim off to the hospital, the officers were ready to leave the area when movement was seen next to the center support of the overpass. Going to investigate, the driver of the hit and run vehicle was found and arrested.

Wayne Schapper recalled a time early in his days of working with the reserves. It was the end of shift and Schapper and his FTO were headed back to the station when they saw one of the canine units struggling with a very large man. Jumping out to assist, the three hundred fifty plus pound suspect was drunk but able to resist the efforts of the one officer. The human half of the unit had the man's right arm and Schapper grabbed his left arm. The dog was in the police car. As they tried to cuff the man, he lurched and all three fell back onto the patrol unit where the K-9 half of the canine unit latched onto the butt end of the suspect through the partially open window. The K-9 had to reach between the two officers to bite the suspect, but it was clear he knew exactly who was what in the scuffle. There was no further resistance.

In 1975, Jerry Joseph and Mike Ward resigned under pressure having been accused of furnishing heroin to contacts while working vice. News coverage of the progress of the case was extensive. The two officers would fight for their jobs, but ultimately lost the battle. The surrounding controversy would force the chief to make many changes within the department.

Sgt. James Backus was suspended pending the investigation of the case involving Jerry Joseph and Mike Ward. Backus was accused of opening a trunk without a warrant and of altering a police report in the case of the murder of Walter Koenig. Backus's partner, Capt. Les Rodman, was exonerated of any suspicion or criminal misconduct. Judge Nat Agliano eventually threw out the conspiracy charges against Joseph, Ward, and Backus. Backus got his job back, but was reduced to the rank of detective, receiving one year probation and a letter of reprimand.

In response to the allegations of misconduct within the department, Chief Roberson ordered heads of the detective and patrol divisions to change places. Some were demoted, others transferred to new positions. The chief wanted to add an eighth beat to patrol and asked for an additional six officers at a city council meeting in July, 1976.

Larry Myers was a sergeant when Reserve Officer Bill Jackson found himself partnered with him. The reserve officer was driving the transportation van at the time and arrived at a scene where the street was covered with police and emergency vehicles. Unable to secure a parking place anywhere in the street, the resourceful reserve parked smack in the middle of a citizen's lawn. When the neighbor came out and complained about this, Jackson quickly apologized. Sgt. Myers heard the apology and promptly informed the citizen that a police action was taking place and they would park the van anywhere they needed to do so. Myers told the man to go back inside his house and stay there. As soon as the man was inside his house, Myers turned to Jackson and said, "You stupid ass, get the van off the man's lawn!" Jackson came to admire Myers in many ways other than his decision to support his reserve in front of the citizen and give him his chewing out in private.

Steve Perryman was working with Mike Barnes when a fight call came over the radio. Barnes arrived first at the scene on Sorentini with Perryman close behind. Perryman saw Barnes as he walked up to the house where it appeared a big party was taking place. As Perryman got out of his car and started to join his partner he saw a juvenile walk up behind Barnes and hit him in the back of the head with a two by four. Barnes went down hard and didn't get up. Perryman took off after the kid, and was able to hit him once with his flashlight before he took off running. Perryman gave chase and kept up with the youngster, but couldn't catch him. A young man jogged up next to Perryman and inquired if he was trying to catch that guy and if he needed help. Winded by that time, Perryman said, "Yes." The helpful citizen took off like lightening and tackled the suspect. Perryman arrested him and took him into the station where Lt. Moss inquired if the officer was, "sure" he had the right person. When Perryman replied that he was "pretty sure," the lieutenant instructed him that wasn't good enough. He had to be one hundred percent sure. Asking if there was any way the officer could identify the suspect, Perryman replied yes, and asked him to raise his arms. The suspect could not lift his arm and was badly bruised. Perryman had broken his collarbone with the hit from his flashlight. Lt. Moss was finally satisfied that Perryman had arrested the correct person for the assault.

Miss Kitty

Miss Kitty, a fifty-six year old prostitute, was interviewed by the *Californian* in 1976. Claiming to have been hustling since the age of thirteen, she discussed her ability to stay in the business without the support of a "man." Prostitution was rampant on Soledad Street, and police even arrested a city councilman, who was later acquitted of soliciting charges. Miss Kitty was remembered by Joe Gunter and John Carr, as a polite and cooperative hooker who did not use drugs and was not a drunk. Her mysterious disappearance years ago caused both Gunter and Carr to believe she had been murdered.

Another regular guest of police, Mary Bamber, was involved in a shots fired call one night following a car stop involving a car that matched the description of a robbery suspect's car. Bamber, wearing overalls and boxer shorts, was screaming that Larry Waller had shot her when Perryman arrived on the scene. Bamber, who had been driving a VW, had been shot by a bullet that had gone though the engine compartment and the firewall and caught her sitting forward in her seat. Hitting her in her butt, the bullet struck her wallet in her pocket. When officers pulled her overalls away to see the injury, they found the perfect impression of an eagle made by a silver dollar she carried in her wallet.

A "Man with a gun" call came in at the Capri Club at Rochex and Main one night. Perryman was one of the first units to arrive at the scene. Francisco Gabriel, a 6'4", 280 pound person known to officers, was hanging out at the club known for being a place for gang members to party. The club was packed that night as usual, and Perryman started to arrest the man with a gun in his pocket. The man was Gabriel's friend and he did not want him taken away. He started a fight in the parking lot which eventually worked its way out to the street. Perryman was at his limit fighting Gabriel down and dirty in the street. He got a chance to glance up, trying to find where his back up partner, John Gates was and why he had not come to his assistance. Standing in the street, waving his arms, Gates was directing traffic around the fight. When Perryman asked him later why he had not stepped in to help make the arrest, Gates said, "You had him under control, so I was just directing traffic away from you."

Steve Perryman was one of five officers chosen for the first newly formed motor unit. The five also included Pat Duval, Clyde Clark, Larry Waller, and Ron Candiloro. Going off to the CHP academy, Perryman shared a room with Waller who was obsessed with passing the difficult program. Of the twenty who started, only eleven would graduate. It was a very high pressure school and Waller would sit on his bed at night, covering his head with a blanket, holding a cigarette in his mouth and sipping a Dr. Pepper. One day the instructor, trying his best to trip up the students so he could kick someone out, led them on a long "follow-the-leader" ride, trying everything he could to trip them up. Waller was in the first position behind the instructor and made no mistakes. When they pulled back into the academy, the procedure was for them to pull in one at a time, parking in a straight line. The instructor would then circle his unit around to face them for final comments. Larry Waller's unit was first in the line and the officers dismounted for dismissal. Waller, however, had forgotten to put down his kickstand and his bike fell sideways starting a chain reaction that eventually led to all the bikes resting on their sides.

Waller was one of the best in the class and Perryman would ride only a short time with the motor unit before being promoted to detective. Keeping him in the motor unit after his promotion because of a grant situation, Perryman became the first motorcycle riding detective, a position he enjoyed for several months before being formally transferred.

The news in 1976 was dominated by the crime rates in Monterey County. Ten murders in the county areas and six in Salinas were reported. At least seven of these were considered to be gang related. The year's worst crime, as stated in the *Californian,* was the robbery and stabbing of Alisal Paint and Hardware store's female clerk, Diane Ballesteros. A young mother of three, she was paralyzed from multiple stab wounds to her neck and head.

Salinas Police Chief Roberson was quoted as saying, "I still believe in punishment and I don't think we're getting enough punishment. There are many loopholes today that allows the criminal more ways of escaping detection and /or apprehension." Salinas also made national news with federal and local police arresting narcotics dealers associated with both Mexican-American bars and drug distributing rings.

BACON BOWL HISTORY

On October 23, 1976, the first annual Bacon Bowl was held between the Salinas department and the Sheriff's Department. That year, the Sheriff's Department won, scoring thirty-four to the Salinas officer's nineteen points. The game was played at the Salinas High School stadium.

The second annual game, between the "County Mounties" and the "Blue Knights," was held on Saturday, August 27, 1977. The Blue Knights won that game, 26-12. Coached by Frank Bernardashi and Mike Hebert, the officers took control of the field. The third Bacon Bowl was held on August 26, 1978. The Sheriff's team won the game, twenty-seven to nineteen.

In April 1977, Chief Roberson tried to curb the problem of massage parlors catering to prostitution clients. Armed with statements by two of his best detectives, Joe Gunter and Frank Bernardasci, the chief met with owners of several parlors. Gunter is quoted in the *Californian* article, "I was solicited by a masseuse at one of the parlors." The proposed ordinance would provide for unlocked doors, six inch by six inch windows in each cubicle and the right for police to inspect without obtaining search warrants.

When Reserve Officer Ron Ralph took a suspect to the emergency room for a jail check, the drunk was combative and refused to cooperate with nurses or doctors. Hospital staff restrained the man with leather straps on a gurney and signed him off. The man continued to be combative so Ralph and his partner wheeled him over to the jail still strapped to the gurney. When they arrived, a deputy asked what he was supposed to do with the man. Ralph informed the deputy that SPD had done their part and the suspect was now the property of the county jail staff. The jail nurse checked the suspect in and Ralph wheeled the empty gurney back to Natividad Medical Center.

The reserves saw their share of tragedy as they worked alongside Salinas officers. Bill Jackson remembers responding to a call one night on Park Place where a man had been stabbed by his wife. There was blood everywhere and the officers tried to put pressure on the wound located just under his rib cage. There was nothing they could do because the knife had knicked the bottom of his heart and he died in their arms.

When Officer Jerry Gowin and Reserve Officer Ron Ralph arrived at a Garner Avenue house one night, a very elderly lady was not breathing. Gowin took the head and Ralph the chest as the officers started CPR in an attempt to revive the woman. With the first compression, Ralph felt the fragile rib bones break as he pressed down and felt as if he had killed her, even though she was already dead.

An arrestee who had a minor wound was taken to the hospital for a jail check. He was screaming about police brutality and was demanding photographs be taken of his minor injuries. Dr. Gonzalez was the emergency room doctor that night. When he had had enough of the fuss and mouth of the suspect, the doctor put his hand on the man's chest and said, "Do I look like a photographer? I'm a Doctor!"

Tim Nihiser became the first crime prevention officer for the city in 1977. The Crime Tip Line which cost $25.60 per month was installed in November 1973, and was getting calls on an almost daily basis on the line. Instead of the despised coin meters to control parking in downtown, police assistants were hired to mark cars and issue tickets. During the rodeo that year, police assistant

Robert Crouch was featured in the *Salinas Californian* which printed a photograph of Crouch using his chalk stick to mark the hoof of a horse parked under a one hour parking sign downtown.

CHIEF ROBERSON RETIRES

Chief Roberson announced his intent to retire after thirty-two years with Salinas. A full blooded Indian of the Choctaw and Cherokee tribes, Roberson began his law enforcement career by guarding German SS troops and Japanese prisoners of war in an Iowa stockade. After three years with the Watsonville Police Department, he moved to Salinas as a juvenile officer. He received many promotions and was considered a great chief. Interviewed at his son's home on Christmas Day 2004, Chief Roberson recalled the best part of police work being his days as an investigator. He enjoyed not knowing how his day would take shape and still recalls certain homicide cases he worked. He still looks like a chief of police.

MAN KILLED DURING ROBBERY STAKEOUT

Officer Ernest Nielsen shot and killed Thomas Lee Sanchez, a robbery suspect during a robbery stakeout at the Cork n' Bottle on East Alisal Street. A string of robberies led to Salinas police staking out various stores. Sanchez committed an armed robbery during the stakeout, coming out of the store with a gun he then pointed at Officer Nielsen. Nielsen shot and killed the suspect.

Rodeo week always brought out not only fans but criminals as well. Using two policewomen as decoys, officers made numerous arrests for prostitution and soliciting in the Soledad and Lake Street area. The newspaper published each man's name and most of their home addresses when it reported the vice busts in the "Law Enforcement Log."

Gang activity was on the rise with a series of shootings involving Nuestra Familia members. There had been eleven murders since February 1976 when Detectives Gunter and Myers were sent to investigate a gang-related shooting at the InterHarvest cooler. One of those murders had taken place at the carnival in 1976. Jack Rice had been shot while at the Foley and Burke carnival. His wife, Gloria Rocha Rice was stabbed to death on July 21, 1977, almost exactly one year after her husband's murder. Found in the East Lake Street alley, Mrs. Rice had been stabbed over one hundred times. Three murders were being investigated in the first six months of 1977, and Detective Captain Roy Hanna was quoted in the newspaper as saying, "We can't emphasize more the value of citizens calling police when they believe a crime is in progress or have information." Those words are as true today as they were then.

The Salinas Police Department's pistol team of Sgt. Ray Jackson, Walt Christensen, Frank Kuehl and John Batton broke the record for the Police Olympics, earning a gold medal. Christensen was the top gun with a perfect 300 score. The summer of 1977 was a good one for the pistol team. Officer Rick Moore won an individual gold in the marksman category, and Instructor Henry Yoneyama won a fifth place bronze. Moore was, "Top Gun," with a perfect 300 score. Fay Patterson won second place in high jump, Mike Schroeder placed sixth in shot put and Tommy Huff was ninth in motorcross.

TWENTY-FOUR

THE FERGUSON YEARS

Fred R. Ferguson was appointed Chief of Police on August 1, 1977. He took over a department of eighty-five sworn officers and almost as many support personnel. One of the first and most unpopular things the Chief did was to go around town to all restaurants and shops informing owners that officers would not be allowed to accept half price meals or gratuities from their establishments. The chief met his match in the owner of Roy's Drive-In who told the chief not to interfere in his business. He said Roy's was privately owned and what he did or did not do or provided to anyone was none of the chief's business.

In December 1978, in an article written by Rick Rodriguez in the *Salinas Californian,* Detective Captain Les Rodman and Lt. William Nelson, (a twenty-two year member of SPD), discussed the way the high numbers of burglaries in the city were related to the narcotics users in the area. The 1978 year was a busy one for the police department. Officers answered over 57,437 calls that year, an increase of over eight percent from the previous year. A huge increase in the number of burglaries and theft led to an increase of forty-nine percent, as the crime rate nearly doubled that year. Chief Ferguson's proposal for a police car wash, to cost $48,200, was made and denied. Chief Ferguson argued that clean police cars were important to police image and morale. The car wash would have been behind the department.

By 1978, the city and police began to discuss getting the ACJIS computer system and motorcycle officers were added to patrol school areas at certain times of day. Those motor officers were: Sgt. Pat Duval, Officer Clyde Clark,

Officer Steve Perryman, Officer Larry Waller and Officer Ron Candiloro who retired in 2005 as the senior member of the division.

According to Police Chief Fred Ferguson, the Salinas Police Department had one hundred fifteen officers answering ten percent more calls than in the previous year. Citing everything from poor construction to carports to "high crime areas" as the reasons for the difficulties faced by the police department, Ferguson also discussed a shortage of clerical assistants in the department. Graffiti was becoming a problem, and the addition of five new motorcycles yielded many more traffic citations in the city. Not everyone was happy about the increase in the number of tickets.

Lt. Tom Brooks graduated from the 116th FBI National Academy in March 1979, the same year the Supreme Court modified the Miranda ruling. The department also joined the CJIS network that greatly increased the speed with which warrant checks could be made. While the public waited in long lines or tried to find gas stations that actually had gas, the country braced itself for the stiff price of $1.02 per gallon, at that time the highest in the nation. In May, a line of sixty-five cars waited at the Chevron station at Laurel and Natividad to get gas. Officer Jim Mount instructed Explorer Scouts in the art of traffic direction. Mount, the coordinator for the Explorer Scout program, turned traffic lights downtown to flashing yellow to provide the opportunity to teach his students.

Bill Olea was the first commander of the newly founded SWAT team in 1979. Active from 1979 through 1998, the specially trained officers were deployed on a number of sensitive scenes over the years. Combined with the Violence Suppression Unit between 1998 and 2003, SWAT would become an independent unit again in 2003.

It was also during the late 1970s that officers began the switch from revolvers to automatic pistols. Finding themselves outgunned by criminals, officers ordered Smith and Wesson Model 59's, .9mm automatics. Later, in 1993, they would upgrade to the Sig Sauer .45 automatics many carry today.

The detective unit was constantly working cases that required extensive surveillance. Gary Edwards and Rick Metcalf were working a long term surveillance one night. Edwards, constantly concerned about his appearance and his weight, had purchased a box of diet and energy bars and brought them along. Hungry, Edwards ate ten or twelve bars, thinking the entire box contained only five hundred calories. Fifteen minutes after his "snack," Edwards was transported code three to the station bathroom where he was sick for some time. Edwards also liked to use his personal van for sting operations with prostitutes. He talked Steve Perryman into being a decoy one night, putting him in the driver's seat and hiding himself directly behind the driver's seat, covered by a very large pillow. Perryman picked up a prostitute known as "Peaches." As they drove around discussing the conditions of the agreement, Perryman suddenly began to hear something from the back of the van that sounded like laughter or snickering. Peaches noticed it too and was looking in the back seat asking what was back there. The snickering continued and got louder and she asked again. Perryman suggested to her that it might be one of his children's toys, activated by the motion of the van. She bought it, and the laughter/snickering continued until after the arrangements were made, when Edwards popped out from the behind the pillow, nearly scaring the poor prostitute to death.

Letha Phillips was hired as a crime analyst with the goal of crime prevention. Studying police response time and the need for beat boundaries to be changed, her job was described by Chief Ferguson as a "management tool." Crime patterns, times and methods were all studied under the grant received for the crime analyst position. Graffiti had begun to pop up all around town. Captain Roy Hanna attributed some of the malicious mischief to the current farm labor strike, but most damage was probably done by juveniles. The eastern part of Alisal, beginning at Laurel Drive accounted for over fifty percent of the malicious mischief calls. While one officer per beat had previously been assigned, more patrol units were being detailed to see if a high profile presence would help the problem. Closter Park, the site of numerous fights, drinking and graffiti was costing the taxpayers in overtime for police. Chief Ferguson told the City Council that high density housing and crime were directly related, as he asked for $122,850 to replace nineteen old police cars. The chief also wanted newer weapons for his men, a better dispatching system, and non-lethal laser type fire power.

Lt. Moss and the Chalk Marks

Don Moss wanted his officers to work their shifts. He would often go out to the Alisal and mark the back doors of businesses with colored chalk. Part of the officer's regular duty was to go around to every door and check the businesses. The Lieutenant would actually go back and check to see if the officers had made the checks and removed the marks. If they had not, he required them to write a report to him about what had kept them from their duty. Gunter, always the innovative officer, engineered a way to put up a thin line of wire in the front of the buildings. When he drove by, if the wire was still up, he knew the lieutenant hadn't been by to mark. If the line was gone, he knew he had to get out and make the checks.

CANINE UNITS ADDED

Chief Ferguson pitched the value of canine units to the City Council in June 1979, adding they would not be in service until the end of the farm strike. A total of $13,353 was budgeted for the two dogs scheduled to begin working in January 1980. Officer John Martorano was pictured with "Max," his new partner as the city announced the addition of the highly trained and valuable canines.

Canines weren't the only addition to the department in the late 1970s. With a two-year grant from the state, SPD purchased five motorcycles and hired four officers and a sergeant. In the first six months of the program, three fatalities were included in statistics that showed an increase in the accident rate. Traffic citations were being issued, with 4,674 in the first three months of 1979. A map at the department showed the clusters of accidents were on North and South Main Street, Laurel Drive and the civic center area. Chief Ferguson reported that half the accidents in the city occurred on South Main Street, blaming the narrow street. Citizens considered themselves "victims" of the radar guns used by the motor officers and complained bitterly, writing letters to the editor.

The Salinas Rodeo continued to provide opportunities for overtime. The entire department was on duty during the 1979 rodeo and seventy-one outside law enforcement personnel were hired. The Colmo del Rodeo wreaked havoc in the city as officers blocked streets, arrested drunks, and patrolled the carnival.

Racial unrest and fights with weapons closed North Salinas High School in March 1979. School resumed the following week under tight security. Tensions between Latino and Anglo students resulted in a rash of guns and knives being brought to school. Many students stayed home, afraid of the threats and fist fighting atmosphere. The trouble spilled over to the El Sausal Junior High where hundreds of students were pulled out of school by frightened parents. Students eventually started a Peacemakers group and the rumors died down after the Easter break.

The year 1979 was marked by the riots and strikes of the farm workers led by the UFW, (United Farm Workers) and Cesar Chavez. Local growers and shippers tired to quell the violence and get strikers back to work and Salinas officers were on the front lines of the battle. The city would pay over $80,000 in overtime to officers by June that year, and with no end in sight, Chief Ferguson assigned twenty-three officers and their supervisors to a full time special strike force. Picketers took over neighborhoods, vandalizing both private and police cars and property. Gunfire and roaming gangs of angry field workers brought back memories of the strike of 1936. Sheriff's deputies went on strike themselves in the middle of the melee. Two Salinas officers received injuries related to working the strike lines, and strikebreakers were the victims of angry strikers as were growers as their fields were ruined by strikers under cover of night. Governor Jerry Brown came to town to voice his support of the UFW protestors. Meyer's Tomato, the largest tomato grower in the nation was the first to sign a contract. Bud Antle's agreement for the five dollar per hour minimum wage came soon after. By the time the UFW claimed victory, some growers were out of business and others had signed agreements with the union, putting workers back into the fields, paying them the five dollars per hour ordered by the union.

Officer Michael Barnes shot and wounded a suspect at the corner of Laurel and North Main Streets when the man reached for a handgun during a fight. Barnes had a suspect in custody and was in route to the office when a man carrying a purse ran in front of his patrol unit and jumped into a car. The prisoner remarked to Officer Barnes, "It looks like that guy took somebody's purse." After stopping, Officer Barnes ordered two men out of the car where the fleeing suspect had gone. The man ran, Barnes gave chase and a handgun fell out of his clothing. The suspect swung at the officer who shielded his face with his hands, but still saw the suspect reaching for the gun. He fired one shot, hitting the suspect in the thigh. The purse it turned out, belonged to the suspect's wife. John Herrera was charged with multiple counts including battery on a police officer, being a felon in possession of a handgun and three enhancements.

Officers Richard Radford and Jim Culligan were sent to the hospital for decontamination procedures after they helped at a crash scene where a crop duster went down. With pesticides on their uniforms, the officers were provided with hospital issued pajamas. They gamely put on their gun belts, badges and revolvers and went back to work where they were needed. They were needed for a variety of crime throughout the city. Even with John Bohannan and Fred Schloss chasing the hookers out of town, drugs, false alarms and trouble at the schools kept the officers busy during their shifts. Officers also were spending their time in court. Civil suits were nothing new to police officers, who had been sued going back to the 1930s. Officers Michael Barnes and Rick Moore were found not negligent by a jury in a case brought by a woman who claimed excessive use of force.

1980 began with a rash of assaults, robberies, and stabbings. Statistics showing the increase in violent crime included nine homicides in 1979, compared to only two in 1978. Armed robberies had increased from 104 in 1978 to 124 in 1979, and there had been eighty-five strong arm robberies in addition to those. A dying victim of a shotgun blast told officers just before she died that she believed she had been set up by friends in an NF, (Nuestra Familia) hit. Chief Ferguson discussed getting out of the funeral escort service provided for years by the department, suggesting the funeral homes take over that service. By March, another murder had taken place behind Marion's Club, the victim dying of stab wounds. The crime wave continued with shootings and stabbings. A juvenile was arrested in April for the arson of an old home on Romie Lane. Owned by the Monterey County Historical Society, the house had been used as a Haunted House at Halloween, with proceeds from ticket sales going towards underprivileged youth activities through the Jaycee programs. *Salinas Californian, April 11, 1980.*

DUMB CROOK STORIES

Vandals and thieves broke into planes at the airport in May 1980. Damaging several planes the thieves left footprints, which would not have helped police were it not for the wallet one of the juveniles left in a vandalized airplane. The owner of the plane found the wallet while examining the damage to his property and gave it to police. Using the information in the wallet, police located the house and mother of the suspect, examined his shoes and determined him to have been the culprit. *Salinas Californian, May 13, 1980.*

An officer, sitting in his patrol car one night near the Denny's Restaurant on East Blanco Road, was surprised by a man who, after walking by the patrol car, returned to the side of the car and tried to break off the antenna. The officer promptly arrested the man.

Burglars entered the Trigger Hill gun store through the roof one night, throwing mostly handguns into boxes they packed for easy transport. A silent alarm brought police to the gun store, where witnesses to the late night burglary were able to provide good details about the thieves and their clothing. Eight hours later, Officer Charles Lincoln stopped at Denny's on De La Torre for a cup of coffee and recognized two of the men from the descriptions given by witnesses at the scene. After a brief chase, he was able to arrest them. *Salinas Californian, September 15, 1980.*

TWENTY-FIVE

MURDERS ROCK THE CITY AND OTHER STORIES OF THE 1980s

Two murders in less than twenty-four hours rocked the city in 1980. Closter Park and a car at 701 East Alisal, Loma Linda Park, were the scenes of the two apparently unrelated murders. Another man had been shot, but survived. Within four days that month there were four murders, bringing the total for the year to eight homicides by September. Detectives Gunter and Enni were still working on a murder from 1978. They had elicited information from the suspect about the location of the murder weapon. Originally arrested and then released for lack of evidence, the suspect had taken the detectives to the approximate location where he had buried the weapon. The rural area of San Juan Grade Road was an impossible search site until the detectives brought in professional metal detector operators. Within a few minutes of initiating the search the weapon, a .22 Taurus, was recovered making the whole thing worthwhile according to one detective. *Salinas Californian, September 25, 1980.*

Gunter and Enni seemed to be on the job at all times in the 1980s. When a man was robbed and stabbed the two detectives questioned witnesses at the scene. Recognizing the nickname of a suspect they had arrested the year before on a robbery and whom they knew to have been only recently released, they stayed in the area of lower Soledad Street on a hunch. Their hunch paid off when they saw the two suspects in the robbery/homicide. One threw the bloody knife as he saw the detectives approaching. The other had the victim's wallet in his pocket. Both had the victim's blood on them and tried to blame the other for the murder.

Police would be able to solve several robberies in south Salinas after Lyon's was robbed one night in September, 1980. Sgt. Larry Myers, after trying to arrest the suspect after a chase, was forced to shoot the man when he reached into his pocket, causing the officer to fear for his life. Suspected in several recent robberies, the accomplice told officers she and her boyfriend were pulling just this one more job before moving on.

The frequency of drug sales near high schools was cause for worry as car burglaries increased in the city. Officers worked to rid the city of dealers, but were kept busy by other crime. Pelted by bottles and can throwing partygoers, police were forced to use the police dogs and mace at the American Legion Hall, where a birthday party turned ugly. Several suspects were bitten and arrested after fighting with police who were called by the private security company to assist after a fight between guests broke out. Within days, Detective Gary Edwards would be investigating yet another murder. The victim had been stabbed and was discovered at Rider and Del Monte.

There were only three female officers out of the one hundred twenty-seven sworn in 1981. Sharon Castillo was the senior patrol officer at that time and had quite a history as an officer. Sharon Castillo and her beat partner, Bob Krentz responded to Atlantic Street in 1980, where a man was holding a .357 on a porch with two wounded people at his feet. Castillo drove her vehicle into the line of fire to rescue a four hundred pound woman and to provide cover for Krentz. Krentz took cover behind the patrol car and Castillo went behind the house to check for armed men or hostages. Jewell Charles appeared on the porch armed again and refusing to disarm. He exchanged shots with Krentz who shot him. Charles was killed with a single shot.

THE ROSE GARDEN

High grade Mexican heroin was making its way to the streets of Salinas and Salinas officers along with agents from federal and other local agencies worked together to find the source. Operation Rose Garden sought out the distributors rather than the lower level street dealers. Salinas had earned the reputation of the center of heroin distribution early in 1975. Undercover officers worked out of the old fire station on Alvin Drive naming the house the "Rose Garden." By November 1981, multiple arrests had gone smoothly and heroin was in short supply in Salinas.

Shift work could sometimes result in difficulties with an officer's internal time clock. Working third watch, Perryman remembers pulling up to a traffic light towards the end of a long shift. He remembers stopping at the light and next feeling someone was watching him. Looking up, he saw a female citizen staring at him from her car in the next lane. His foot still on the brake, the officer had fallen asleep at the wheel. To this day he has no idea how long he was there before realizing what happened.

In 1981, Chief Ferguson wanted to try a new way of capturing fleeing suspects. He was always trying to figure out new ways to work or looking for new equipment. The chief looked into the use of the "net," a system that could be used to stop an out-of-control suspect or someone who was running. Teenagers and cruisers on South Main Street were the rational behind the new laws prohibiting loitering and a curfew restriction early in 1981. City parks had suffered from repeated vandalism and residents complained of loud car radios late at night. Warnings were issued to youths and parents, but more than three in one year could result in fines up to $500 and/or six months in jail. During the first week of enforcement, police filled out twenty-four citations.

Officer Larry Herrera was on patrol one afternoon when he was confronted by a man at Alisal and Salinas Streets. The man pulled out a hunting knife and lunged towards the officer, according to witnesses at the scene. Officer Herrera ordered the man to put the knife down, but he came within inches of the officer, who was forced to shoot him with his .357 magnum revolver, shooting him in the hand in which he held the knife. Gunter was on the scene for the investigation, during which the suspect continually mentioned Christ and Charles Manson. *Salinas Californian, February 5, 1981.*

Serious traffic accidents were part of every officer's daily work. Pedestrians hit by speeding cars made up the bulk of the serious injuries officers saw on an almost daily basis, with victims both children and senior citizens. Drugs were also becoming more and more evident and Salinas police, using undercover officers, were successful in making major arrests and confiscating marijuana, hashish, cocaine and a variety of pills. More than one rapist was at work in the city and seven rapes had been reported by early May 1981. "Operation Lookout" was a program set up by the Women's Crisis Line and Salinas Jaycees to teach women about home safety and prevention.

Truant high school students were the focus of "TABS," the Truancy Abatement and Burglary Suppression program to be headquartered in the post office by Captain George Garwood. Working with the high school district, police hoped to curtail truancy and the crimes that commonly accompanied youths not at school. The first day officers scooped up twenty-seven truant kids. The second day netted only fifteen due to staffing issues in the program. Citing statistics Chief Ferguson pointed out that 62% of daytime burglaries took place within four blocks of school. *Salinas Californian, April 2, 1981.*

Alarming statistics were also out for the 1979 year. A 41.4% increase in rape was the biggest increase in the city while the homicide rate was the same as the previous year. Because officer's time was so valuable and costly, Chief Ferguson proposed charging for repeated responses to false alarms at both residents and commercial properties. Asking for a $20 fee after one mistake in each three month period Ferguson showed city council members the figures for March. Of 382 alarms requiring an officer respond, only 1.7 percent were found to be valid.

Detective Larry McCrumb worked on white-collar crime in the city, discussing the problems of stolen business checks from employers such as Bud Antle. Officers Jim Huggins and Jim Hayes patrolled the one hundred block of Main Street, and included sweeps of the two hundred and three hundred blocks, as well. They looked for drunks, drug users, and people who "had nowhere else to go."

Fred Schloss had been promoted to detectives after a number of years with SPD. Partnered with Henry Yoneyama, the two worked vice in plain clothes on Soledad Street. They thought themselves pretty savvy as they pinned their badges underneath their lapels and went out to find a 647b candidate for their project. They found a pretty girl and talked and talked, but they could never figure out if they had the elements necessary for an arrest. Schloss called it their "learning curve." Life was interesting with Yoneyama, who was known for wearing a baseball cap with a strawberry on it, earning him the nickname, "Oliver Henry." One night Yoneyama went alone to Frank's Bavarian Inn to enforce the football pool law. He succeeded only in getting himself kicked out of the bar.

THE GREAT PISSER CASE

Schloss was working vice with John Bohannon, and trying to bust prostitutes one night when they were called to the Townhouse after a couple rented a room and arrived to find a working girl with a client. Everyone was gone when the two detectives arrived, so they staked out the room, expecting the girl to return. They put towels down in the bathtub so their feet would not make any noise and waited. Soon the phone rang, and the detectives knew the working girl was checking to see if anyone answered. They stayed in the tub. A few minutes later there was a knock on the door, but still, the officers stayed in their position. When the door opened, two girls and their clients stepped into the room. Schloss and Bohannon could hear the activities in the other part of the room and tried to keep from laughing. When one girl came into the bathroom to use the toilet, they were unable to contain themselves, and she suspected something. Throwing the curtain open, she shrieked in surprise at finding the officers. The skinny girl fell right into the toilet, butt first, hence providing the name of the case. The two detectives were able to turn her and made six arrests out of their evening's work.

The vice unit was also used to make busts in local bars. Undercover work was risky and required the officers learn a different language and culture in order to be effective. While the sergeant discouraged it, officers felt they had to drink when working in bars where they got a lot of good leads from bartenders. Their bar tab was upwards of one hundred dollars per week. They never had a lot of bar busts due to the laws at the time, but they did cite bartenders at the Caravan for serving obviously intoxicated people. Gary Edwards worked with Fred Schloss on the bar detail and both received letters of commendation for a two week period that netted fifteen suspects. Edwards and Schloss would later work narcotics together. Schloss said his ten years in narcotics were the most fun of his career.

THE GREAT CHICKEN SHIT CASE
SEARCH WARRANT STORIES,
AND MORE STORIES FROM THE 1980S

The burglary unit Fred Schloss was part of also included Max Hauser and Glen Rouse. Burglary cases involved serving a lot of search warrants, as did narcotics. Schloss recalled the house they had to search where the woman had been raising chickens. Allowed the run of the house, the chickens had roosted up high and their droppings made for a slimy and smelly job. They dubbed the case the, "Great Chicken Shit Search Warrant." Max Hauser, Glen Rouse, and Fred Schloss often confiscated stolen goods during the search warrants. Sometimes, if the owners could not be found, those items would be sold at auction. At one search, the detectives found numerous VCR's, but struck out, finding no drugs. One year later, at the auction, a little old lady purchased one of the VCR's for fifty dollars. After she paid for it, she put her hand into the slot for the video to pick it up. Out fell two ounces of cocaine!

Al Ruiz was with Fred Schloss when the two seized a car, placing it in a fenced yard for protection. They figured it for a good bust, but found nothing. Several days after the bust, the two detectives went to the yard to have another look at the vehicle. Sitting in the car, they noticed a small hole in the dashboard. They inserted a paper clip into the hole and a hidden compartment opened revealing $10,000 in cash.

Detective Kills Suspect During Search Warrant

Detective Tom Huff shot Enrique Stanley Thomas after Thomas's dog attacked the officer during service of a search warrant. Huff shot the dog, then chased Thomas into a back apartment. Thomas slammed the door on Detective Huff's left hand, forcing the Detective to shoot through the door, killing Thomas. Detectives Gunter and Perryman ran to Huff's aid after hearing the shots fired and found the suspect laying down inside the door, with his hand inside the cushions of a couch in which they found a gun.

Salinas officers called to appear in a federal trial in San Jose, were staying at a hotel. The city attorney, Steve Lankis, had told them their room key would, "get you anything you want." Jim Toft was there with his wife. Bob McKeen, Monty Roecker, and Steve Long were alone. The group dined at Original Joe's and returned to the hotel, where the three single guys started calling Toft's room. Deciding to send an outcall massage girl to Toft's room, they had a coin toss to see who would be the one to call. McKeen lost the toss and was to make the call. Looking for the biggest ad in the phone book he called and tried to set up a girl, sending her to Toft's room. The phone call entailed more questions than they had anticipated, questions about just what the client wanted. Meanwhile, back in Salinas, Gunter received a call from the San Jose Police Department, asking if he knew his officers were calling for a girl and telling him they had called a sting operation and SPD officers were now right in the middle of it. The traveling pranksters took the heat when they returned. Undeterred from their fun, they continued to have a good time. They would drive around in their patrol units with paper bags over their heads, eye holes cut out so they could see. The "Unknown Policemen" would enjoy the surprised expressions on the faces of citizens as they pulled up to traffic signals. They worked hard when it was needed and enjoyed the slow days when they could.

In spite of media coverage of the many dangers of a career in law enforcement, Salinas had a good response to its Explorer Scouts program. In 1981, the Salinas delegation of twenty-four was the largest at a training program put on by the Marine Corps Drill Instructors at Camp Pendleton. The legal rules of law enforcement work, survival, and safety were some of the topics taught at the difficult course. One Salinas scout, Vincent Canales, then eighteen years old, was number two in the class of two hundred-fifty. Scouts learned about traffic control and search and seizure laws as part of their week long training. Jim Mount was the chief advisor to the Scout Explorer Post 201 in Salinas at the time.

As the time for the rodeo neared, violence in the city and against officers was escalating. An attempt to issue a mere citation for a minor with alcohol at a party, erupted into a near riot with dozens of officers being called in from outside agencies to assist. Disputes about the riot would lead the news for days and concerns about problems at the upcoming night parade were well founded. Lt. Tom Brooks hired fifty officers from outside agencies to assist with the Colmo del Rodeo Parade, held at night and with a history of violence.

The ten most dangerous intersections in town were listed in August in the local paper: Blanco-Sanborn and Main Street was the top of list, with twenty-three accidents in six months, and was followed by Alisal and Sanborn. Laurel and Main, Main and Acacia, Main and Alvin, Main and Romie, Market and Monterey were some of the others. The list did not include the bloodiest intersection in town, East Laurel and St. Edwards. In one two month period, three accidents were responsible for two fatalities and three injuries.

THE DIABLO CANYON ASSIGNMENT

Sgt. Jack Springer was in charge of ten Salinas officers sent to help guard the Diablo Canyon nuclear power plant in San Luis Obispo County in September 1981. The officers were issued dog tags at the National Guard facility at Camp San Luis before being bussed to the location to protect the power plant from expected protestors. Stationed first at a back fence and later at a gate, officers assisted with making arrests of mostly peaceful protestors, who told them "We love you." Officer Jim Huggins said the guard assignment was "like being at a three-ring circus." *Salinas Californian, September 21, 1981.*

While some officers were away guarding the power plant, others were injured in a battle with residents at 1415 Del Monte Avenue. Still others were beginning new positions as School Resource Officers. Don Cline, Rocky Ugale,

Jim Higgins, and Jim Hayes worked in plain clothes carrying only police radios as they tried to develop relationships that would help stop juvenile crime. Chief Ferguson had to defend his decision to implement the program citing the success of the truancy program, TABS in lowering crime off campus but telling citizens that on-campus crimes and fights were continuing and even escalating. Don Cline was "Officer Bill," talking to elementary school age children and giving them a positive view of policemen. Demonstrating how handcuffs work, letting children hold his badge, and giving tours at the station, Cline tried to make the children see the personal side of police officers.

THE DYNAMIC DUO

Legends in their own time, Joe Gunter and Andy Enni shared the Officer of the Year award in 1982. Partners for four years at the time, the two had a knack for solving homicides through good detective work and a network of informants that has never been equaled. Gunter was also part of the first team to enforce the laws against gang members. Along with Kyle Kimm, John Bohannon, and Fred Schloss, the team would go to Cindy's for dinner after having worked their regular assignments during the day. After dinner, they went out to their cars, donned their vests and equipment and headed out to find gang members. They made twenty-eight fresh arrests in two weeks and were able to clear one homicide within twelve hours. Another homicide was quickly solved after a night at the Blue Boar Inn. Gunter and Schloss had met at the bar and were drinking and talking about their day. Gunter's pager went off, informing him of a homicide and rather than calling in his partner, Schloss went with him to the scene. The two worked the case that night and arrested the suspect.

Cooperation with other departments sometimes required learning a "foreign" language. When Rick Lack came to Monterey County as the head of the FBI office, Salinas detectives and dispatchers had to learn to understand his Arkansas accent. The ultimate professional, Special Agent Lack would often ask dispatchers for directions to the most recent bank robbery location, usually on Main Street. There, he would meet up with Detective Gunter and others. Lack always said, "I love working bank robberies in Salinas because they're going to catch the guy and the FBI can get all the credit for it." Special Agent Lack worked alongside many Salinas officers and detectives over the many years he headed the local field office. During the Christina Williams investigation, the FBI called upon Salinas detectives to follow up the many leads in their jurisdiction. Lack, who retired in 2004 to head up a large statewide security firm, continues to live in Salinas and remains one of the legends of local law enforcement.

OFFICER DOWN

Officer Dennis Pardini was shot on Halloween day after a high-speed chase involving a stolen car and kidnapped woman. Anthony Archer jumped onto the hood of Pardini's patrol car after the officer rammed the stolen vehicle to get it to stop. The suspect fired his .41 magnum into the windshield, hitting the officer who was able to get several shots off at the suspect. Archer then ran into a barn and, surrounded by officers, killed himself. Chief Fred Ferguson credited Pardini with saving the victim's life. Pardini, who had formerly been with the Fremont Department, had been with Salinas for six years at the time of the shooting. The Chief was at the scene and rode in the ambulance with the wounded officer. Lt Mike Gibbons remained at the scene, awaiting word with the other officers on Pardini's condition. After making sure the officer would survive, the Chief returned to the scene, after first making a stop at a cocktail party being given by his wife. It was believed at that time that Pardini was the first Salinas police officer to be shot in the line of duty.

WANTED: POLICE CHIEF

Chief Ferguson retired after eight years in Salinas. His temporary replacement was Vic Collins, who took the position on February 28, 1986. The city included 17.75 square miles and 138 sworn officers that day. Two canines were to be added to the police force, the idea of outgoing Chief Ferguson. The *Salinas Californian* ran an article regarding the search for a new chief in Salinas; "Wanted: Police Chief, strong leader. Must be able to fit in and improve the department's relations with the Latino community."

TWENTY-SIX

CHIEF JAMES CORRIGAN

James R. Corrigan was the man for the job and was appointed Chief of Police on August 18, 1986. Captain Tom Brooks retired soon after, having served thirty-one years with the Salinas Police Department. He had worked as an officer, instructor, Sergeant, Detective, Lieutenant and finally, Captain.

Chief Corrigan had been the chief of Santa Paula's department prior to coming to Salinas where his salary was $59,352. During the interview process for the chief's position, Corrigan had indicated he had some ideas about the use of undercover officers in schools to combat the massive drug problem. In 1988, Corrigan hired Mike Groves and Andy Miller, both unknowns in Salinas. He sent them to an academy outside the area, refusing to even allow the two recruits to step into the department. The two men had no contact with anyone from the Salinas department and made no visits to Salinas during their academy training. The day after they graduated, they went to Modesto where they participated in a drug bust. Given their badges by Chief Corrigan, they were told to, "Look at them, then put them away for six months."

The two young officers were just out of the academy and began their careers in Salinas as undercover officers. Groves was assigned to Salinas High, Miller to North Salinas High. They played the difficult part of drug scene high school kids well, and were responsible for many arrests. Groves was even seen by a teacher when he made a buy at school and was sent to detention. He recalls being paid overtime for the time he spent in detention that day. No one knew the two men and only the superintendent of schools knew their identities. Groves remembers the stress of trying to look and act like a druggie teenager, when he was, in fact, a twenty-three year old straight and narrow police officer. He was always surprised in the years after his identity was exposed that those who had been arrested had no hard feelings towards him. On breakout day, his one request was to be able to wear his police officer's uniform, something he had never yet been allowed to do. Chief Corrigan brought his full uniform to the school and Groves changed in the library. That morning, he had his hair cut and he looked so different that when officers brought in the suspects he had been "friends" with during the operation, they didn't even recognize him. One long time drug dealer, James Parola, was one of Groves' first busts and had long been wanted by local law enforcement because he sold to kids. Parola got a seven year sentence for selling six joints worth under twenty dollars to children.

Chief Corrigan, in an attempt to boost the morale of the department, started the "Turkey Shoot," a tradition that would become one of the most popular and successful morale boosters in department history. In the days before Thanksgiving, every police department employee, officers and staff, would be allowed to shoot in the basement. Provided with one target and able to purchase additional targets for one dollar, employees tested their skill. The front side of the targets was blank, but on the back were random numbers that could not be seen by the shooter. Bullets were supplied by the department and the shooters would add up their score when they retrieved their target and could see which numbers they hit. Many, wanting to get better scores, bought and shot multiple targets, often spending more money on targets than it would have cost to purchase the turkey itself! Chief Corrigan would then take all the money and buy turkeys, awarding as many as he could buy to the top scoring employees. Guille Cedillo recalls what fun the event was and how it really brought the department together and lifted morale. Many have asked to get the event back today.

Salinas Police Arrest Kidnapping Suspect

Salinas was the end of the road for a kidnapping suspect who had snatched a young girl off a school bus in Los Angeles. The SWAT team was dispatched to its fifth call of the year to the Casa Linda Motel and successfully tricked the suspect, arresting him and taking his .38 caliber weapon.

Rick Moore was a twelve year veteran in 1986, when he, as a member of the SWAT team, responded to a hostage situation in north Salinas. A female victim was forced to walk in front of the suspect who had a .38 pointed at her. Moore was able to pull the victim to safety while the rest of the team arrested the suspect. He was commended for his outstanding work by the Jaycees. Sgt. Jim Toft also had his day in the news after intervening as the hostage negotiator in a five-hour standoff where the subject had been firing shots off. Sgt. Toft was successful in getting suspect David Rodriguez to eventually walk out to the officers.

Vicky Gray joined only four other women on SPD when she was hired in 1986. Pat Hanna, Sharon Castillo, Cassie McSorley and Terry Heffington were the females officers at the time. Vicky remembers hearing about how two female trainees had been flushed just before she hit the streets with her FTO, J.W. Wilson. She worried that she would not make it but between J.W., Rick Moore, and Don Watkins, she made it through and joined the department as a regular patrol officer. Gray recalled one of the first pursuits she had with J.W. Wilson in the early days of her training. They attempted to stop a vehicle traveling east on Bolivar. During the ensuing pursuit the occupants were throwing out beer cans and the passenger bailed out of the moving car. J.W. called it in and Dave Williams, hearing the call, asked for a description of the suspect who had bailed. J.W. replied with his typical drawl "He just looked like a rolling ball of flesh." New officers were on the receiving end of many jokes in those days. When J.W. decided he and his trainee would go to the restaurant at the Laurel Inn for their two-seven he told the new Officer Gray to park in a particular location. After fifteen minutes they returned to the car to find the window smashed out and the shotgun missing. Glass was scattered on the ground around the driver's door. J.W. told the new officer she must have really messed up and she better call it in to the Watch Commander, Yoneyama at the time. Just before she did J.W. popped open the trunk, retrieved the shotgun and rolled up the window. It had all been a set up.

Officer Gray was the first female officer to become pregnant while on the job. She continued as a patrol unit through her sixth month before she was assigned to the front desk. Told not to "do" anything and specifically not to attempt to make arrests, Officer Gray hated the desk duty. One day, a woman came in who was found to have a felony warrant. In those days there was no glass at the front counter and officers spoke face to face with visitors. An attempt to delay the woman from leaving resulted only in the woman becoming agitated. Officer Gray was eight months pregnant at the time and the woman was catching on to her efforts to delay her. The suspect took off, running from the department. Officer Gray was not willing to lose the suspect and jumped over the counter to pursue the woman, arresting her.

Terry Heffington and Vicky Gray responded to a 459, (burglary call) in progress in North Salinas one night, and were the only units available because everyone else was tied up at a big fire in South Salinas. The two female officers were in a foot chase trying to catch the suspects as they fled around the neighborhood. Larry Manalo and Sam Tashiro were at the scene in South Salinas and heard the foot pursuit on the radio. When Manalo asked Tashiro if he thought they should send someone, (a male officer), to help the "chicks," Tashiro replied. He told Manalo that, "They knew this was a man's job, a tough job when they took it and they are just going to have to handle it."

Officer Dan Aguirre Shot

Officer Daniel Aguirre was thirty-nine years old when he was shot three times during a search for a man with a gun near the California Club. Aguirre was able to return fire and killed the gunman. Officer Aguirre was a nine year veteran officer and was seriously injured. At that time, it was believed he was only the second officer to be shot in the line of duty. Captain Ron Scott told reporters that the suspect had a long history of violence and drunkenness. Aguirre spent over two weeks in the intensive care unit at the hospital and had several surgeries to remove all the bullets in his body. Acting Chief Vic Collins updated the city on the improving condition of the officer.

Jesse Gilpas started working at SPD in the summer of 1986, as a janitor. By 1990, he had moved into vehicle maintenance. Jesse was paid overtime to clean out the insides of the cars on weekends. His superiors generally chose the cars in the worst condition for him to work on, and he would go through the interiors trying to clean them. At that time, some of the car seats had plastic over them for protection. Jesse, wanting to make the cars look the best possible and to please his superiors, sprayed the seats with Armoral until they sparkled one day. A few days later Jesse was called into the office of Captain Hanna who asked him if he was the one who had cleaned out the cars. Worried that something like a shotgun might be missing from one of the cars, Jesse admitted to being the one who had cleaned them. Apparently, Sgt. Larry Manalo had entered his vehicle and slipped off the seat when he got in. The Armoral had done its job too well and the seats were as slippery as ice.

Jesse Gilpas was still a minor when he was asked to work as a decoy with Detectives Russ Porter and Fred Schloss. They made some busts around town and Jesse's confidence grew. When the detectives suggested they go into a Chinatown bar to test their luck, Jesse readily agreed. The detectives strapped a microphone on him and sent him inside with instructions to tell them on the mic when he was served so they could come in to make the arrest. Inside, sitting at the bar, Jesse ordered and was given a beer. Holding it in his hand, he said into the mic, "I've got the beer," which he repeated many times. The music in the bar was so loud the detectives couldn't hear him as he repeated himself and people began to look at him with more interest than he wanted. With people in the bar watching him, Jesse held out as long as he could. Finally, he lifted the glass and took a drink of the beer. When the officers finally came in to see what was going on, they decided there would be no prosecution of that case.

Dave Shaw was five years old when his father, Larry Shaw became a police officer in 1971. When Dave joined the department as a reserve officer in 1987, the two made history as the only father and son to work as officers in the department at the same time since the very early days of the department. Other father-son teams would come later with the Barnes family and Justin and Pat Duval. The only known father-daughter team was that of John and Kim Butz. One of the younger Shaw's first traffic stops was for a minor violation. Questioning the driver who said the car belonged to a friend, he believed the very cooperative and polite man. There were no "hot sheets" then and everything appeared clear. The next day, Officer Glen Rouse stopped the same car and ran the history. Finding the car was stolen and finding Shaw had stopped it the day before, the veteran officers had a field day giving Shaw a hard time about his error.

Shaw remembers Lt. Carr always carried a five-shot .38 caliber weapon when he was inside the station. Carr, proficient with all guns, was adept at removing his weapon holster and all, when his presence was needed, especially in a holding cell. Shaw recalled how you just knew someone was really in trouble if you saw Carr coming down the hall taking off his gun, holster and all, with one swoop of his hand and slamming it into a locker. According to Shaw, the lieutenant could remove his gun and holster and get it into a locker in a flash.

In June 1987, a vintage 1928 photograph of the Salinas Police Department made the cover of *The Monterey County Lawman*. The long awaited range at Toro Park was open after many years of delays and a match was set for August between the San Jose Police and the MCPOA members. In an effort to try to get more members to attend meetings, the board brought in LAPD Detective

Charlie Sosa to speak on street gangs in September 1990. At that same meeting, Officer Earl Reynolds was given the Award of Merit for his part in dissolving a major drug ring as part of his assignment to the McNET, (Monterey County Narcotics Task Force). *The Monterey County Lawman, September 1990.*

In 1990, SWAT was an on-call team of twelve with Rick Moore as the sergeant in charge. Mike Groves joined SWAT after a few years on patrol following his Salinas High drug busts. SWAT had no vehicles at that time and used the regular police cars. They had tactical uniforms, but no special vests, just the regular patrol vests. They had no special equipment, no night vision goggles or special radios. One cold night, they were watching a house on Towt Street looking for Daniel Rocha for gang activities and drug sales. They finally got to him in the attic, where he was hiding.

Steve Long, president of the Salinas Police Officer's Association since the mid-1990s, and a board member for over twenty years, came to Salinas in September 1980, as a reserve officer. Long had been a military policeman in the Army and security manager at Penney's before being hired as a regular officer. He worked the first federally funded DUI program with Monty Ruecker for one year, and recalled that it was, "a lot of fun." In 1990, Long joined the gang suppression unit, staying with it when the name was changed to SET. Still a unit member when the Gang Task Force was initiated and when the name was again changed to VSU, Long is believed to be the only officer to work all four gang units. He spent two years in enforcement before spending another three years in intelligence. Returning to patrol for a short time, he then became a CSI for over seven years.

Long recalled being at the station one night when officers were working a DUI checkpoint. Larry Shaw, Dave Shaw's father, was the watch commander that night. When Long saw an officer struggling with a drunk as he came into the back door, then being hit in the face by the handcuffs the prisoner had on, Long jumped into the fight. The only way to control the subject was through a choke hold, which Long applied, temporarily putting the subject out. He felt someone behind him, and looking over his shoulder, found Monty Ruecker on his backside. The two men began laughing hysterically which loosened Long's hold on the drunk. The drunk, coming to quickly, began fighting again. On top of the drunk, Long was laughing because Ruecker was on his back, in a most hilarious scene. Long said of those days that, "Everyday was the same thing…we had so much fun."

1990 began with the SPOA, (Salinas Police Officer's Association) in contract negotiations, a shaken baby case and a shooting at North High. By the end of January, there had been gang shootings, a false kidnapping story by a juvenile female and a rape in Central Park. Glenn Rouse, as president of the SPOA, addressed the possible tax measure. The outbreak of the Persian Gulf War led to a small reprieve in crime, as Americans were glued to the television, watching reports of the war. By February, as detectives worked on a gang murder that occurred in December, traffic officers investigated the death of a school crossing guard, hit by a speeding and inattentive driver while carrying a stop sign and assisting pedestrians. The death spotlighted the Pajaro Street thoroughfare and officers used radar to try to get drivers to slow down. Steve Long and Kelly McMillen began foot patrols in Oldtown after complaints about the aggressive behavior of some panhandlers made both merchants and customers wary.

Chief Corrigan was delighted to tell the press that the crime rate had dropped, presenting the 1989 statistics for comparison. "I am absolutely convinced that as we target the hoods, the crooks, the pimps, the whores, the hypes in town, that is the only way we can expect the crime rate to drop. We've been doing that for three years and the crime rate had dropped. We'll do it again this year," the chief stated. *Salinas Californian, February 6, 1990.* It was a slight drop only, but a step in the right direction for Salinas. The next day, Detective Andy Enni would be investigating two bodies found in the trunk of a car parked on Rider Street. The two victims were "border boys," who brought drugs from Mexico, and police believed the murders to be the work of the NF, who wanted to takeover the entire drug market in Salinas. Short staffed, the officers of the SPD continued to work on crime during intense labor negotiations, but reduced moving violation traffic citations, writing only sixty-five in February where they had written over fifteen hundred in January of 1988, down ninety-six percent.

Short fifteen officers in 1990, those on duty were stretched to their limits. Service calls had increased forty-eight percent since 1977, according to records. With twenty officers on duty during the peak night hours, that meant only one officer for every 5,100 residents, a vast change from the earlier statistics. On a Saturday night early in April 1990, Officer Gilbert Bacis was one of only ten officers on duty, meaning one officer for every ten thousand residents. That night, he answered ten calls in six hours, from minor incidents to an assault. He participated in arresting a suspect with a knife, interrogated gang members, responded to a spousal abuse at an NF hangout and talked to a group camping out in a motel parking lot. It was a slow night.

Statistics reported by the California Bureau of Criminal Statistics in 1990 included the salary of an officer in Salinas, $2770 per month. There were 1.36 officers per thousand population. *Salinas Californian, April 10, 1990.*

Out of three hundred who would apply for the fifteen open positions, only one hundred-fifty would show up for the physical agility test. Most of those would continue the process, but sixty failed the written exam and thirty-four failed the oral. Forty-six remained before they took the psychological exam, which knocked out all but nineteen. Those nineteen decreased during the medical exam, vision test, background and lie detector portions of the investigation. Three would take jobs with other departments. Salinas would send three to the academy out of the original three hundred that applied. More openings were to come as Ron Scott left to take over as chief in Livermore.

Kidnappings, shootings, drive-bys and gang activities shared the news with Dorothea Puente, the landlady who faced murder charges for killing her tenants in Sacramento. Her trial would eventually end up in Monterey County. Revenge killings between gang members kept police busy and by July, another murder had taken place on the east side, along with two unrelated and non-fatal shootings the same day. East Salinas stores battled what they considered an undeserved image of a crime-ridden area responsible for drugs and gangs. But crime was everywhere.

In a tragic case in which a three year old boy had died from a head injury inflicted by his father in 1989, the father changed his story at sentencing, and asking the judge for leniency. Convicted of murder in a non-jury trial, Bruce Bredeson remains in prison following the denial of his first petition for parole in 2005.

While the supervisors argued about saving the courthouse lawn, another gang related murder took place in East Salinas. Guns were not the only weapons used in homicides that year. A stabbing victim died one week after being hospitalized. He had been stabbed on Rossi Street and walked to the A-1 Ambulance headquarters on Market before collapsing. Victims were being hit by gunshots while inside their homes and citizens were complaining about the six shootings and two murders East Salinas had seen in a two month period. There were robbery and rape investigations to be done in addition to the homicides and assaults. Two stabbings in South Salinas and a rash of burglaries and vandalism brought the violence into an area previously untouched by gang crime.

Officer Leonard Wilson, sued by a drunk driver weighing 250 pounds for brutality, was cleared by the U.S. District Court of the 1985 allegations. It took the jury only fourteen minutes to free Wilson from all criminal charges. Another stabbing in east Salinas brought the third death in three months there. As undercover officers were making buys and seizing heroin and cocaine in large amounts, three shootings in one day left one more dead. Extra patrols were added in an attempt to combat the gang related shootings. Since May, there had been seventeen assaults and shootings, with six deaths in East Salinas. City council members wanted more police presence on the street and believed the department should have one hundred-fifty to one hundred sixty officers, based on the 1.5 officers per thousand residents rule.

Detective Joe Gunter, working the most recent homicide, convinced the suspect to come to the police department and turn himself in after speaking to him on the telephone. The suspect gave Gunter a full statement as to how he had shot the victim and why, putting an end to that investigation.

Officer Bob Serratos was sitting in his patrol car on Garner Avenue when a primered Chevy passed by, shooting bullets out both sides of the car, hitting the police car with one. Not the intended victim, the officer was unhurt. Motor officers, reassigned to patrol units to help with the shortage of officers, were only a band aid on the swelling problem of gangs. The overtime bill jumped sixty-seven percent in September, according to Finance Department statistics. From $45,810 in July to $71,906 in September, the media speculated whether the $26,000 difference made any difference. The hiring freeze prevented the department from replacing employees, and those still there had to double up on their jobs, thus leading to the increase in overtime costs.

Their hard work paid off in the end with leads and arrests in several high profile cases. In one incident, the SWAT team was called in when a subject failed to show up for a court appearance. Daniel Rocha was wanted on drug and domestic violence charges. After a seven hour standoff, SWAT had to fire tear gas into the house on Towt Street, then search the entire residence. Removing an exterior wall, the found Rocha in the attic, hiding under insulation. Two other raids had taken place that day, with drugs, money and parolees located and confiscated. By December 7, 1990, Salinas had seen ten homicides. A murder in late December would bring the total to eleven homicides for 1990, up from seven in 1989.

TWENTY-SEVEN

CHIEF DAN NELSON

Previously the chief of the East Palo Alto department, Dan Nelson took over a department of one hundred thirty-five officers who answered 80,000 calls and covered eighteen square miles of city. With degrees in public administration and administration of justice, the new chief's salary was just under $68,000. He came from a city with a high crime rate, out of control drugs and a murder rate three times that of Oakland, where personnel cuts and lack of funding plagued the police department. Chief Nelson vowed to get out and meet the people of Salinas and felt his officers should do the same. He would be supportive of the PAL program and was expected to have an "open door" policy in his office. *Salinas Californian, March 1991.*

Stabbings and gang activity forced police to arrange special patrols at the Northridge Mall. While officers patrolled there, others served papers on gang members, notifying them of the new law providing for stiffer penalties for those convicted of any gang related crime and civil penalties for property owners who knowingly allowed gangs to congregate on their property. Guns stolen from local gun shops were showing up at local crime scenes and in the hands of gang members. Police proposed forcing gun shop owners to lock the weapons in vaults at night and some complied, having been the victims of the previous burglaries. Roger Milligan told reporters that Salinas had no ordinance or standards for gun stores and suggested the deterrent of vaults might help. *Salinas Californian, May 12, 1991.*

The gang war was heating up and shootings were becoming common. City council members thought buying equipment and setting up a gym would ease the tensions in the city. The situation was escalating as nine shots were fired near Closter Park, where children were frightened as they played nearby. When "Boyz N the Hood" opened at Northridge Cinemas, officers were on duty when fights broke out and suspects were arrested after shots were fired, hitting a young girl. Days later, Nuestra Familia member Daniel Ray Mendoza, in court for a traffic violation, was killed after he grabbed a bailiff's gun and was shot by other officers in the courtroom. Chief Nelson put officers on foot patrol in gang ridden East Salinas, hoping that high visibility would deter gang activity and crime. Pablo Casteneda was wanted for questioning in a robbery-homicide that had occurred on East Market Street. The Moreno brothers were arrested after selling a pound of cocaine to undercover officers, who later found three pounds of cocaine, worth $48,000, $3500 in cash and two handguns. A substation of the East side was still being considered in 1991, and a tax initiative was to be put on the ballot the following year.

Chief Nelson and
The Last "Policeman"

Dan T. Nelson was appointed Chief of Police on April 22, 1991. With him, came changes in the department. Art Garcia had started with the department in 1964 as a patrolman. There was no academy or training for him and he started patrol with Roy Hanna trying to educate him. One year later, and feeling the responsibility to serve his country, he asked Chief McIntyre for permission to leave the department so he could serve during the Viet Nam War. Understanding the patriotic man's duty, he released him, telling Garcia his position would be held for his return to duty after his military service. Garcia, believing he might not return from the war, was unconcerned with a future job and spent several years in the military. When Garcia returned in 1968, he went by the department to visit his old friends. The chief pulled his badge out and plunked it down on the desk, telling him he was going to the academy immediately. Garcia would leave one more time, this time to help with the start up of the Dick Bruhn's uniform department with Don Thompson. Two years of inventory control and cost analysis were enough to send Garcia scurrying back to the department after a call from Roy Hanna, telling him they wanted him back. This time, Garcia had to go through some background investigation, including a polygraph given by Paul Scott. Garcia would patrol the Alisal area for the rest of his career. He worked under five chiefs, McIntyre, Roberson, Corrigan, Ferguson and Nelson. When the department changed the badges, moving away from the "Policeman" designation, changing instead to, "Police Officer," Art Garcia refused to turn his old badge in. The chief called him into his office, telling him he was the last man with the "Policeman" badge and he had to turn it in. Garcia reluctantly handed over his badge, asking the chief if he could buy it. The chief gave it back to him, saying it would be taken care of. Art Garcia was the last "Policeman" in Salinas.

The city council refused to place a proposal for an $80 per house tax that would raise funds for a substation in Alisal and more officers on the November ballet in 1991. While a majority of citizens supported the hiring of additional officers, council members felt they needed more time for those citizens to understand the proposal. Others felt a substation was unnecessary and inappropriate for a city the size of Salinas. *Salinas Californian, August 7, 1991.*

Rick Moore was a sergeant that year and spoke to the media when a firebomb was thrown into a home in the 400 block of California Street. A woman was burned in the incident, which police were investigating as one of several recent firebomb incidents. Gang attacks were escalating, with four incidents in an eight-hour period, one the murder of a teenager on Sanborn Road. Salinas was not the only city fighting gang crime as Gonzales and Seaside were also having shootings and stabbings. In Salinas, officers responding to what they thought was a drive-by shooting, became targets themselves as they approached the house of the reporting party. Paint chips flew by the face of one of the officers in a close call. The suspect was inside a house and SWAT had to be called. After seven hours of negotiations, the man, despondent over family issues, finally put down the .9 mm gun and surrendered to the officers. *Salinas Californian, September 2, 1991.*

The Police Activities League was founded in 1991. The first activity sponsored by PAL was a softball game between the Blue Knights of SPD and the Vagos team, which included members of the gang and others. The Vagos, believing the officers could not beat them at softball because they could not beat them out on the streets, were disappointed to find the officers more than capable. The gang members had challenged the police before forming their team. Crediting a team that had worked together longer than the Vagos team, Glenn Rouse, a board member of PAL and a Salinas officer, said the next PAL event would be a fundraiser to include only law enforcement members. *Salinas Californian, October 14, 1991.*

The homicide rate fell in 1991, with only seven in Salinas of the twenty-seven countywide. But 1992 began with violence in a drive-by shooting on

California Street. Officers hoped Measure A on the ballot would help pay for additional new officers to fight crime that was increasing all over the city. A teenager was shot while at the Foster's Freeze in East Salinas and officers were on the lookout for a suspect in a 49'ers jacket. The suspect, a Norteno, was arrested within days and the victim, a member of the Vagos street gang, knew and argued with his assailant. Gangs were not the only ones battling in Salinas as the tax measure stirred controversy and distrust. Asking for a $50 per year tax on each residential lot, the idea was to raise funds for thirteen patrol officers, two gang intelligence officers, four DUI patrols, one SRO and miscellaneous other support services. Citizens spoke out with both the pros and cons of the tax and homeowners argued they should be the only ones to vote on the measure since it only taxed them. Chief Nelson spoke of anticipated better response times, the cost in time and manpower of DUI cases, and the need for more School Resource Officers at schools. Still hoping to open a substation in East Salinas, the city council and citizens argued about the need for, and cost of, a substation. Councilman Robert Taylor chastised the council saying they should be cutting back expenses instead of taxing the citizens. There was talk of a utility tax if the measure failed. The Editorial in the Californian pointed out the loopholes in Measure A saying the city was spending on high level salaries that could go towards police services and that there was no guarantee funds from the measure would be used for police improvements. *Salinas Californian, February 29, 1992.* In the end, voters voted the measure down and speculation was that voters simply did not trust the system. The measure was shot down in every precinct in the city.

Crime, however, took no break. A female suspect robbed the Bank of America on South Main Street just weeks before "American Me" opened at the Northridge Cinema, requiring extra security. A teen was shot in the back at Fremont and Carr Streets and tension at Salinas High and Alisal High resulted in a number of fights. Salinas officers were called to help probation officers patrol at Salinas High School as the gang related tension increased. Central Park was the site of a gang fight and stabbing. The legacy of the Rodney King case and the ensuing verdict led to local activists insisting on a police review commission. As Leonard Wilson wrote an opinion entitled, "Don't Stereotype Police Officers," others condemned police without cause or evidence. Officers were trying to curtail the growing crime problem on South Main Street. Citing "numerous beatings, clubbing attacks and gang fights" that were directly related to cruising, a new ordinance was proposed with a $500 fine for anyone passing a check point more than twice within six hours. *Salinas Californian, May 29, 1992.*

Officer Eric Wallace hit the streets in August 1992, looking for money to support what would be the city's second canine officer. "Max" had been purchased and trained by the officer but was not on duty because of the cost of supporting the canine officer. Wallace's walk netted him $2000 in cash and pledges of another $1000, half what he needed to support his partner for three years as an officer.

Terry Heffington had been a Salinas officer for seven years when she was confronted by a man who tried to cut her with a piece of broken glass. Backing up sixty feet in the street Heffington tried to talk the man into putting the glass down. He continued to jab at her, coming within cutting distance before she fired at him. He survived surgery.

Saying the woman had it coming, a man gunned down his wife after violating a restraining order several times. After shooting her with a shotgun, he made the couple's two young children look at the body of their mother.

By November 1992, there had been fifteen homicides in the city. The fifteenth victim was a sixteen year old boy killed by a gunshot in East Alisal. Not since 1970 had the city seen such a statistic. 1970 had previously been the year with the highest number of homicides, eleven, a number that had been duplicated in 1982 and 1990. Unfortunately the fifteenth victim was not the last of 1992. By early December, police were looking for Armando Santa Cruz for the gang related murder. In a December 7, 1992 article in the local paper, Brian Contreras told Salinas that the shooting would not end the truce the gangs had at local schools. He said the gangs, "had an understanding there will be no weapons at high school." *Salinas Californian, December 7, 1992.*

Within days, William Baxter, a teacher at North High was shot three times in the corridor of the school. The gang suppression unit that had operated since 1990 had been shut down early in 1992, but was reactivated in September. Officers Jesse Herring, Paul Guzman, Kyle Kimm, and Sgt. Roger Milligan were doing all they could to fight the gang intimidation problem and find witnesses. Statistics told a bleak story. There had been ninety-one shootings into inhabited dwellings or cars, one hundred seventeen assaults with firearms, and sixteen murders, eight of which were clearly gang related. Most of the one hundred-thirty robberies were thought to be gang-related and the gang members were getting younger. On December 15, 1992, the department opened a small field office at the Northridge Mall.

Salinas officers began the 1993 year with the arrest of murder suspect Armando Santa Cruz. Public support however, was not to favor the department for long. Officer Eric Wallace was forced to shoot a man carrying a pistol grip sawed-off shotgun after he threatened the officer and pulled the gun out of his pants. LULAC continued to call for a citizen review board, accusing police of abusing Latino residents of Salinas. The editorial in the *Californian* supported giving citizens a role in internal investigations. Tensions between some citizens and police on patrol led to arrests after officers were pelted by rocks and shots were fired towards them. Mayor Styles defended Officer Wallace's actions and the department saying "The attempt on the life of Salinas police officers brought a measured an effective response that led to some arrests without major incident or further violence." Captain Scott Miller would hold the *Californian* responsible for the anger towards police and the subsequent near riot that resulted and the paper received many calls from readers complaining about the lack of support for our police. *Salinas Californian, January 16, 1993.* Wallace was cleared of any wrongdoing after an investigation by the District Attorney's office.

In February 1993, the *Salinas Californian* editorial predicted that by the year 2000 gunfire would be common in Salinas unless the community worked together to change things. Teams of armed robbers were hitting multiple locations in one night, terrorizing store owners and employees. A woman was murdered in her South Salinas home and became the first homicide of the year and the push was still on for a citizen's review board.

Officers played in a charity basketball game held at Hartnell College. Officers Candi Apple, Eric Smith, Brandon Hill, Vince Maiorana, Jesse Herring and Captain Balanos and Corporal Don Cline joined CSA Bert Morales on the team. Morales, who liked to say he "walked differently," used a wheelchair to get around. His duties during his three years with the department included translating into Spanish, clerk duties, and answering the phones. The SPD team would compete against a well-known Santa Cruz team, the Rollercoasters, all of whom were disabled and who beat the SPD team sixty-seven to sixty-four. The SPD team used borrowed wheelchairs for the game which raised about $2000. *Salinas Californian, March 22, 1993.*

Captain Roy Hanna retired in 1993 after a career spanning four decades. Starting at SPD in July 1962 after a very short time spent as a Soledad prison guard, he was from Gilroy and had attended Hartnell College. The biggest problem in his early days of police work, according to Hanna, was rounding up the drunks on Soledad Street. His starting salary was a whopping $419 per month and his training was a short two weeks of riding with a superior. Hanna noted how much police work and the city had changed since his early days with the department.

One necessary change came shortly after Hanna's retirement date. Officers, clearly outgunned in the streets, needed better firearms. Until this time, the .38 caliber Smith and Wesson had been the official weapon of the department. In May 1993, the department switched over to a more powerful gun, the .45 caliber Sig Sauer semiautomatic pistol. The city council had to authorize the purchase of one hundred new Sig Sauers at a cost of over $57,000. Officers preferring the old revolvers would be allowed to continue carrying them. *Salinas Californian, May 12, 1993.*

Assistant Police Chief Vic Collins also retired in 1993. Starting as part of the group of officers hired just prior to the annexation of the Alisal area, Collins was one of the first officers to patrol Alisal on January 6, 1964. He was dispatched to the first injury accident that SPD responded to in Alisal after the annexation. No replacement was planned for Collins as Salinas City Manager Mora planned to save money by leaving that position and others, open after retirements. After twenty-nine years as an officer, Ray Jackson would also retire, as would Lt. Mike Gibbons, Sgt. Larry Manalo, and Cpl. Don Watkins. The loss of five veteran officers and their experience would be felt by the department as they faced increased gang violence that included shootings and slashings.

The teen arrested for the shooting of the North High teacher was found guilty of attempted murder just days after another murder took place on East Alisal Street. Men in ski masks and gloves robbed the McDonald's on North Main and a man working on his car on Del Monte Avenue at noontime was shot. A fight on Mae Avenue left one dead from a stab wound and another man was arrested after beating another with a candlestick, fracturing his skull. By July 1993, numerous and violent attacks were frequent and bloody. A man was shot while stopped at a light, a street vendor was stabbed, a man was beaten with a golf club by a fourteen year old boy during a party and there were several violent robberies in one weekend. Pizza parlors were robbed, drive-by shootings were common, and the FBI arrested two men found stealing clothes at the Northridge Mall after it was determined they were involved in pipe bombings at an NAACP office in Washington.

The Nestle Chocolate and Confections plant closed after thirty-two years in Salinas, displacing one hundred-seventy employees with only sixty days notice. Many who had worked there for decades were shocked. Meanwhile, robberies had increased during the first seven months of 1993. One hundred sixty-two robberies occurred in Salinas between January and June, an increase of twenty-seven percent over the prior year.

Cassie McSorley had been the highest ranking female with SPD for some time. As a sergeant for four years, she was promoted to the position of Lieutenant in 1993, by Chief Dan Nelson. With the department since 1982, she credited her promotion to the rank of lieutenant with her, "really strong work ethic." McSorley was one of only five female officers in the department at that time. A graduate of North Salinas High School, McSorley told reporters she planned to spend her entire career at SPD. Promoted to the position of Deputy Chief under Chief Ortega, McSorley now heads the Investigation Division of the department. *Salinas Californian, August 5, 1993.*

Chief Nelson was calling for a new era in his police force, making promotions to fill vacancies left by retirements. The new younger generation of supervisors and administrators included Sergeants Tracy Molfino, Don Cline, Bob Eggers, Manny Perrien, and Leonard Wilson. Newly promoted Lieutenants were Steve Hood, Cassie McSorley and Rick Moore. The new Captain was Larry Myers.

While the robberies continued, the shootings and stabbings brought the department to the limit of its manpower. In one night four people were shot and one was stabbed in separate incidents occurring on Rider Street and East Romie Lane. Another gang related murder left yet a juvenile victim dead. Alexander "Chino" Chang was found shot and stabbed before being set on fire at the dead end of Kilbreth Avenue. Officers reported that both the victims and the suspects were getting younger and gangs were becoming more organized.

Anthony Heredia and Cpl. Brent Sweeney began bike duty in September 1993 on Cannondale 21-speed mountain bikes. Hoping for higher visibility and a community policing approach, the bike patrols would spend much of their time in the downtown area where merchants had been complaining about peddlers. Still a hot topic, overtime parking continued to spark anger among downtown merchants and shoppers. New laws prohibited moving cars from one timed space within a lot to another without a specified distance or time between parking events. Once again it was the all-day parkers, known as the "shufflers" in Oldtown that caused the most problems and took up the spaces so badly needed for shoppers.

Shots erupted at Sherwood Park during a football game between two rival gangs. The game was supposed to be a program to keep the peace between gang members, but resulted in one fourteen year old suffering from stab wounds that left him in critical condition. The gun battle surprisingly did not result in any gunshot wounds, although at least twenty shots were fired. Mayor Styles opposed the Salinas Football Organization, doubting its ability to have any impact on the gang war and concerned about further violence. Promoter Daniel Villegas was hopeful the league would continue. *Salinas Californian, October 12, 1993.*

THE HALLOWEEN MURDERS
FOUR HOURS OF TERROR

The following weekend seven people were wounded and seven others were in custody following the exchange of shots on Trazado, Sieber, and Williams Road and East Market Street. Guns were confiscated, casings were located, and victims were treated. One week later two teens were killed and four others injured in a Halloween night shooting spree on Cedar Street. Another man was found dead, shot in the head on Rider Avenue the same night. A fourth man would die from the injuries received during the Cedar Street shooting. The "four hours of terror" had begun at 8:57 p.m. on a Sunday night and ended at just after midnight Monday morning.

Citing the ease with which juveniles or adults could purchase weapons, Captain Scott Miller was quoted as saying, "There's just this endless supply of guns." Most were stolen weapons. The violence continued with the firebombing of a residence on East Alive Drive where six were injured. *Salinas Californian, October 1993.* Another firebombing within two weeks hit a house on Surrey Way and a third attack took place on Rockhaven Court bringing the gang war to the new Creekbridge subdivision. "The community has to do something to fix itself," said Chief Dan Nelson. Gangs were ruling the streets and people were afraid to leave their houses. More officers were needed and the department hoped to fill ten positions left vacant for some time. The department was authorized one hundred thirty-seven officers but had left vacancies because the city wanted to save money. Proposition 172 had just been passed and it was hoped some money would be made available to hire officers to fill some empty slots. The Gang Task Force assigned sixteen officers from various agencies and two prosecutors to follow cases brought by police. They made twenty-six arrests in a ten day period in November 1993. Over the

Thanksgiving Day weekend eight commercial robberies rocked the city, from South Main Street to Sanborn Road. By December, the substation opened in the Del Monte Plaza in Alisal. By the end of 1993, officials hoped Salinas would receive a large grant from the U.S. Justice Department that would help hire additional police to fight the gang situation that held the city captive. The department would need every advantage as they faced the next five years that would include a predicted rise in gang activity and an unprecedented number of homicide investigations.

TWENTY-EIGHT

P.C. 187 – THE 1990s

The *Salinas Californian* printed the predictions of local people for the upcoming year. Brian Contreras of the Second Chance Youth Program said, "I predict 1994 will be less violent than 1993." He couldn't have been more wrong. The gang task force was due to disband but Chief Nelson felt it was needed and should continue. After much pleading the task force would survive, but lost several officers, able only to add a part time air patrol in the form of a helicopter. The first homicide of the year was clearly gang-related. An argument led to a fight and a man was shot at Cooper and Towt. The second homicide of the year would shock both police and residents. Eighty-two year old William Vaught was stabbed to death in his home of forty years on Williams Road. The crime would haunt detectives assigned to the case. By March 1994, there had been five homicides. Crediting citizen cooperation with helping solve the seventh homicide of 1994, Detective Joe Gunter thanked the citizens who gave him the information leading to arrest of two suspects. The shooting of a school crossing guard caught between rival gang members enraged citizens on all sides of Salinas. Saying it was a miracle no children were hit officers arrested a fifteen year old the following day. On the same day that a Grand Jury met in Los Angeles to consider an indictment against O.J. Simpson, Chief Nelson introduced his new concept of community oriented public safety. The somewhat quiet summer was over when three shootings were reported within one hour late in July. Citing statistics that showed how the number of police officers had not kept up with the expanding population in Salinas, police were stretched to the limit. With only one hundred thirty-seven officers, the number had remained the same since 1975, but the population had increased by almost 40,000 citizens. *Salinas Californian, July 30, 1994.*

When Vicky Gray was promoted to corporal in 1994, she soon was assigned to the detective division where she worked with a number of different partners. Her memories of working with "Daddy" Joe Gunter are vivid as it seemed the two detectives were always in a fight with someone. It seemed everyone wanted to take on the old guy and young girl thinking they could win, but the two officers always got their man. They had only mace at the time, no tasers or other special equipment. Gray recalls how it seemed that every DUI stop they made resulted in a fight that ultimately had both officers tumbling with the suspects on the ground. The two detectives took some gibes from other officers when a photograph of them walking away from court appeared in the local newspaper one day.

When a juvenile working in a summer program for Second Chance was gunned down on the street in broad daylight by a bike-pedaling assailant, council woman Gloria De La Rosa expressed disappointment and frustration. But, it was only the beginning. In a five hour period in August three people were injured in five drive-by shootings. Police were unsure if the shootings were related. Victims were taken to hospitals as police investigated. The twelfth homicide of the year took place on the afternoon of August 21, 1994. Shot in the head on Elkington Avenue, he was the second teen killed in gang-related violence in a two week period. Two other teens were arrested but the violence continued. A produce packer opened fire at the Fresh Choice plant on Abbott Street with a .30 caliber high-powered rifle killing one man and injuring another. A late September shooting left another young man dead, the fourteenth of the year. Killed while cleaning out the family car in his own driveway, Jose Alvarez was shot from behind. Two days later two more were killed after being shot in separate incidents. By October third, the city recorded the seventeenth murder of 1994, as a man was shot as he stood in his living room on San Benito Street. Officers were working overtime to try to quell the violence. Three months were left in the 1994 statistical year and already the city had a new and unwanted record for homicides.

It was not long before the eighteenth homicide put Salinas on the map as one of the most violent cities of its size. While the city reeled from the violence, more shocks were in order. When a man was gunned down outside the Harvest Queen Bar on South Main Street, South Salinas residents started to grasp what was happening in their city. The bowling alley hired security, worried about the safety of their customers. Halloween brought extra patrols as officers anticipated problems as East Salinas families marked the anniversary of the triple murders of 1993. The gang task force was disbanded in November just days before the city recorded the twentieth homicide of 1994.

In one of the most horrifying scenes Salinas officers would ever encounter, a triple homicide with three family members killed and a toddler wounded by gunshots took place in a garage on East Market Street, bringing the homicide total to twenty-three for the year. As the wounded baby girl lay in the hospital detectives worked to find those responsible. The case would take years to process with the suspects fleeing to Mexico, arrests and trials taking many months to complete. Early in December, with the death of Victor Lomeli, Salinas recorded the twenty-fourth homicide of the year in what has been to date, a sad record for the city. There would be more shootings even some injuries, but no more homicides. Two more deaths were the result of overdoses.

On December 29, 1994, Officer Tim Wheelus was cleared in the shooting of Rigoberto Ramirez. Ramirez had cut and burned himself before charging at the officer who repeatedly ordered him to drop the sharp glass he brandished. The year had taken its toll on Salinas, the county, and the officers who served. Fort Ord had closed after seventy-seven years as an army base, where many Salinas officers had served in the military. Of the twenty-four persons murdered, twenty-one, eight of them teenagers, had been shot to death on Salinas streets. One survivor, a mere baby shot multiple times as her family was murdered around her, continued to struggle for her life.

Predictions for 1995 were optimistic. With twelve new officers set to be hired, bringing the force to one hundred fifty, Lt. Robin Stuart hoped to see a better year than 1994, but refused to make any predictions about the level of violence. Mayor Styles said the city was in "good financial shape," and the hiring of additional officers and cooperation between schools and the city would have positive results. *Salinas Californian, January 2, 1995.*

Unfortunately, by the end of the first month of the year the city would see the first homicide of 1995. Sergio Herrera was shot once in a gang-related incident after answering the door of his Del Monte Avenue apartment. Barrios Unidos and Second Chance directors would object to homicides being labeled as "gang-related," saying it, "makes it sound a lot worse than it really is." *Salinas Californian, January 31, 1995.* Police had no time for arguing semantics as they continued to work to solve the record setting number of homicides from 1994. Eighteen of the twenty-four cases had been solved by the end of

January, a seventy-five percent solve rate the detectives were proud of. The remaining six cases involved suspects who had left the area and unwilling witnesses, the bane of all gang related investigations.

April Fool's Day brought the second and third homicides of the year in separate incidents only ten minutes apart. The Los Arcos Restaurant parking lot and the Lakeview Apartments were the scenes of the latest murders, the victims both receiving multiple stab wounds. The new cases did not keep detectives from working the older cases and late in April, they arrested three men linked to the 1992 murder of Adam Najera. Familiar with the suspects, Paul Meza, Phillip Montoya, and Job Nan, police now had witnesses who told them the victim had angered the gang members. The Najera homicide had been one of seventeen in 1992.

Out of control students at Alisal High nearly rioted and an officer was beaten during a fight at the school. Twenty-six officers responded to the fight thought to have been the result of charges pending against Eric Lucio for the Halloween murders of 1993.

It was May before the fourth homicide of the year was seen. Gabriel Orozco was shot in the head while standing outside his Garner Avenue apartment. Danny "Parrot," Sanchez had already been convicted in the Alexander Chang murder case when he was charged with the 1992 murder of Timothy Patterson. Investigators went to Pelican Bay where Sanchez was doing his time to advise him of the new charges.

In June 1995, the city implemented a "wellness" program, giving a $500 bonus to any officer who could pass a fitness test and causing a great deal of controversy. Arguing that good health prevented sick days and injuries, the city had no rules requiring police or fire employees to stay in shape. The editorial questioned the wisdom of the program and suggested that staying in shape be made a requirement for the job, not a "perk." *Salinas Californian, June 7, 1995.*

Charlene Zuehlke was bludgeoned to death by her husband in their Stockton Street home before he drove to Jack's Peak and dug a grave for her body, in the first homicide related to domestic violence that year. South County was seeing an increase in gang violence, shootings and malicious mischief. Juvenile case filings were up considerably and speculation was that gang activities had increased after the murder of a King City High student in January.

Good press was always welcome in the department even when the story was sad. In June, a young dog was found in Carr Lake. Tied to a bale of hay, someone had tried to drown the animal, tying her legs and body to the hay with rope and wire. Officer Tim Wheelus was quick thinking and borrowed a boat from a rental store, paddling out to try to save the distraught animal. The rescue was difficult but Wheelus was able to free the dog with the help of an SPCA employee in scuba gear. Wheelus was pictured in the newspaper as he sat in the small boat, his hand on the dog's head as he tried to comfort it during the rescue process. *Salinas Californian, June 23, 1995.* A $500 reward was offered for the conviction of the person who had left the dog to die.

Utz had come to the department in September 1994. The canine partner of Eric Wallace, Utz was an especially valuable addition to the force. In 1995, Officer Tony Heredia got a new partner when Rix, a three-year old German shepherd joined SPD. It was the first time SPD had two canine units on duty in fifteen years. Utz would have an outstanding career in Salinas, assisting in numerous arrests and being injured in the line of duty. He would eventually retire, moving with Officer Wallace when he went to Northern California.

THE LAST MAN OUT

Art Garcia was a veteran officer when a call regarding a stolen car interrupted briefing one night. A baby had been asleep in the back seat when the car was stolen and police were searching for the missing child. A woman doing laundry that cold night had turned the car and heater on, placing her baby in the back with the first load of laundry, then returning into the Laundromat for the last trip. When she returned, the car and baby were gone. Tips led to many officers heading to Chualar Canyon Road because a known parolee with a history of car theft was found hitchhiking on the highway near Chualar. Garcia felt the car and baby were nearby. He drove around the small town of Chualar, searching for the car, with an intuitive feeling it was close by. Hours passed and officers were being called back to town. Garcia, his gut instinct very strong, refused to go in. Sam Tashiro was sent out to bring him in, but still, he refused, sending Tashiro back to town, telling him he would come in soon. Tashiro told him to hurry in to the station because he was, "the last man out." Garcia, tired and worried, prayed for the baby before he switched on his high beam lights as he readied himself to leave the area. Spotlighted in front of him in the bright lights was the car he had been looking for. Rushing over to the car which had been partially hidden backed in between two mobile homes, he found the child asleep and safe in the car seat. Garcia held the bundled baby close as he was driven in to the hospital. An article written in the *Salinas Californian* called

Officer Garcia, "The Last Man Out," because he was the final car out searching that night. That article later spurred another writer to publish the story in January 1995. "You're never alone – even when you're the last man out," was the last line in the story that appeared in the January 1995 edition of the *Guidepost.*

While the shootings and homicides made the headlines, accidents still claimed the lives of many Salinas citizens. In one short month, both a baby and an elderly woman were run over by family members backing out of their driveways. A baby in a stroller was crushed to death when a driver accidentally hit the accelerator, trapping the stroller between the car and a building. Six weeks after the Charlene Zuehlke murder, the city recorded the sixth homicide of the year with the death of John Dunn.

Criticized for not having enough Spanish speaking officers, the department tried recruiting minorities in an attempt to diversify. But, conscious of their desire to hire only the best, SPD recruiters did not take just anyone. Don Cline, then in charge of the personnel division told reporters, "I would not want to see us sacrifice our standards for the sake of diversity...Just because you have a shortfall doesn't mean you grab the next person who happened to fit that category." *Salinas Californian, July 29, 1995.*

An argument between a nineteen year old victim and a sixteen year old suspect led to the eighth homicide of the year. The 1992 triple homicide and shooting of the baby remained an active case. Bounty hunters from Salinas went to Mexico and found one of the suspects, bringing him back to Salinas for the reward. Daniel Covarrubias-Sanchez had been the subject of an extensive manhunt because it was believed he was involved in the triple murder.

A new wing opened at the county jail. Costing ten million dollars to build, the one hundred ninety-two bed wing was dormitory style and would house only low risk or non-violent offenders who were serving sentences.

Officer Candi Apple took over a new beat in August 1995. She walked the Acosta Plaza area as part of her duties after the city won a grant for extra police services. Having been a patrol officer in the Alisal area for some time prior to her new assignment, Officer Apple was well aware of the gang problems and knew many of the people who lived in the area. The community was delighted with her presence and she towed away abandoned and unsightly vehicles, ordered gang members to disperse, and was the police presence that the neighbors had been calling for. Officer Apple gave out Peace Builder's Citations, helping to combat the image of police officers most East Alisal kids had and trying to give the children a positive role model, thereby making the community safer. She was also instrumental in organizing and implementing a program against drunk driving. "Every 15 Minutes" was a two-day program that brought a simulated crash to a high school where students watched as emergency crews worked. Every fifteen minutes one student was taken out of class, representing a person killed in a drunk driving accident. Officer Apple had been with the department for seven years when she was recognized for her outstanding work. Named as the Salinas Police Officer's Association, (SPOA) Officer of the Year in 1997, Apple made a difference in the community she served.

More shootings in different parts of the Alisal would leave several injured and one fourteen year old boy dead. Daniel Estrada was shot once in the head while on Toro Avenue and another juvenile was in custody, charged with the ninth homicide of 1995. Within days of that murder, a transient was found stabbed to death and in an advanced state of decomposition near the Sanborn Road railroad tracks. Andy Miller collected flies and maggots for examination by an entomologist. He kept the bugs, along with part of the victim's liver, in his overhead in the detective offices, where it could be smelled throughout the division. Murder number ten had just been recorded. By November, the fourteenth murder had officers working overtime on investigations. Shootings alone were escalating, with nine victims shot in one incident outside of Portuguese Hall. In contrast, Monterey had seen no homicides in 1993 and only one in 1994. While the nation's crime rate fell, Salinas defied all statistics and saw unwelcome increases. Police had put all the narcs and gang officers on a robbery detail after the number of robberies swelled. Finding that most of the robberies had been related to gang activities, the robbery task force seemed to work and Salinas saw a drop in armed robberies between 1993 and 1994.

It was late November when the city saw homicide number fifteen. Shot in the head while driving on Natividad Road on a Tuesday afternoon, Miguel Jimenez was only seventeen years old when he died. As if the gang activities, robberies and murders weren't enough, Salinas officers saw the spread of Methamphetamine within the city during 1995. Meth labs were moving into the city at an alarming rate and had been found in homes, hotel rooms and even cars. Detective Gerry Davis was part of the team working on stopping the spread of the drug. Using informants and making buys, the team was successful in finding both the manufacturers and users. Toxic chemicals, the by-product of meth production, worried both police and citizens who had to pay for the clean-up.

Two vacant traffic officer positions left city drivers with little prevention and enforcement. Dana Cornelison was one of only two officers assigned to traffic control in late 1995. Photographed in the newspaper using his radar gun to catch speeders on West Alisal, Cornelison had his hands full. Citizen complaints about speeders had officers scrambling to cover an entire city while recruiters tried to hire new officers, train them and get them on the streets. The shootings continued and arrests were made, too many to document. On the positive side, the police officers and firefighters bought toys for needy children for Christmas as they did every year. Gathering donations of food and toys, the officers and firemen would distribute them to thirteen hundred kids just before the Christmas holiday at a party held at the Alisal Community School. The holidays held more investigations in store for detectives as seventeen robberies took place during the first ten days of December. Armed robbers accosted citizens on the street and bank robbers hit two banks in two days. When a citizen wrote a letter to the editor asking Chief Nelson, "Where is the police chief?" and "What is he doing about the violence?" the Chief responded. Encouraging citizen inquiries and providing his phone number, the chief tried to explain his duties and the many functions of the department. Citing the PAL, (Police Athletics League) program, the School Resource Officers, (SROs) at schools, and the Violent Injury Prevention Coalition, he discussed the department's involvement with the Peace Builder's organization. Telling the author of the letter that officers had arrested 7,044 people as of September 30, 1995, he defended his officers and the job they were doing. After listing the numerous ways in which the department was addressing crime and violence the chief closed his response by asking the author, "Where were you?" and "What are you doing?" *Salinas Californian, December 15, 1995.*

Constantly criticized by some citizens, the department continued to try new tactics in fighting the violence. The gang task force was free to roam the entire city looking for gang members and the problems they caused. Kyle Kimm told a ride-along reporter that "There could be one hundred Salinas police officers assigned to track gang activities, and they still wouldn't be able to cure the city's gang problems." *Salinas Californian, September 2, 1995.* The department, in cooperation with race car driver Alex Padilla, tried a "guns for jackets" program. Citizens could turn in guns and receive a racing jacket with no questions asked. Thirteen weapons were turned in to officers. A grant of almost one million dollars would fund the creation of the fourteen officer Violence Suppression Unit.

Seven officers were awarded the "10851" award for their work in locating and recovering stolen vehicles. Lance Miraco, Robert Griffin, Tony Chaffee, John Butz, and Matt Maldonado, Sgt. Eggers and Ono Solis were all honored for the recovery of one hundred eleven stolen vehicles and thirty-seven arrests between June and September 1994. The most often stolen vehicles at that time were the mid-1970s and early 1980s Buicks and Oldsmobiles. The parts of those cars were interchangeable, making them valuable to the thieves. Salinas did not have many luxury or sports cars at that time. *Salinas Californian, September 28, 1995.*

The early months of 1996 brought a wide variety of crime to Salinas. Rival gangs squared off again and a man was in critical condition early in 1996. Members of the newly funded Violence Suppression Unit joined a dozen detectives and crime scene officers investigating the shooting that had taken place in the 1000 block of Del Monte Avenue. John Avery was kept busy with fingerprinting the scenes of various bank robberies. By February, five banks had been robbed. Gil Bacis, the SRO at Alisal High School, told reporters that fights on campus were, "nothing out of the ordinary." Lt. John Carr refused to speculate on the possible penalties a local supervisor might face in court following his arrest by Salinas officers for drunk driving. He had sped through East Alisal, hitting a fire hydrant and two poles after leaving a campaign party held on Main Street just days before he faced an election. While the number of homicides had decreased in 1995, Chief Nelson was cautious about celebrating the apparent reduction in crime. Robberies were up, but citizens felt more confident than the 1994 year when twenty-four murders were the main headlines in news.

Willing to go to any lengths to stop the injuries and deaths caused by drunk drivers SPD had a billboard made, warning citizens of the welcoming committee they would meet if they chose to drink and drive. Featured on the billboard were Officers Fay Patterson, Rick Sorratos, and Detective Vicky Gray. Wearing full uniforms and with a serious look of determination, the billboard was located at the busy corner of East Market near Pajaro Street. The day the billboard went up, Officer Eric Wallace's partner, Utz, was honored by the MCPOA, receiving the Officer of the Year Award for 1995. It was the first time a canine had been selected to receive the prestigious award.

Twelve new officers hit the streets in March 1996. Mark Lazzarini joined his identical twin brother Mike, who had been with the department for five years before his brother joined up. Bringing the force to one hundred forty-one sworn officers, the department was still down ten officers. Todd Swinscoe also joined his brother Chris as an officer. Chris Swinscoe had been with the department twelve years when he found his brother alongside him in police work. Other new officers hired during that year were Jeanne Allen, Kevin Orepeza, Steve Denison, Leo Arsitio, Manual Loza, Royce Heath, John Murray, Gary Dahl, Keith Blanchard, and Wayne McLaughlin. They would all be put to work alongside senior officers who would train them for some time before they were ready to patrol on their own. There were plenty of training opportunities as Great Western Bank became the eleventh victim of a bank robbery in April that year. The arrest of one suspect had officers believing they had solved at least eight of the bank robberies.

The Cost of Murder

The cost of murder was the subject of a study by the Peace Builders Business Task Force. Hoping to shock people with the true cost of a homicide the study showed that one murder, that of the young man shot while driving his car on Natividad Road, cost taxpayers a total of over $572,000. Life saving efforts had cost $8,000, repairs by Pacific Gas and Electric to downed lines and efforts to restore power was an additional $10,000. $20,000 covered the cost of the prosecution of and defense of the defendant in the case. The highest cost, however, was the $420,000 tab for incarceration of three teenagers to be imprisoned at CYA until they turned twenty-five. Criminals, however, either didn't read the article, or didn't care as the third homicide of 1996 took place in May. By June, the anticipated rise in summer crime had come. In one weekend one man was shot during a fight on Sanborn Road, one was stabbed repeatedly on Garner Avenue, and two were pistol-whipped during a robbery attempt. The weekdays were no better as gang members robbed a man then chased him down and shot him as he played basketball at Jesse Sanchez School on Monday. Tuesday, three people were injured in another multiple shooting on North Sanborn Road. While the state crime rate was the lowest in twenty-five years, Salinas bucked the odds and had seen an increase in violent crime in 1995.

Lieutenant John Carr retired on July 1, 1996 after thirty-two years with the department. He continued to work periodically as a watch commander for the department and as the Range Master for the MCPOA. As a board member and active retiree John, who retired as a Lieutenant, still lives in Salinas. Both his sons are officers with other departments. Carr had been a key officer hired during the Alisal annexation process and became one of the best known supervisors in the department. His blunt comments were history in the department. He had once told a woman stopped for speeding and given only a warning, "I would hate to have to put a toe tag on you." Carr also had his opinion about what it took to be a police officer. "It takes a very special individual," he said. "You have to be sixty percent humanitarian, thirty percent adventurer and ten percent jerk." *Salinas Californian, July 2, 1996.*

Bill Keyes, who has worked as a Community Service Officer since 1975, has towed over 112,000 abandoned vehicles off the streets of Salinas. Bill has seen just about everything in his time and recalled the time when he hooked up a car from the front of 37 Soledad Street. The tow truck took it about half way to the yard when the rear axle and differential just fell off in the middle of the street. Bill has trained twenty-five people to take his place, but continues to serve the city to this day as a part time CSO. He just cannot be replaced.

OFFICER EDGAR SHOOTS KNIFE-WIELDING MAN

Officer Jarrett Edgar was forced to shoot Bulmaro Reyes after the suspect first tried to stab the clerk at the 1-2-7 Liquor store, and then charged at the officer when he arrived on the scene. The officer backed away as far as was possible prior to the shooting. The man, previously convicted of an assault with a knife, died of a single shot. The security video in the store showing the man lunging with the knife at the clerk, was released after complaints that the officer had acted inappropriately. However, backed up against cars, Edgar had no choice in his actions and he was cleared after an investigation by the District Attorney's Office.

GUARDING THE PRESIDENT

President Clinton was elected in November 1992. In 1996, he came to Salinas, speaking to crowds outside the old courthouse buildings. Salinas officers worked with the Secret Service agents and planned for the safety of the president. All off-duty officers were called in to help with crowd control and traffic issues. Streets would have to be closed down to insure the safety of the President, but officers were not complaining. President Clinton praised Salinas for the anti-gang efforts, calling our city a role model for others. Stopping in at Chapala's Restaurant after the reception at the courthouse, Clinton was seen by a thrilled local admirer, George Coe, a realtor who happened to be having lunch there that day. Not since 1901, when President McKinley's train made a stop in Salinas had the city been honored with a visit by a president. The aftermath of the president's visit would be marred for years as arguments ensued over payment for the cost to the city.

Local officers had set up a curfew center and credited it with lowering the number of juveniles out on the streets after curfew. Lt. Steve Perryman told reporters that no one juvenile had been brought to the center on more than one occasion. "Parental awareness has developed from this and hopefully, parents are taking a little bit more of an active role in what their children are doing," Perryman said. Strict house rules made it clear that the center was not a fun place to be. *Salinas Californian, September 11, 1996.*

Daniel Solis was pronounced dead after being shot while attending a party on East Alisal Street making him the fourth homicide of the year in 1996. Two more shootings in September left one dead and one injured. And some victims, their bodies never found, never made the official count. One man had been missing his son and fearing him dead since 1992, worked with Detective Gunter to try to solve the case, even offering a $25,000 reward. His son had testified against a drug dealer in Yuma and the father feared he had been killed in retaliation for his testimony. Although many missing people were missing on purpose, Gunter still had fourteen open cases, nine juveniles and five adults, whose cases dated back to 1986.

Federal grants would help put computers in patrol cars, but couldn't deter the number of murders in Salinas. The third shooting in less than twenty-four hours left one more homicide victim a sad statistic. Williams and Garner was the scene of the next homicide, the eighth of the year. "Operation Cease Fire" sought to stop random and dangerous gunfire in city streets during the holiday season. Officers tried to educate the public about the dangers of firing weapons and bullets that could pierce roofs. But it was a stabbing victim that would claim the next life in Salinas. That murder was followed by the fatal shooting of a female, the second homicide in less than twenty-four hours. Abused for years, the woman had been killed by her husband leaving two young boys without any parents after police were forced to shoot and kill him after he turned his gun on them following a chase. PAL tried to make the holidays a little brighter for the two boys by purchasing bicycles for them. The bicycles had been purchased at Target, the store giving the officers a discount.

Early in 1997, the city was horrified when a ninety-two year old man was beaten to death in his home on Beverly Drive. Daniel Cisneros was able to give details of the beating and robbery to officers before he died at the hospital, but unable to make any identification. Detectives had suspects, but without additional evidence, they were unable to make the case. It remains an open homicide investigation to this day. Earlier in the month, a woman was murdered and found under a mattress on Deer Street. Days after the murder of Daniel Cisneros, another female would die of a gunshot wound as she rode in a car near Lunsford Drive.

Utz, the canine partner of Eric Wallace, was seriously injured during a struggle with a suspect. His jaw broken during the fight, Utz continued to hold onto the subject until Wallace could restrain him. After two months of recovery, Utz returned to work. *Salinas Californian, March 14, 1997.* He and his partner were needed as the shootings continued with a frequency that placed them out of the main headlines of the news. Four were injured in two different shotgun attacks and another man was killed after being shot once in the head, making him the fourth homicide in 1997. The shootings were almost as common as the stabbings in those days and explosives were becoming another weapon of choice. Officers had become familiar with firebombs during 1994 and 1995. Now they had to learn about pipe bombs, plastic explosives, grenades, and fuses. Police believed there were twenty-six gangs operating in Salinas with approximately one thousand five hundred members but only three gangs were believed responsible for the bulk of the crimes.

Duty during the month of April included traffic control at the main post office, where citizens scrambled to mail their tax returns at the last minute. The curfew program was working and both the department and probation officials asked the city council to continue to finance the curfew center for another year. Chief Nelson traveled to Washington D.C. to push for a juvenile crime bill that would emphasize prevention rather than punishment. He returned to Salinas where merchants were complaining about drive-by shootings affecting their trade. The manager of Kentucky Fried Chicken in East Salinas told reporters, "People think East Alisal is a bad area...There are parts of East Salinas where there is a lot of gang activity. But I just don't think East Alisal and the business area is as dangerous as people think. I feel safe here." *Salinas Californian, June 3, 1997.*

On June 12, 1997, the city council discussed a $17 million dollar budget for the police department, including one hundred ninety-eight positions. Other news included the return to the earlier days of Salinas City, as Steve Perryman discussed the introduction of horseback patrols for parks and special events. Sirhan Sirhan, the convicted killer of Senator Kennedy, was denied parole for the tenth time. In custody since the 1968 murder, Sirhan told reporters he now believed he was innocent of the crime. *Salinas Californian, June 19, 1997.*

High risk sex offenders suddenly became more visible with the introduction of the Megan's Law data released to the public. Over four hundred fifty registered sex offenders were located in Monterey County. All but two of the high risk offenders resided in Salinas. Schools, worried about security after several nearby shootings, even hired private security. A dead body, another murdered victim, was found near Virginia Roca Barton Elementary School in September, discovered by a member of the parent patrol. The locations of the many shootings and dreaded violence ping-ponged around town. This made it nearly impossible to predict when or where they would occur. It seemed no neighborhood was exempt from the warfare. From the East side, to the West and North, the shootings continued. In September, Detective Gunter was photographed covering the body of Martin Soza, who had been shot in front of his home on Bolero Avenue, the ninth homicide of the year.

The Police Athletics League was active, contacting and playing with kids, raising money with barbecues and other events. Tim Wheelus, on a bike paid for with donations, started a downtown beat. The eleventh murder of the year took place in October. An unintended victim had been shot when the suspect fired at someone else. Stabbed multiple times, the city's thirteenth victim died in his car on Williams Road. It was only a few days before the fourteenth victim was found just off West Market Street, beaten to death.

Jose Manuel Zepeda became the seventeenth homicide of the year as he rode in a car fired upon by an unknown person on Rider Avenue. While the seventeen murders appeared to be unrelated, four two-man detective units were working overtime to try to solve the crimes. While some were clearly gang-related others were not, or there was not enough information to make a determination. Detectives spent Christmas Eve investigating the eighteenth homicide of the year, the second drive-by and the third murder of the month. There would be a fourth. Manuel Mendez, found in his car near the Stone Mountain Carpet Mill by an employee, had been shot in the neck. Putting twelve additional officers out on the street following the latest shootings and murders at a cost of $15,000, officers were able to arrest thirty-five gang members and confiscated five guns. Three of the four December murders were gang-related and the city council, now responsive to the need for more officers, voted to release the additional funds.

There were nineteen murders in Salinas in 1997, a sharp increase from the

1996 statistics. Hoping there would never be a repeat of the twenty-four murders of 1994, most the result of a gang war, detectives were stretched to their limits. Gary Edwards retired from the police department and Dan Nelson was still the chief. Tom Huff was a sergeant, and Alan Styles was the mayor.

Community Service Officer positions were used for parking control during the late 1980s. Parking and traffic had long been a source of problems for the department and there was a history of citizen abuse of the law and the CSOs. Watching a suspected abuser of the time limitations on Howard Street, Jesse Gilpas and other CSOs caught a woman spraying her car tire with a spray bottle to remove the chalk mark. They waited until she was one-half block away before placing a very expensive ticket on her windshield.

Jesse Gilpas went to work in the Evidence Room when Walt Hays and Diana Mendoza were still there to train him. Walt had been in charge of evidence for over fifteen years. A World War II veteran, he was generous with his wisdom, training Jesse to take over. Jesse recalls a television set brought in to evidence. Riddled with roaches, the bugs spread throughout the evidence room before moving on to infect the entire downstairs area of the police department, including the break room. Diana and Walt had to "bomb" the entire downstairs area to get rid of the nasty creatures.

By March 1998, the fifth homicide of 1998 had local authorities worried about a repeat of the record setting number of murders in 1994. Organizations like Peace Builders called for help from the community and a united stand against the violence. The following day another man was in serious condition after being shot outside a market on Sanborn Road. Newspaper stories about the murders ran next to listings of local school's honor roll lists in a bizarre display of extreme contrast.

Molotov cocktails, thrown at a home on Ranier Drive, destroyed a car, giving officers yet another violent crime to investigate. For the first time, the MCPOA award for Officer of the Year was shared by a group of four men from two separate departments. Salinas Lt. Leonard Wilson, Corporal Kyle Kimm, Officer Steve Long, and Sheriff's Investigator Chuck Bardin, were awarded the honor as a group for their work in the arrest and conviction of Matt Rocha.

Russ Hauschild was working in the gang intelligence unit on May 1, 1998. With Greenfield police for six years before a short stint with the sheriff's department, Hauschild had worked patrol and VSU enforcement before taking the intelligence assignment. He was sitting at his desk, working on his computer late that afternoon when his partner, Mike Lazzarini, told him that Roy

Rodriguez, wanted on a number of warrants, was in the vicinity of a robbery and shots fired call. Hauschild went with his partner to see what Roy was doing. Officers had contained him with a perimeter and Roy was perched on a roof on East Market Street. The officers pleaded unsuccessfully for Rodriguez to come down. Eventually Rodriguez made a run for it and a foot chase ensued. Hauschild, catching Rodriguez, was stabbed during the arrest. Off duty for weeks during his recovery, he returned to full duty and is currently the sergeant in charge of the Personnel and Training Unit, where he is enjoying learning the administrative end of police work.

The Investigations Division was working with FBI agents on a big case in Salinas in 1998. One of the FBI agents had a habit of leaving her identification papers around the office and misplacing her documents on a rather regular basis. Tired of picking up after the federal agent, officers kept her documents one day. Wiring Eric Wallace with a transmitter, they asked him to make a traffic stop on her as she left the department that afternoon. Stopped only yards out into the street and asked for her driver's license and identification, the federal agent became more and more flustered as Wallace questioned her. Asking why she was stopped, and being told she had been speeding, the agent told Wallace she was FBI and that he could call her boss. She then told him she was armed. Wallace, incredulous that an armed federal agent would drive around without identification, chastised her and asked if she really wanted him to call her supervisor. Dialing his cell phone, Wallace then handed her the documents and the transmitting device, letting her know the joke was on her. She used the transmitter to send her own message, "You x--x- x--x holes!"

In 1998, the city was counting on the opening of the Steinbeck Center to do for Salinas what Cannery Row had done for Monterey. The home of the first Mayor of Salinas was moved from Romie Lane to Market Street near the train depot, where it was expected that thousands of tourists would arrive on trains from San Francisco to roam downtown shops, eat lunch and spend the night at a first class hotel across from the Steinbeck Center. The Intermodal Transportation Center was going to be a hub of activity including trains, buses and taxis. As of 2005, that has not happened.

While officers investigated shootings early in January, the 10-20 Life Law went into effect, upping the penalty for crimes in which a gun was used. A man stabbed while at a party at the home of a local city council member, sued for damages and an East Salinas store owner was killed during a robbery. Thirteen of the nineteen murders from 1997 remained unsolved and the police asked for help from the community. The trial of Daniel Covarrubias for the 1994 triple homicide began the same week President Clinton denied the allegations of Monica Lewinsky. It was also the week police would be called to a home on Navajo Drive, where the body of a missing boy was found buried beneath the house.

Jeanette Reynolds was working as a Community Service Officer assigned to the Investigations Division in 1998. One of her assignments was Missing Persons cases, something she felt needed a sixth sense. There were three hundred eighty-one missing persons cases by August 1998, and Jeanette was sending out letters to families who had previously reported someone missing in an attempt to close out files where those people had returned. She sent one such letter to the DeNoyer family who had reported a sixteen year old boy missing in 1984. While most turned out to be runaways who returned home after a short time, others required more work. The family had moved out of the house but the new owners read the letter shortly after making some repairs under their home. While under the house making the repairs, a family member noticed some tennis shoes in the dirt. After receiving the letter, further inspection of the shoes showed socks attached and police were notified. The body was identified as that of the young man who had previously lived there and had been reported missing. Detectives worked to find out what had happened to Christopher DeNoyer and eleven days after the discovery of the body, officers arrested the step-father of the victim of the homicide.

One day later police were investigating the third and fourth homicides of 1998. Both were victims of gunshot wounds. The Salinas paper ran an editorial two days later, calling the homicide rate in Salinas, "intolerable." It was only mid-February and already there had been four murders. In all fairness, one of those murders had been committed years earlier, that of Christopher Denoyer, but the discovery of the body in 1998 was counted in the statistics for that year. Recalling the record setting year 1994, the editorial called for the people of Salinas to prevail over the violence. *Salinas Californian, February 11, 1998.*

The homicide rate did not seem to affect the number of other violent crimes in Salinas. Robberies were escalating and the suspect in a child beating case was found and arrested on Homestead Avenue. County courts were stretched to their limits as fourteen homicide cases worked their way through the system. The triple murder of 1994 was pending trial after many delays and the Preliminary Hearing in the DeNoyer murder, the victim having been found fourteen years after the murder, was scheduled. County cases pending included that of an eleven year old girl murdered in her Gabilan Acres home, and the robbery-murder of a jewelry store owner in Marina.

Sergeant Dan Perez and Officers Juan Ruiz, Jon Smith, and Wayne Vance were cleared by a federal jury of charges they assaulted a man and denied him medical aid during and after an arrest. Although the criminal case against the man resulted in an acquittal, the jurors felt the officers had acted appropriately during the 1995 incident. *Salinas Californian, April 8, 1998.*

The city was considering civil injunctions they felt would help stem the rising number of gang incidents. Gang members found loitering in selected areas after being served with the injunction, could be arrested. As the city discussed the use of the injunction law, a sixth man became the latest homicide victim. By late May 1998, sixty-three injunctions were ready to be issued to known gang members. The names of the first sixty-three Vagos members who were served were released in June and published in the newspaper.

Shootings continued during the summer months as the city discussed shutting down the curfew center. A shooting and a stabbing occurred within minutes, unrelated to each other and both on the East side of town. Christina Williams disappeared from her neighborhood in Marina that month, and many law enforcement agencies were involved in addition to the FBI with running down tips regarding her disappearance. Salinas detectives worked closely with the FBI and Rick Lack to try and find out what had become of young Christina. Eighteen months later, her body was found off Imjin Road and the case has never been solved. It remains an open investigation to this day.

Prices for gasoline were once again on the rise. The Alisal Beacon station had regular gas for $1.11 per gallon, while the Valley Center Chevron was charging $1.29 per gallon. There was an investigation by the State Assembly Consumer Protection Committee as the prices started to soar just as the summer months and time of travel plans approached. *Salinas Californian, May 7, 1998.*

The month of May 1998, was one of the wettest in the history of Salinas. 1997 had been an unusually dry year, with only .05 inches during May. Over two inches of rain fell on Salinas during May 1998, appropriate as the citizens of Salinas and the rest of the world mourned the death of Frank Sinatra.

Anna Caballero announced her intention to run for Mayor of Salinas. A councilwoman since 1991, she wanted to represent the city and felt the position of mayor was best served by someone with a history on the city council. *Salinas Californian, June 23, 1998.* Shortly after her announcement, the

Steinbeck Center opened with a gala celebration marred only slightly by a wave of burglaries in the Old Town area. Accused of not patrolling the downtown district, Sgt. Pat Duval informed citizens that officers made regular patrols in the downtown area on every shift, calling it "one of the most well traveled parts of town." *Salinas Californian, June 26, 1998.*

In July, the eighth homicide victim of 1998 had refused medical aid offered after he was beaten on Sanborn Road. Walking home after refusing to talk with police or go to the hospital, the man died of a ruptured spleen and liver damage one day later. Another man died that week, the victim of a hit and run drunk driver on probation for a prior DUI.

Salinas High had just gone through a complete renovation when an angry young man took his frustration out on the school, causing $40,000 in damage. Schools were no longer as safe as the city would have liked. A seventeen year old boy was beaten and robbed while walking across the Hartnell campus.

Two separate shootings early in July 1998 left one dead and three wounded. Later that month another man was gunned down on Williams Road, shot in the chest. Kevin Oakley, a deputy who worked in gang intelligence, began the process of the certification of gang members throughout the county. Deputy District Attorney Chuck Olvis hoped the certification process would mean longer sentences for those convicted of gang-related offenses. There were ten criteria for the certification process, including the admission of gang membership, the wearing of colors, possession of drawings or letters, tattoos relating to a particular gang, photographs with gang members using signs, and having a name on a gang roster. The pros and cons of the injunction process and results were argued among many citizens and leaders in the city.

The robberies and shootings kept officers busy at all times of the day and night. When a shooting victim died six months after the assault, another homicide was added to the statistics for the prior year, 1997. In August 1998, the city saw the thirteenth homicide of the year, the victim shot in a drive-by shooting. Within days, there was more violence. Michael Castillo was found shot to death late in August, making him the fourteenth homicide victim of the year.

THE BEANIE BABY CAPER

Tipped off by an elderly man complaining of unauthorized charges to his bank account, Detective Joe Gunter found himself working with Carmel Detective Pete Poitras. The unauthorized charges had been made at stores in Salinas and Monterey. Finding a woman was ordering Beanie Babies and paying for them with stolen credit card numbers taken from the trash of a Carmel hotel, the two detectives set up a notification system with a store in Salinas. When the woman had car trouble and could not pick up her stolen items, the detectives volunteered to deliver her Beanie Babies. The woman was shocked to discover an empty box when the detectives arrived at her door. Her home was full of over one hundred plastic wrapped Beanie Babies. *Salinas Californian, August 28, 1998.*

Sgt. Jim Toft was in charge of the traffic division in 1998 when citizens complained about speeding drivers near schools. After a near miss where a crossing guard was almost hit in front of Fremont School, officers were deployed to stop the speeding violators. Officers Robert Hampton and Greg Rivera handed out tickets for offenses including speeding and ignoring the red lights on school buses. In 1998, the fine for passing a school bus while the red lights were activated was $406, much more than the $270 fine for running a red light. *Salinas Californian, September 11, 1998.*

Salinas officers were a big hit at the El Grito festival in 1998 as they signed trading cards with new photographs. The most sought after card featured the motor squad parked in front of an F/A-18 Hornet jet. Ron Candiloro was a senior officer with the motor squad and his son, a Navy fighter pilot, had flown the big jet into the Monterey Airport for a high school reunion. *Salinas California September 1998.*

There were seven female officers by 1998. Terry Heffington had once been a clerk in the Sheriff's Department and was now a sergeant in Salinas. The department was trying to diversify to better reflect the community they served. Several bilingual officers had left to work in other departments and more were needed. *Salinas Californian, August 8, 1998.* A testing session was scheduled for an upcoming Saturday in hope applicants would start the background process.

Officers were beyond busy on the weekend of September 20, 1998. In separate incidents around the city there were two drive-by shootings, five stabbings, and several robberies. A young girl was sexually assaulted the following day. October gave no break to police who continued to respond to robberies and shootings, both accidental and by home intruders. Shootings were so common they were usually found only in the *"Local Briefs"* section of the local paper. Bank robberies plagued many of the Main Street area banks and a violent home invasion robbery on Garden Way was investigated. In the days just before Halloween, one man was shot five times at the Boronda Manor apartment complex and a sixteen year old high school student was stabbed and beaten in what appeared to be another gang-related incident.

By the third day of November police had arrested numerous high level gang members suspected of involvement in the shootings of two people in an apartment on Soledad Street. Charged with conspiracy to commit murder after the incident which left one man dead, high ranking members of the Nuestra Familia were arrested and eventually charged with multiple counts, including violations of the RICO acts. They remain in prison today.

The violence continued with the shooting of yet another man on Hebbron Street and a stabbing on Abbott Street. Once again, robberies and shootings were noted only by brief paragraphs in the local news. Road rage shootings, domestic violence assaults, and robberies at motels did not prepare Salinas for what was coming. In November 1998, a seventy-seven year old woman walking home from a dental appointment near San Jose and Alameda Avenue was beaten, robbed, and shot in one of the most shocking and horrifying events in the city's history. Three days later the owner of Margarita's Place was shot down and killed in front of his bar at 153 South Main Street. It was thought the second daylight attack was related to the earlier shooting where two juvenile males were the suspects.

The mood of the city was glum and senior citizens changed their routines, afraid to go out for the daily walks in what had formerly been considered on of the safest neighborhoods in Salinas. Martial arts instructors offered self-defense classes for seniors at reduced rates as police examined a bicycle left at the scene of the Margarita's shooting for evidence that would help find the perpetrators. A $10,000 reward was offered and the public was beginning to understand that their help was needed in solving the cases. The two suspects were convicted of multiple charges in both shootings.

The department had thirteen openings near the end of 1998 and was trying to recruit new hires that would stay with the city. Sgt. Dan Perez and Corporal John Batton were working on the recruitment drive that had started months earlier. A television commercial featured the highlights of police work in Salinas and the website provided instantaneous information to potential officers. Two hundred had taken the physical agility test in August, but only forty were able to continue the process of the background investigation. The field was narrowed to only eight candidates as the testing and background procedure continued. Five were hired from that group; three of them were lateral transfers.

It was the holiday season again and Jim Toft, having started a toy collection program in 1986, was still in charge of the SPO, (Salinas Police Officer's Association) and the SFA, (Salinas Firefighter's Association) collection and distribution program. In 1986, two hundred toys had been collected and given to needy children. In 1998, that number had increased to more than 12,000 toys. *Salinas Californian, December 11, 1998.* When a young boy's Sony Play Station was stolen just after the Christmas holidays, the SPOA stepped in to purchase another one for the grateful child. The family's home had been burglarized while they visited relatives. Corporal Bill Gaston had taken the report and found a way to make a difference for this family.

The December meeting of the MCPOA in 1998 honored Russ Hauschild He had recovered from the stab wound he had suffered during the chase of a suspect and was back at work. The MCPOA awarded Hauschild the Medal of Valor at their annual dinner in Seaside. Hauschild was quick to credit team work for the success of the Salinas department, saying "It's never an individual effort with us." "We are a team and if we ever separate from that philosophy, we will fail." *Salinas Californian, December 17, 1998.*

Just after midnight the morning of New Year's Day, officers responded to the first shooting of the year. Of the eighteen murders in 1998, seven remained unsolved as the new year began. Detectives worked the 1998 cases and continued to receive new ones on a daily basis, shootings and attacks being a regular part of life in Salinas.

Technology was coming to patrol units, with computer systems that would allow officers to quickly access car registration without having to contact county communications. In 1998, dispatchers had handled over 140,000 calls often handling multiple requests from officers and delaying response time, a danger to the officers.

Steve Hood left the department early in 1999 after seventeen years of service to take on the position of Captain in the Petaluma Department. Hood had been one of the officers responsible for writing a grant for funds and implementing the Violence Suppression Unit. He had been recognized for his work when President Clinton visited Salinas. He was also the recipient of the Medal of Valor from the MCPOA and other several other awards. *Salinas Californian, January 19, 1998.*

Chief Dan Nelson had been the top cop in Salinas for eight years when he made the decision to retire in 1999. Nelson had worked as an officer in both Richmond and East Palo Alto before coming to Salinas in 1991. When he left Salinas, he had over thirty-three years in law enforcement and planned to work on his golfing skills in Palm Desert. Fifty people applied for the chief's job in Salinas. By April, the list had been reduced to six potential candidates.

It was March before the city saw the first homicide of 1999. A single gunshot wound to the chest killed the young man as he walked on Pacific Avenue. A number of shootings followed within weeks, leaving one dead and many more injured. Officers were making headway in some cases and arrests were made as the investigation into the multiple shootings continued.

Some relief was available to the officers who helped raise funds for the Special Olympics with their "Cops and Lobsters," Tip-a-Cop program. Tips and donations were given to officers who served dinner at the Red Lobster Restaurant in Salinas and t-shirts were sold. Fifteen officers participated in the event that was supervised by Officer Chris Swinscoe. They raised $1200 during the lunch meal and hoped to double that during the dinner meal.

The decision to end a city contract with the SPCA for care of animals was made in April 1999. The city council decided a permanent solution was needed and recommended staffing the Salinas Animal Shelter on Hitchcock Road with nine employees at a projected cost of $250,000.

"Police Line" was the brainchild of Sgt. Tony Heredia and Officer Chris Swinscoe. They had attended a seminar about a police show and thought it would benefit Salinas to have a similar show. Produced by Hartnell College's TV production class, the weekly show ran on KMST through the Monterey County Office of Education. Swinscoe would be joined as host by Officer Bobby Phillips. With live interviews, telephone calls, and information useful to all citizens, the show's first interview was with retiring Chief Dan Nelson. *Salinas Californian, April 27, 1999.* By February 2001, the show had aired ninety-four broadcasts, with many positive remarks about the information it presented to citizens.

In another tragic case, a domestic situation ended in the death of two people, shot and killed by the jealous husband of a woman involved with another man. Detectives Gunter and Gerry Davis found the suspect shortly after the murders and elicited a confession. When a second murder took place within months at the Margarita Place Bar in Old Town, police quickly arrested three suspects. Public outcry and the concern of the department finally led to the closing of the bar, where numerous acts of violence and problems had persisted for some time.

In June 1999, the city set the budget for the upcoming 1999-2000 year. With the police department leading the list of expenditures at $17,849,500, it was hoped the addition of at least twelve new officers including traffic safety positions would help fight both the violent crime and traffic problems the city and the officers faced on a daily basis.

TWENTY-NINE

CHIEF DANIEL ORTEGA

*Chief Daniel Ortega
Courtesy of the
Salinas Police Department*

Daniel M. Ortega was sworn in as Chief of Police on July 1, 1999, saying, "We must all work together toward long-term solutions." His early years had been spent as an officer in Stockton where he was raised. After four years there, he went to San Jose where he started a curfew program and worked on a gang abatement program. The new chief had also been the executive director of the PAL program and the commander of the Violent Crime Unit. He vowed to be "visible and accessible," and has kept that promise to both his officers and citizens of Salinas.

One day after Chief Ortega took command of the Salinas Police Department, officers from San Jose on a stakeout in Salinas where they were watching a robbery suspect, shot and killed the man at a convenience store on Sanborn Road. Salinas officers and detectives would have to investigate the shooting that had happened in their city. They would also have to investigate one of their own as an off duty officer was suspended after being accused of waving his pistol at a truck driver in another county.

Justin Duval was sworn in by Chief Ortega in August 1999. The son of Sgt. Pat Duval, a twenty-six year veteran of the force, the younger Duval had quit a job as an auto mechanic to enroll in the academy in Gilroy. He worked as a deputy in the county jail for one year before transferring to the Salinas department. He is now an officer with the Redding Police Department. Pat Duval retired, moving to Redding with most of the family and Justin, choosing to make the change to be nearer his family.

Four Salinas recruits were honored and recognized for their outstanding achievement in the Gavilan Police Academy. Michael Batchelor was honored as the "Best Overall Police Recruit." John Sabino won the award for best in the physical and practical exercises. He ranked highest of all recruits in driving, shooting, and all physical aspects of the training. Angel Gonzalez and Lalo Villegas served as part of the class honor guard during the graduation ceremony. Salinas Police Chief Dan Ortega was the keynote speaker. *Salinas Californian, September 21, 1999.*

Chief Ortega wanted the public to recognize patrol units in the streets and had the forty-five all-white vehicles re-painted in more traditional black and white colors. For over forty years Salinas patrol units had been all-white. The all white cars made Salinas police cars stand out from other, more standard cars and many wish they were still around. The change from the old white to the new black-and-white colors took some time and only a few of the original all white cars remain in the fleet today. It took some long time citizens quite awhile to get used to the new look. The chief also authorized new badges to celebrate the California sesquicentennial.

During a SWAT operation with a barricaded suicidal subject, members of the SWAT team tried to subdue a man who attacked them with a knife after many hours of negotiations. Shots were fired and Corporal Stan Cooper was accidentally shot in the leg by a bullet that went through a wall, striking him as he held his post. The suspect was killed in the confrontation. Cooper returned to work after recovering and has worked a number of different assignments within the department.

The Thanksgiving Holiday was no vacation for officers and detectives working on two shootings involving rival gang members. The holidays were marred by the memories of the multiple shootings and murders that had taken place throughout the city. Once again, Jim Toft worked to collect over 16,000 toys to give to kids who would not otherwise have had much of a Christmas.

The number of homicide victims was down from 1998, but 1999 had been hard on everyone in the department and on the public they served. The last murder that year took place at a car dealership on East Alisal Street, the victim the owner of the business, leaving the city in a haze of disbelief and trying to find a way to stop the violence.

The new millennium dawned with little irregularity in spite of pessimistic predictions of computer problems and subsequent shortages of food and other products. In Salinas, Lt. Robin Stuart told reporters the New Year's Eve night had been very peaceful. Other than numerous DUI arrests made by the "Avoid the 17 Campaign," the first hours of the year 2000 were quite routine. The calm did not last and the shooting of three men on Short Street brought the gang problem to the news once again.

The murder rate in Salinas had dropped and credit was given to the cooperation of witnesses and good old fashioned police work. Sgt. Sam Tashiro recalled his first day on the job as a Salinas officer in 1967 when he retired in 2000. Half the department showed up to recognize him when he walked in to the department on the last day of his thirty-two year career. Tashiro had been a field supervisor and a watch commander during his years with SPD. Recalling the greatest moment in career as the moment when he was sworn in as an officer, Tashiro also spoke of the saddest day. Bill Darby, a patrol officer and former partner of Tashiro passed away after fighting a battle with leukemia. Tashiro was known for his habit of chewing on cigars and for giving the troops advice on health matters. The best advice he ever got was from Lt. William Lucero. Lt. Lucero cautioned the young Officer Tashiro, telling him to "Look toward the future and do the best that you can."

One hundred thirty members of many police agencies including the FBI, Monterey Police Department, Monterey County Sheriff's Department, CHP, CDC and State Parole joined together to investigate high level gang members. In January 2000, the task force raided a number of homes based upon federal indictments against the suspects. Multiple charges were brought against the suspects, varying from conspiracy and distribution of heroin to gang-related murder. Eleven defendants were listed under the indictments which were the product of a nine month joint investigation.

Salinas was still short twelve officers, with many veteran members of the department at retirement age. As the department searched for new recruits, two more shootings left victims hospitalized. By March 15, 2000, five separate shootings had occurred within three days. The next day an Alisal High School football player became the first murder victim of the year. Thefts, robberies and shootings were escalating. Two women were shot in robberies and Mayor Caballero and Chief Ortega asked witnesses to come forward. The second homicide came within the week, the victim shot in his car in the Lake Street area. Once again, Salinas citizens and police were stunned when a gunman was caught on video tape, shooting a female clerk at a 7-11 store during a robbery. It was only days later that a third murder victim was killed while sitting in his car on Ukiah Street.

The father of the man sentenced to life in prison for the double murder of his wife and her boyfriend, was shot in the back of the head and murdered only days after his son was sentenced. Garner and Rider was the scene of the next homicide when a man was driving his car when he was shot and killed.

Citizens demanded more patrols, many blaming the department for the acts of the suspects. The truth was, police were doing everything they could to track down and arrest anyone connected to gangs or crimes in the city. While community members met to discuss ways to eliminate the violence, six gang-related shootings and three fire bombings kept police running code three from one end of the city to the other. Two people were even shot after leaving a rosary for a murder victim at a mortuary. Police were forced to step up security at the funeral the following day.

During a peace march on the afternoon of April 17, 2000, two more teenage boys were shot on Elkington Avenue. Five weeks of violence led to town meetings to try to answer questions and brainstorm answers as city leaders and the community pondered whether everything that had been done over the past fifteen years to combat gangs and the violence they brought, had gone to waste. The decision was made to bring back the gang task force.

On a lighter note, Chief Ortega's photo made the newspaper as he tried out one of the new police-equipped mountain bikes to be used at the Bicycle Rodeo at the airport. Eight Salinas officers were recognized for their recovery of stolen vehicles, receiving their "10851" pins during a ceremony where they received special pins commemorating the number of vehicles recovered. Officers Paul Cervantes, Sheldon Bryan, Dave Shaw, Tim Wheelus, Bill Hickman, John Butz, Bobby Phillips and Wayne Vance, all received pins for recovering various numbers of stolen vehicles.

A homicide on Homestead Avenue broke the quiet of the neighborhood and a thirteen year old boy was killed by gunshots while standing in front of his house on Winham Street in May 2000. But, the deadliest day in Salinas history took place several days later on a Monday. Three people were killed by gunfire on May 30, 2000. The only other time three people were murdered in one day included the Halloween night gang fight and the triple homicide of the family on East Market Street, where only the baby had survived. In both those instances, the triple murders had resulted from a single incident. In May 2000, the three deaths were the result of three separate and unrelated events. There were more shootings in the days ahead and classes had to be locked down at Alisal Community and Alisal High Schools after a man had been shot in the vicinity and collapsed on the school lawn. Two more teens were shot on Galindo Street, leaving them with serious injuries.

In addition to the shootings and murders, officers and detectives were investigating a series of robberies around town. Many small liquor stores and similar types of businesses were being hit, some more than once.

New officers, even those born and raised in Salinas, struggled to learn all the streets. The city was growing and new communities peppered the north and east sides, with new streets and street names, along with unusual patterns for those streets making it hard for even veteran officers to find some locations.

PAL was nine years old in Salinas and sent kids to a summer program in the Ventana Wilderness for the second time during the summer of 2000. The week long camp taught children about mountains and farming, similar to a science camp. They rode on horseback, went kayaking, and explored the mud flats at Elkhorn Slough. Keith Blanchard, head of the PAL program at the time said, "It's building confidence and trust in law enforcement," as well as a love and respect of nature.

The second multiple shooting in three days claimed the lives of two more victims and others were injured. The attack warranted only a very short clip on the local page of the paper Monday morning. The tenth homicide of the year was believed to be gang-related.

Once again, South Salinas was rocked by violence when a man murdered his wife after she fled the house during a quarrel. Officers arriving at the scene after receiving calls of screams and shots fired, found a woman lying on the front lawn. SWAT had to be called out as officers could not reach the victim. The suspect was still armed and inside the home. The standoff went on for hours and the Monterey County Sheriff's Department SWAT team had to be called in to relieve tired Salinas officers. Salinas SWAT would return after a rest and threw a phone into the suspect. After a record twenty-seven hour standoff, during which Salinas officers had negotiated with the suspect and were finally able to remove the victim, Gary Cooper walked out of his home and surrendered. More than fifty neighbors had been evacuated out of two story houses and over fences during the incident. It was a tragedy Salinas would not soon forget.

There were many new restaurants and stores in the recently built Westridge Shopping Center. Applebee's Restaurant was a popular hang out for many Salinas citizens when it became the scene of a shooting late one night. Two off-duty Sheriff's Deputies were able to detain a woman found in a truck they followed after hearing the shots. The case would take months to get through the system, with unsubstantiated allegations made against the department and defense requests for special testing of the evidence.

A man on house arrest and previously sentenced to probation, admitted to having shaken his four month old son to death. Both banks and customers were being robbed. Well's Fargo and Union Banks were common targets and the knifepoint robbery of a customer in a drive-up window line at Bank of America was another example. While some residents were fearful of walking the streets of Salinas, terrorists bombed the U.SS Cole, a Navy destroyer, killing seventeen seamen.

A thirteen year old boy at Washington Middle School was found with two homemade bombs. School Resource Officer Sheldon Bryant and a probation officer put the explosive in their office before evacuating the entire school.

The fifteenth homicide of 2000 was investigated in November. Beaten with a bat, the female victim never regained consciousness and even though police had some witnesses to the crime, they had no idea of the motive or perpetrator.

Cramped in their thirty-five year old building, the police department was bursting at the seams. The building had been modern and accommodated the officers of the 1950s, but with growth in both sworn and support personnel, it was just too small. Community Service Officers were stationed in the post office. The Violence Suppression Unit was in the old fire station, later found to be contaminated and dangerous. Figuring a new station would cost in excess of thirteen million dollars, the city did the shuffle to make space for officers.

Twenty minutes after a man shot a co-worker to death at Valley Fabrication, he called 911 to surrender. Joe Gunter was in the last days of his career as a police detective and was partnered with Tim McLaughlin. The two drove to the location behind Star Market where the suspect gave himself up and Gunter located the weapon in the trunk of his car. The Abbott Street murder was the sixteenth of the year.

One day later, the climbing homicide rate climbed even higher as the seventeenth victim was killed during a drive-by shooting on Garner Avenue. Again, Detective Gunter was there heading the investigation as he would be at the tragic scene of the eighteenth and last homicide of 2000. Judi Schlem was removing Christmas packages from her car in an apartment parking lot on Iris Drive when she was the unintended victim of drug dealers and a gun battle. She was in Salinas to visit her daughter who lived in the apartment complex. Her son and husband were scheduled to graduate from the Correctional Training Facility Academy in Soledad. They were to start work at Pelican Bay Prison after their graduation. The suspects were both located and found guilty. The death of Judi Schlem was the result of a confrontation between drug dealers. It had been another difficult year for officers and citizens.

In December, three new members of the police department were shown with their partners. Faruk and Klief were bi-lingual, German being their first language. Brutus had been raised and trained in the Bay Area. Officer Marty Persijn stood with his new partner Faruk. Officer Bill Gaston was working with Klief and Officer Ken Ellsworth's new partner was Brutus.

When the Grand Jury report came out early in 2001, it advised against the formation of a citizen's review board. Saying the police were doing a good job of reviewing complaints against themselves, the Grand Jury made some suggestions the department implemented to make citizens feel more comfortable.

During the first two weeks in February, the city saw a rash of shootings. In five separate incidents, three were wounded, but there had been no homicides to date. Three more shootings in early March brought the total number of violent shootings to ten. On March 11, 2001 Salvador Casteneda was killed in the first fatal shooting of the year. SPD arrested three suspects within days.

Detectives were working on several homicides and multiple shootings when they were called to Cap's Saloon on West Gabilan Street in May 2001. A man sitting at the bar had been shot in the back of the head execution style and police were able to quickly identify a suspect. The suspect had a prior record and was thought to be in Oklahoma. Detectives Gunter and Gates coordinated a search with law officers in Oklahoma City and surveillance was established there. When the suspect was seen, Gunter and Gates flew to Oklahoma to pick up the suspect, who later confessed to the gang-related execution. It was not the first murder to take place in Cap's and the bar eventually lost its liquor license because of the violent history.

When a black bear appeared in the Abbott Street area one morning, it was seen by early morning walkers and produce workers. It galloped from the Sanborn Road area to Abbott Street, jumping fences and eventually breaking into the Hertz Equipment building by crashing through a plate glass window. While it was unusual for a bear to make its way into town, Salinas did have a history of several such incidents. Fortunately, this time the end of the story had a much better outcome than that of the story of Salinas Sam many years earlier. Gabe Carvey was on duty and watched the bear as he ambled through town. Voluntary evacuations were done to secure the safety of nearby homes and officers surrounded the Hertz building. When attempts to tranquilize the bear by Fish and Game officials were finally successful, Charlie Sammut, the director of Wild Things, volunteered to transport the animal to the Los Padres National Forest. The team work of Salinas officers, Fish and Game and Wild Things employees resulted in the successful return of the wild animal to a habitat better suited to his needs. *Salinas Californian, June 2, 2001.* Six months later, another bear found her way into Maple Park, jumping from yard to yard on Alameda Avenue and Romie Lane. Once again, teamwork between Salinas officers, Fish and Game and Wild Things resulted in the safe return of the animal to the wild.

By the end of June there had been six homicides. Three shootings in one week had the city on edge once again. The violence continued with the stabbing murder of a man at the El Rodeo Club parking lot. Officers and detectives were making arrests and investigating at a fast pace, trying to keep up with the growing numbers of assaults. When a witness to a robbery tried to intervene to stop the robber, he was shot.

In the summer of 2001, Lt. Leonard Wilson was promoted to Captain. A gang intelligence officer, Wilson was a well-liked leader who had been with the department since 1984. The newest lieutenant credited his success to the support of his co-workers and family as he looked forward to his new duties. Sgt. Kelly McMillan was promoted to Lieutenant and had been a SWAT leader and supervisor of personnel and training. Corporal Ono Solis was promoted to Sergeant. With the department since 1989, he had worked a number of different assignments prior to his promotion. Officer Vince Maiorana, hired in 1990, was promoted to Sergeant. His experience included patrol and narcotics work in addition to being a training officer. Corporal Mark Clark was promoted to

Sergeant after working as an FTO, SWAT member and Violence Suppression Team member.

Vicky Gray, with the support of Chief Ortega, organized the mounted unit in 2001. The horse unit has six members and works various assignments like the Christmas Parade and Northridge Mall and the Law Enforcement Memorial held each year in Sacramento. The unit traveled out to the east side where they handed out violence prevention tip line cards in what Sgt. Gray believes was one of the most successful assignments for the unit. Sgt. Gray had one of most unusual experiences as a police officer while sitting on her horse at the back of the rodeo grounds during the California Rodeo. Patrolling the grounds, she was quite surprised to see a kangaroo hopping and bouncing along. Calling in to county communications that she was in pursuit of a loose kangaroo she and her horse went after the animal that was headed for the rodeo grounds. There was a circus on the other side of the grounds and the animal had escaped. Sgt. Gray and her steed, trained as a cutting horse, were able to corral the kangaroo and trap it in a corner until the trainer arrived. Picking the scared kangaroo up, the trainer carried it away like a babe in arms. Now in charge of the SRO program, Sgt. Gray believes the GREAT program helps youngsters develop a rapport with officers and enjoys seeing the beautiful projects some of them turn in at the completion of their classes.

On the morning of September 11, 2001, terrorists launched a horrific attack on the people of the United States. Hundreds of New York police officers and fire fighters were among the dead. To honor those who had lost their lives in the attack, Salinas police officers and firefighters quickly organized a memorial and fundraising event held at the Steinbeck Center. Many events were canceled throughout the country because of the attacks and the Salinas International Air Show was held under high security and without any flying airplanes. Emergency services formed a parade in honor of those who had died in New York. Salinas residents joined people around the world mourning in the aftermath of the attack and subsequent rescue efforts. SPD had long been prepared for major emergencies like earthquakes and officers had already had some training in terrorism response. More training would come as the city, county, state, and country prepared for higher level security at all levels.

The terrorist attacks on America were no deterrent to criminals in Salinas and the shootings continued, as did the murders. Officers faced an increased population and newly opened businesses that created increased opportunities for crime. Still looking for enough officers to fill out the department, those who were on duty were working many hours of overtime with few breaks. There were days when officers were unable to take a lunch break or even a coffee break as calls stacked up and pended for hours.

Salinas had grown at a faster rate than the state average in the first six months of 2001. While some crimes had shown a decline in the same time period, others had shown an increase. While the homicide rate had slowed, the city still showed twelve homicides by June. Twenty-five rapes and over two hundred robberies joined over four hundred assaults in making up the statistics for Salinas. *Salinas Californian, October 11, 2001.* The history of gangs in Salinas was legend, but one the city hoped to eradicate. The reputation for violence was hurting the city's ability to attract new businesses. Officer Brian Link spoke out about the impact gangs were having on Salinas. "For a city our size – and I'm not trying to give Salinas a bad reputation – that's what we are known for," Officer Link told reporters as he discussed how crime and violence was destroying the quality of life in Salinas. *Salinas Californian, November12, 2001.*

Officer Brandon Hill was a longtime PAL leader when he responded to a call of a domestic problem on Sanborn Place. The male subject in the dispute had been calmed down by the time Officer Hill started to leave, but became distraught and tried to jump off a train overpass. Hill caught the man just in time and was able to hold onto his wrist while the man's brother grabbed a part of his jacket. Calling for help, they two held the man until other officers arrived to assist in pulling him to safety.

Washington Mutual Bank at 425 Main Street was robbed by a man with a tattoo on his left earlobe on a Tuesday morning in mid-December 2001. The statistics for 2001 were coming out in late December and once again, Salinas had a high murder rate. With twenty-eight homicides in the county, Salinas accounted for fifteen of those. At least ten of those fifteen were gang-related. Domestic violence accounted for most of the remaining five.

THIRTY

Gunter's Last Day and A New Era

Thirty-two years after he walked into SPD as a young officer, "Papa Joe" Gunter was ready to retire. On January 4, 2002, Gunter was partnered with Dave Shaw and his last day as "David 1" was anything but boring. The two detectives were out and about looking for a bank robbery suspect. They had an idea about where he hung out, and they were driving around looking for him when they contacted a male and female on Murphy Street. Neither detective recalls why they chose to contact the two, but something made them curious. Jody Wright was also in the area and drove by. The male subject decided to run when he saw the patrol unit pull up. Gunter grabbed the male subject and the fight was on. Shaw, trying to assist, jumped into the fight which had both detectives on the ground tumbling with the fighting subject. They ended up underneath the bumper of the car, dirty and disheveled, but with their man in custody on warrants and dope charges, not to mention fighting with the officers. Turning him over to Wright, they continued looking for the suspect in the bank robbery. When they rolled into the Rianda Street area, they came upon two guys burglarizing a vehicle. They took custody of those two and once again went looking for the bank robber. It comes as no surprise that the two detectives located the bank robber and arrested him before Gunter left the department for the last time as a detective. All and all, both men agreed it was a great last day. Gunter returned three days later as a background investigator and continues to serve the department by investigating applicants.

By 2002, the Salinas Police Department was seriously recruiting for new officers. They were finding it difficult to replace retiring officers and their experience. Retired detectives Joe Gunter and Gary Edwards went to work on backgrounds of applicants and the department placed a full page ad in *The Monterey County Lawman*, listing the many benefits of working for the elite agency. New recruits were offered $2955-$3592, while laterals and academy graduates were offered $4096-$4979. Bilingual pay, three percent at fifty, a uniform allowance and twelve paid holidays were things the officers of the early department would have approved of and found helpful. With medical retirements, full retirements and the high cost of living in this area, the department tried to find a way to entice both experienced and young officers to stay in Salinas.

Victims themselves were often uncooperative in providing any information to officers. With only limited information in many cases, officers and detectives followed up on what had become almost daily reports on shootings within the city. Not only were they facing danger from the human criminal element, but officers were many times forced to contend with aggressive dogs and their owners. Officer Jason Mellow was bitten by a loose pit bull and was forced to shoot the dog after it attacked him twice.

When an eight year old boy was caught in the cross-fire between two rival gang groups, the city once again reeled from the news. This incident was not the first time a child had been injured by gunfire. In fact, six months earlier a young girl had been hit by gunfire as she attended a baptism and no one had forgotten the infant who had survived the triple murder of her family some years before.

Schools were locked down on an almost regular basis as gunfire could be heard throughout the city day and night. Some shootings resulted in property damage or minor injuries to victims, but others left people dead and families in shock. Mayor Caballero called the week of March 18, 2002, "appalling," referring to the two fatal shootings and numerous other gang-related shootings that had wounded seven others that week. SPD officers arrested ten people and guns were seized as the city participated in the Youth Crime Gun Interdiction Initiative which traced and tracked guns taken from the juveniles. School Resource Officer Dave Lara tried to connect with elementary school age kids as he taught the Gang Awareness Education and Training program, (GREAT) at local schools. Many believed early intervention would keep juveniles from gravitation towards the gang life.

The fourth and fifth homicides of 2002 took place in April, just days before local officers from many law enforcement agencies in Monterey County met in

Marina for the Law Enforcement Memorial Service. The eighth annual service memorialized officers killed in the line of duty. Eleven officers had been killed in California in 2001 and those present also remembered the officers killed in the attack of 9-11.

By mid-May, Salinas police were working the sixth homicide of the year. Counterfeit money was circulating, banks were being robbed and carjackings were becoming more violent. The public was beginning to see the need for cooperation and arrests in one murder case were made after information was provided to officers about the suspect and his whereabouts. Identify theft was causing grief for victims of mail theft and credit card fraud.

Use of restraint became a big issue after two cases where suspects had died after being restrained following chases. The use of the "TARP" restraint was brought under fire and the actions of department members were questioned. Reviews of the cases found officers acted appropriately in restraining the men one of whom had been delirious because of cocaine intoxication and a clear danger to the public and the officers. The officers involved in the arrest were cleared in the subsequent investigation of the incident by the District Attorney's Office. Alternatives to the TARP procedure eventually led to the purchase of hobble devices.

A summer weekend in June was marred by five shootings and one stabbing that left five men wounded. Monterey Bay Bank and Washington Mutual Bank were robbed within days of each other in July and three more men were injured in five gang-related shootings. Another woman was killed by her ex-boyfriend in a brutal stabbing attack in her home.

New officers and veteran detectives saw the first triple homicide in over nine years when three men where killed in a parking lot on Williams Road. The three victims were drinking when a gunman shot each of them multiple times. One thing was certain – this was another gang-related homicide. A quick arrest was made.

In October 2002, the department was short twenty-four officers. Four officers were in the academy and others were on the street with training officers, still in their probationary period. High speed car chases, robbery reports and shootings were giving the new officers a lot to learn and there had been fourteen murders by mid-November. The number of shootings and murders was nothing new to the city, but many of the detectives were new to the division and the cases were coming to them faster than the eight-man team was working overtime. One recruit was fired after it was learned he was living with a seventeen year old juvenile female that he had met when he had worked previously in juvenile hall.

Thanksgiving Day brought no relief. A nineteen year old man was shot while playing football. The murders continued, with two the following night in a parking lot off Alvin Drive. Chief Ortega requested help from the CHP and MCSO in patrolling city streets. A teenager from Fresno was arrested for the Thanksgiving Day murder. The final homicide toll for 2002 was nineteen.

As a token of appreciation, a nine foot evergreen Christmas tree was given to the department after officers recovered it from a thief. The sixty-five dollar tree had been stolen from the Crown Packing tree lot and the company wanted the department to have it in appreciation for the work officers did all year long. *Salinas Californian, December 10, 2002.*

THE RAIDER NATION

When the Raiders won the AFC championship game, chaos ruled the area of North Salinas. Fans cruising, honking horns, and shouting at each other frightened residents along North Main Street, Chaparral and Curtis Streets. Traffic was so congested that no one could get through. Police blocked the streets and forced businesses to close in an attempt to get people to leave the area. SPD had to call for assistance from several other departments as they tried to restore order. Departments from Greenfield, Soledad, Monterey, Del Rey Oaks, Marina, CHP and even CSUMB were called in to help. The department needed to re-evaluate its crowd-control plan before the Super Bowl date came.

The loss to the Tampa Bay Buccaneers did nothing to quell the celebrations of the Raider Nation. Over one hundred law enforcement officers were in place to handle the expected crowd, including the horse patrol unit, motor units and a helicopter. Ten arrests were made for minor violations such as drunk in public but the gridlock of traffic was something that it seemed no amount of planning could prevent. 49er fans taunted Raider fans and gang members sported the colors, but the celebration continued as fans showed they were not sore losers. *Salinas Californian, January 27, 2003.* Reserve Officer Dave Cole was riding with Reserve Officer Ron Ralph that night. Ralph was driving, racing from one call to the next with a frightened Cole sitting in the passenger seat. After one harrowing trip, Cole considered never riding in a police car again.

On February 20, 2003, the city saw its first homicide of the year. A seventeen year old boy was shot while sitting in his car in front of the Rodeo Market.

Officers had every reason to believe it had been motivated by gang activity. Other shootings followed and the Comerica Bank was robbed, followed two weeks later by a robbery at the Main Street Union Bank.

TASERS

Hoping to reduce the number of injuries suffered by officers during confrontations with out of control suspects, and hoping to also avoid more lethal shootings of suspects, the chief ordered TASER guns for his officers. The decision was partly due to the deaths of two men who had died after being tarped while fighting with police in separate incidents. Both men had been under the influence of methamphetamine and cocaine at the time. *Salinas Californian, March 27, 2003.*

Opinions about the use of TASERs would vary widely. While most citizens approved of the less lethal method that saved officers from injury, others criticized the department and called for the new weapons to be banned, saying the use of TASERs was violating the civil rights of those arrested and hit with the weapon. The editorial in the *Californian* called for the elimination of the weapons, saying more information was needed. There was no doubt that the rate of injury to officers had declined with the use of the TASER. Seen by law enforcement as a good and effective alternative to more deadly force, the controversy continued into 2005 as officers and chiefs around the county tried to educate those opposed to the weapon about its benefit to both the law officers and the people who forced them to take action.

Several more shootings and murders marred the Spring season in 2003. When a young man was shot at the Valley Center Bowling Alley in April, he became the third homicide victim of the year. Citizens were getting fed up with the robberies and murders and when a man robbed the Monterey Bay Bank at Main and San Joaquin Street, bank employee Brian Barr chased him and watched him try to carjack two different cars. Barr continued to the chase the man, tackling him on Orange Drive as officers arrived on scene.

Police questioned three people for the murder of a former officer's son. A victim of a hate crime, the young man had been killed in Salinas and buried outside the city. Another victim was killed by a single gunshot wound to the head in front of the Quik Stop on Williams Road. Bullets hit the Gavilan View Middle School on a Wednesday afternoon as students sat at their desks. Fortunately, no one was injured in the shooting. Someone poured a flammable liquid on a homeless man behind a store on North Main Street and set him on fire. He died six days later. Firebombings and carjackings led the news as the city got word the budget would have to be trimmed by four million dollars. There were several fatal car accidents to investigate within the city limits and gang activity was suspected in many of the shootings. A woman fatally stabbed her husband during a domestic argument and a man was shot and killed outside the 7-Eleven on Sanborn Road. By August, there had been eleven homicides in the city and five shootings in one weekend were under investigation.

K-9 Brutus was injured during a confrontation with a burglar who hit him with a tire iron. The canine bit the suspect and held on in spite of his injury until his partner could get to his side to arrest the subject. Brutus had a swollen and sore mouth and had to take pain medication for some time, but he returned to duty after his recovery. *Salinas Californian, August 22, 2003.*

A missing person case turned into a homicide investigation when a body was found south of Monterey County. There were five shootings on a Sunday in August 2003, leaving residents of a section of East Salinas feeling vulnerable and the department spread thin.

When a city councilman blamed the chief for gang violence in the city and asked him to resign, the Salinas Police Officer's Association stepped in to support their leader. Calling the councilman's accusation "the most ridiculous statement and request made by one of our elected officials," SPOA Vice-President Kyle Kimm told reporters that "Chief Ortega has led our department with a commitment to reduce violent crime in our community by utilizing every resource available to him." The gang problem was not new to Salinas, the chief was not to blame, and the community knew it and spoke out in support of Chief Ortega. *Salinas Californian, August 28, 2003.*

A series of five shootings in September left one dead and three wounded. Lt. Yoneyama explained how the lack of cooperation from witnesses made the work of investigators more difficult. Once again, the department leaders asked the community to help by providing information about the crimes.

Soon after the latest increase in violence, the city council voted to give back five police positions previously lot due to budget cuts. The chief's recommendation for more officers was taken seriously, as were the words Monterey County Prosecutor Terry Spitz who spoke in favor of adding positions to the department. While some Salinas officers investigated four apparently unrelated robberies in one day, others looked into the cause of death of a man found in back of a hotel. Three more robberies and one more murder took place soon after the council meeting.

A November weekend in 2003 added three more murders to the city statistics. Once again, Salinas saw three unrelated homicides within hours and another man survived after being shot. When the subject of a pursuit pulled a gun out and aimed at Officer Jason Scott, the officer shot the wanted subject.

In early December the homicide toll stood at eighteen when another man was shot in the chest near an elementary school. A fatal accident in the residential area of Riker and Park Streets left both parents and an unborn baby dead. Two young children had survived the deadly crash that was the result of a driver under the influence and speeding.

When a female shopper walking with her children at Northridge Mall was shot during the Christmas season, the newspaper headlines were in the boldest possible print. Police were able to determine that the woman had been the unintended victim of more gang activity. Fortunately, her superficial wounds were not life-threatening.

Of the eighteen homicides in Salinas in 2003, three victims were juveniles and eleven were in their 20s. Eleven were known to be gang-related murders and thirteen had involved guns. Police had arrested a number of suspects in many of the murders.

As community leaders sought an end to the violence and searched for a way to handle the growing financial crisis and gang situation, two first two homicides of 2004 took place before ten days had passed in the new year. Continued multiple shootings led SPD to increase patrols. Overtime was authorized and one councilman wanted to declare a state of emergency in the city. With five gang-related murders in the city before the end of January, Mayor Caballero told Chief Ortega to "use whatever overtime" he needed to stop the gang violence. *Salinas Californian, January 24, 2004.*

Salinas needed more officers and new officers took time to train. In February 2004, the city council restored two positions previously taken from the police department and authorized an additional ten officers. The additional officers would cost the city more money, but the people of Salinas had spoken. The help of a CHP helicopter brought cheers and complaints from Salinas residents. The helicopter was a handy tool for police involved in pursuits, for rooftop checks, and for cover for officers on felony car stops.

Five days after hundreds marched to support peace in the city, two more shootings shook Salinas. Schools were locked down as officers served search warrants on seven homes, seizing sawed-off shotguns and arresting two suspects.

The man who had chased down and tackled a bank robber shot and killed one of two people who were trying to rob him. Two other robbery victims were pistol whipped by their assailants.

The chief was trying to get funding for a joint gang task force as his officers continued to investigate the latest shootings and murders in the city. Car thefts had also taken a big jump, climbing fifty-two percent. Salinas had the second highest rate of car theft in the state.

KLIEF

Officer Gaston with K-9 Officer Klief
Courtesy of the Salinas Police Department

Klief and Bill Gaston made a great team, handling hundreds of calls each year. In one incident, Klief was able to follow a blood trail to locate a suspect. When a woman armed with a knife assaulted an officer in 2001, Klief was sent in to take down the suspect.

Klief was pictured with partner Bill Gaston on a popular trading card which listed his accomplishments. By the age of four, Klief had two years of service to Gaston's thirty with the department and had made one hundred fifty-eight apprehensions. He had searched four hundred fifty buildings, attended sixty-seven training sessions and loved to play fetch and Frisbee.

On May 16, 2004, Officer Bill Gaston and his canine partner Klief, a five year old important member of the Salinas Police Department, were on duty when they were called to Glacier Drive. A knife-wielding suspect confronted officers and the canine, refusing to drop the weapon or stand down. Klief, next to his handler and partner, was stabbed repeatedly by the suspect as he protected the officers from the suspect who was eventually shot and killed by other officers. Klief died of his wounds the next morning, but the officers he had protected had not suffered any physical injuries. The loss of Canine Officer Klief was mourned by officers and department families who shared the grief felt by his partner, Bill Gaston. Klief was given a full memorial service attended by hundreds of officers, canines, and grateful citizens from throughout California. Klief, who had a superior record of apprehensions and assists to Salinas officers, is still held close to the hearts of all who knew and worked with him. Months after his death, Officer Gaston chose a new partner and continues to patrol the streets of Salinas with "Nerro," a large, all black dog who walks alongside his partner with the same pride as Klief, who will always be remembered as one of the greatest canines of all times.

Klief
Courtesy of the Salinas Police Department

By June 2004, there had been ten homicides in Salinas and eight remained unsolved. The two solved cases were those of Brian Barr who had killed an intruder, and the officer involved shooting where K-9 Klief had been killed by the suspect. Early in July, they added another homicide to the list when a body was found on the campus of Natividad Elementary School, dead from an apparent gunshot wound. Leslie Drive, a quiet neighborhood with no history of violence, was the scene of the twelfth murder of the year.

Domestic stabbings, fatal accidents and more shootings took place as the summer months passed. Two more shootings took the lives of cousins near Maryal and Chaparral Drive. Senator Barbara Boxer visited Salinas and promised to help the city fund a joint city-county gang task force. Days after her visit, yet another man was shot to death, the fifteenth homicide victim of the year. Another teen was killed and his girlfriend injured in more gunfire on Acosta Plaza.

The CHP, (California Highway Patrol) joined the MCSO, (Monterey County Sheriff's Office) and the Salinas Police Department to work on a safe-streets operation that included high profile patrolling of the city. "Salinas Safe Streets," as the operation was called, would attempt to suppress gang violence by a noticeable presence of officers in patrol cars and helicopters. In spite of one murder on the first night of the operation, it was believed the high profile presence of the combined forces of the three agencies would make a difference.

When hundreds of citizens watched Chief Ortega sign a pledge to keep safe anyone reporting a crime, five hundred people agreed to report crimes to police when they saw them committed. Shortly after that meeting, witnesses helped officers with information about the person responsible for a gang-related shooting. Officers were able to obtain and serve a search warrant and make an arrest in the case.

Jason Scott was on duty early one evening when he received a call to a house on fire. Officer Scott arrived at the house on Pine Street before the fire department and went into the house to find the elderly resident. Through smoke and flames, he carried the eighty-five year old woman out to safety, risking his own life in the process. With that unselfish act, he became one of the many heroes in the history of the Salinas Police Department.

Today, evidence technicians must get rid of evidence according to very stringent rules. In the process of purging the unclaimed transient property in the evidence room in 2005, Jesse Gilpas and Betty Wilder heard a bag buzzing. Concerned, they worked around the bag, which eventually stopped buzzing.

As they took the load to the dumpster, the bag began buzzing again. Fearing the possibility of a bomb, the two brave evidence technicians opened the bag to find a large plastic bag with a vibrator that could have been used for an Energizer Bunny commercial. The batteries were still going and going and going!

THIRTY-ONE

THE FINEST PROFESSION

Serving the community since even before the inception of a recognized police department in 1903, the men and women in the Salinas Police Department have earned the respect and appreciation of the citizens they protect. With notably few exceptions, they have been a force with integrity, compassion, and determination as they patrol the expanding city keeping the peace, never sure of where their next call will take them or what will face them when they arrive on scene.

The history of this department shows the many obstacles it has faced over the years, the ways in which it was able to surmount those obstacles, and the influence of those who went before. As the officers of today set out on their beats, may they remember those who walked down Main Street in the dark, alone and unarmed, continued to patrol on a motorcycle after losing one leg, were injured, shot or killed in the line of duty and faced many of the same challenges as the officers of today, but without much of the support now provided. May they remember the oath they took and the reason they became law officers when they feel overworked and underappreciated. And most of all, may they be watched over and protected by the spirits of those officers long gone, who set the standards for what an officer of the Salinas Police Department is expected to be.

THE DEPARTMENT TODAY

Chief Daniel Ortega, assisted by Deputy Chiefs Rick Moore and Cassie McSorley, heads up a department of one hundred sixty-seven officers, including fourteen female officers. Fifty-nine non-sworn personnel provide much needed and valuable support services. One hundred and two years after the appointment of the first chief of police, Salinas has little resemblance to the city of 3,000 that covered only one square mile at the end of the 1800s. With a current annual budget of $31 million for the modern department, it is difficult to comprehend the $2.50 per day specially appointed officers made for risking their lives without equipment or training. The early officers, chiefs, and special officers had to have been very exceptional men and women, as are those who serve today. In 1961, the ten department cars traveled 365,339 miles and the three motorcycles another 22,823 miles. The fleet of 2004 traveled 2,336,200 miles, an increase of over sixty percent in the last forty years.

Today, many officers work in special assignments. A mounted unit for special events is one of the few that harkens back to the wild west days of early Salinas. Significant improvements have been made in technology, crime scene investigation, traffic investigations and narcotics and have given rise to specialized units, providing better training for our officers. Canine officers train dogs for use in searches and chases in direct contrast to the officers of the early department who were forced to pay someone to shoot stray dogs in town and then bury them. The 1903 department of three men, who knew each other well having worked together for years, would not recognize the city or the men and women who serve her today. Few memories of the early Salinas City and police department remain today.

Like the early department, our men and women continue to serve in wars, being called to Iraq and hoping to return home, just as the officers who served in the two World Wars, the Korean War and Viet Nam, hoped they would return. Cameron Murphy was only a newly hired officer when his National Guard Unit was called to duty. Injured in a roadside bomb attack, Murphy gave medical aid to a fellow officer before realizing he had been badly burned. Keeping his small team focused, he got them out of danger before receiving any aid himself. He returned to duty to complete his tour. The department awaits his safe return. Officer Wayne Vance, vowing to memorialize his mentor, an MPC instructor who was killed by a drunk driver, made a record two hundred twenty-six drunk driving arrests in 2004. Jason Scott, recognized as the 2004 SPOA's Officer of the Year, risked his life to go into a burning house to save a woman. These are only a sampling of the exemplary work of the Salinas Police Department's officers.

Unlike the early officers, ours now have medical benefits, pensions and rights. A motor officer losing his leg and returning to ride a motor unit with a wooden leg for many years is a story that will never be duplicated, and one that should never be forgotten.

One thing is certain. The Salinas Police Department strived to be the best from the very beginning. It has not lost that designation over the years. The fast paced action of the Salinas department leaves nothing to be desired by those seeking an active career in law enforcement. The best officers today, just as those who walked the streets before them, are those who were born with that instinct and intuition that cannot be taught. Anyone with a good imagination can picture in his mind Chief Stonewall Jackson Smart, sitting atop his horse, Baltimore, supervising the building of his rock pile next to the railroad tracks. Or, reflect on how Butch Beevers must have felt on the lonely drive back to Moss Landing, where he picked up the dead body of Special Officer Rader and brought him home.

The brotherhood of police officers within the Salinas department represents a common interest in, and dedication to, the people of this city. Steve Long, president for the past nine years of the SPOA, (Salinas Police Officer's Association) believes the biggest challenges facing our officers and department today are retention and pay. The officers of today may patrol a larger area than their predecessors and may have better training and technology than those who went before them, but they all share the distinction of having been part of the history of this city. One hundred years from now, the officers of today's department will be the ones memorialized and remembered for their part in making Salinas a department to be proud of. In the words of A. Beldon Gilbert, the director of the Peace Officer's Civil Service Association of California: "...the days of the 'hitching post' type of law enforcement are long past, when an officer was provided only a badge and a gun as the tools of the profession, with no knowledge of vital police science. Law enforcement officers, investigators and police administrators must not only be equipped with modern physical weapons, but must also be trained in the latest methods of crime detection and crime prevention for the enforcement of the law and administration of justice. Enforcement of the law is a profession, not just a job, which requires intelligence, skill and everlasting study and training. The peace officer's objective of honest, intelligent fulfillment of duty, designed to give more adequate protection to the citizens of his community, must be accomplished by raising his own standards in the police profession. With it will come a sense of accomplishment, a higher morale, a greater satisfaction, as well as renewed courage, plus wholesome respect for the effort, and just reward."

This quote was taken from a book published in 1945, and presented to Mae Eisemann by the State Executive Director of the Peace Officer's Civil Service Association of California, in appreciation for her service. It rings as true today as it did sixty years ago, when it was given to the first female police officer to serve in Salinas. The book, entitled, *Peace Officers Home Study Book and Digest of Criminal Laws,* was dedicated to, "the finest profession in the world – Law Enforcement." It was one of the first texts published specifically to educate and train police officers and included practice tests, penal code sections, fingerprint identification instructions, and these words of wisdom, "Every precaution must be taken to keep the criminal from beating the law."

The Salinas department is doing just that. The budget crisis of the twenty-first century has not stopped crime in the streets, nor has it stopped the officers from doing their job. It has made it more challenging for an administration that is forced to spend much of its time dealing with the financial crisis of our time. From the days of 1954, when there were no charges for booking a prisoner, to 2004, when the city must pay $145.69 for each person booked into the jail, the fee is only one example of the increase in costs. When the department moved into its current headquarters in 1958, the still small department had less than half the officers it has today. It wasn't until 1992 that there were dedicated personnel for crime scene investigation. Today there are twelve officers working as Crime Scene Investigators, in addition to a full time criminalist, latent print technician and many part time or temporary specialists. The two black squad cars and one paddy wagon used by officers in the 1940s have been replaced by a fleet of ninety-five vehicles, forty of which are patrol units. Computers began to appear in patrol cars in 1998, and Officer Chris Swinscoe was temporarily assigned to keeping them on line. How the department grows out of this period will have much to do with the future of law enforcement in Salinas. One recurring theme throughout the history of the department is the need to hire more officers as some retire and others move on to other places. The search now, as it was then, is for those very special men and women who will be willing to dedicate their lives in service to the Salinas Police Department and who are willing to become a part of the vibrant history of the place that began as Salinas City so many years ago.

ISBN 141207548-3